1 MONTH OF
FREE
READING

at
www.ForgottenBooks.com

By purchasing this book you are eligible for one month membership to ForgottenBooks.com, giving you unlimited access to our entire collection of over 1,000,000 titles via our web site and mobile apps.

To claim your free month visit:
www.forgottenbooks.com/free245172

ISBN 978-0-266-22530-0
PIBN 10245172

A REPORT

RECORD COMMISSIONERS,

CONTAINING THE

Boston, Registry Dept.

ROXBURY LAND AND CHURCH RECORDS.

SECOND EDITION.

BOSTON:

ROCKWELL AND CHURCHILL, CITY PRINTERS,

No. 39 ARCH STREET.

1884.

CITY OF  BOSTON.

REPORT

OF THE

RECORD COMMISSIONERS.

BOSTON, December 31, 1880.

The Record Commissioners obtained the consent of the City Council this year, to print, as their sixth volume, the Land Records of Roxbury, thereby carrying out the idea of apportioning the work among the various sections of our present city. The second volume contains Boston records; the third, Charlestown records; the fourth, Dorchester records; the present, Roxbury records; and the seventh, now in the printers' hands, will resume the Boston volumes.

The Roxbury book here printed, has, we believe, been taken apart and re-arranged, so that it is no longer possible to say when the record of grants was commenced. Certainly the first entry on our first page, dated in 1639, is not in the same handwriting as the entries paged 1–86, on our pages 12–51. These entries were all by the same hand, and probably the following order explains them : —

Roxbury Town Records Vol. i. p. 9. "Town order for makeing new transcript."

"The town boock wherin most mens lands being recorded [by] gods prouidence being burned. therby much dammedg may [be done?] to seuiriall men. to preuent dammedg as aforesayd [it is or]dered by the town of Roxbury that ther shalbe fife [men] chosen to doe there best indeuer to set down etch mans land giuen them by the town or that may belondg [to] them other ways. and make return vnto the town within three months soe as this may be accomplished for the pshon of dammedg as afore sayd. and allsoe to record hieaways and other town preuilidges. 17. of 11. 1652.

JOHN JOHNSON
WILLIAM PARKE
ISAK MORILL
ED. DENYSON
GRIFFEN CRAFT."

These signatures are not autographs, but a comparison with other pages leads us to the conviction, that this transcript, or book of possessions, was written by Edward Denison at that time.

The other items in the book are dated, and are of the miscellaneous nature generally to be found in old books of town records.

As this particular volume would not make a book of the size of others in this series of reports, the commissioners searched for material to accompany it. The first volume of town records is in proper form for printing by itself, and it seemed unwise to divide it so as to fill out this book. It was, however, believed, that the Records of the First Church in Roxbury were of so conspicuous interest and value as to warrant their selection for printing. Not only are they of interest as being largely the work of that most famous of our divines, the Rev. John Eliot, but they contain many pages of entries of general interest. Mr. Eliot and his colleague, the Rev. Samuel Danforth, happily conceived the idea of entering in this volume a summary of public events, year by year. As public records, therefore, they will be valued by many who have no special interest in the doings of the settlers at Roxbury.

Portions of this record have been printed already. In 1850, the late J. Wingate Thornton, Esq., published a number of articles, in a Roxbury newspaper, concerning the early settlers. A portion of the church record was thus printed, and fifty copies of these essays were issued in book form. During the past two years the whole of the public record of Eliot and Danforth has appeared in the New England Historical and Genealogical Register, with elaborate notes by William B. Trask, Esq. But even this publicity is but partial, and the expense to a collector would be considerable. The greater part of the volume, however, is now printed for the first time, and all of the volume, except a very few pages, is here given.

The following description of the venerable manuscript volume will show exactly what has been done with it. It will be noticed that we have altered the arrangement in one or two points, in order to make the whole more systematic. Thus, at the end, the baptisms and burials, from 1641 to 1688, were written in double columns on each page, under the heading of each year. As we could not print these entries in this form, it seemed best to print all the baptisms in chronological order, and then to treat the burials in the same way.

In the manuscript we find first three leaves, on one of which there is some poetry on Abigail Tomson, and on two of the others some church votes, etc., in 1658. The pagination then begins regularly, but we have not inserted it in the text, as many of the pages have but a few names on each. Probably Mr. Eliot intended to leave room after each name for further notes. On p. 56 (our printed page 86) the entries begin to be more in detail. With page 70 (our page 100) these entries end, and the lists of admissions begin, continuing through p. 81 (our p. 111). Pp. 82, 3, 4 are blank. On p. 85 is the list of five names printed by us on p. 111. P. 86 is blank.

Pp. 87–89 are entries of admission from 1753, printed on pp. 111–114. Pp. 91–96, blank.

Pp. 97–110 are baptisms from 1751–1766; these we have transferred to their proper place, and print on pp. 147–162.

Pp. 111–124 contain votes of the church from 1751–1774, *and are not printed*, as they contain nothing of interest to the public. Pp. 125–138, blank.

Pp. 139–144, baptisms resumed, 1768, etc.; printed by us, pp. 162–169.

Pp. 145–242, blank; pp. 243–4, two pages of accounts A.D. 1672–7.

Pp. 245–249, Eliot's general records, printed on pp. 187–191; p. 250, the note on William Curtis.

Pp. 251–262, Danforth's records, printed on pp. 196–212. Pp. 262–268, Eliot's records, printed on pp. 191–196.

P. 269, Amos Adams' memorandum on our pp. 169–170, ending with the entry of Dr. Porter's death in 1833. Pp. 270–297, blank; p. 298, notes about a legacy; pp. 299–302 are wanting, probably by error in numbering the pages. P. 303, note of a legacy; pp. 304–6, blank. Pp. 307–314, accounts, A.D. 1759–1774, mostly about Col. Lamb's bequest. Pp. 315–6, blank; pp. 317–18, accounts of 1759. Pp. 319–464, blank.

With page 465 begin 34 pages not numbered, of baptisms and burials, written in double columns. We print the baptisms, 1641–1688, on pp. 114–142, and the burials for the same period on pp. 170–187.

Then come 5 pages of persons owning the covenant, 1700–1750, printed on pp. 143–146; then the note by Rev. O. Peabody, printed on p. 146; then 7 pages blank; then pages numbered 519–525, blank; lastly, p. 526, Index.

We have been thus particular in describing the contents of the volume, as it was found inexpedient to print it continuously. Like all such books, entries were made at random, and it seemed best, in printing, to correct the arrangement. If the present members of the church will print the few pages of church votes and accounts, they can feel sure that this invaluable record will be certain of preservation.

Respectfully submitted,

WILLIAM H. WHITMORE,
WILLIAM S. APPLETON,
Record Commissioners.

ROXBURY LAND RECORDS.

[1.] The First day of the Fowerth moneth Comonly Called June 1639 this booke was bought (by the Seaven men then imployed in the Towne affairs) for the entrying of the Towne Lands and other weighty bussinesses being fully Agreed vpon which may concerne the Inhabitants of thes Towne of Rocksbury and payed for the booke Fower shillings.

Edward Bugbie 8 Accres for a great Lott lying vpon the hill bejond the great Pond vpon the lands of Phillip Elliott abuting.

Jasper Gunn 5 Accres and a halfe of meadow and Vpland lying at the end of Beare hill Bounding vpon M^r. John Goare his meadow South east and the other end and two sids bounds to the Comon.

Arthor Gary seaven Accres and a halfe for a great Lott at the great Pond lying next to Edward Bugbie towards Dedham path one end of it abutting to the railes of Phillip Elliott and also fower accres and a halfe at muddy riner abutting to John Perry his highway to his meade.

Thomas Ruggles seaven Accres and a halfe for a Lott abutting vpon Arthor Gary and one end to Phillip Elliotts railes thether side to the Comon Dedham path going through the same, and Fowr accres and a halfe at Muddy Riuer in two p'ts three Accres want [*] pole betweene two p'cells of ground giuen to Thomas Grigges and one Accre and a halfe and 7 pole abutting to Arthor Gary and Robert Prentice.

Samuel Chapin his lot upon which Georg Alcocks lot N°. 6 in the 3^d division is entered.

[2.] Philip Searle sen. and Jonathan Torry transfer their right of the halfe of the Nipmug Land Granted to the Generall Court to the Town of Roxbury which did belong to the stayers, unto Roger Adams and his heirs forever he or they discharging all the charges equitably required by reason thereof.

[3.] Robert Masson hath sould vuto William Perkins two Accres and a halfe a Roode of Broken up ground in the Calues pasture adioyning to the lands of the said William on the one side therof and to the Lands of ^{Wm} Denison one the other side therof with one end abutting on the highway and the other end vpon the marsh paid for it twelue pounds and tenn shillings the sixteenth day of March 1639.

Witnes. JOHN STOW

p me ROBERT MASSON.

Gregory Bexter hath sould vuto William Perkins his howse and buildings therevnto belonging, with seven p'cells of Land namly three Accres of broken up ground one the back side of the howse, and two Accres and halfe a Roode in the Calues pasture between Joshua Hewes and William Webb. and Sixe Accres of Fresh Marsh vpon John Stow and Fower Accres vpon the meeting howse hill, and Eight Accres of Salt Marsh vpon the Lands of Samuell Hagborne and Isaae Morrell on the other side. And Seaven Accres at Stony Riuer Mr Thomas Weld one the one side and William Denison on the other And Nine Accres at the greate Pond adioyning to the land of [Blank] Cheney paid for it one hundred Forty sixe pounds and Ten shillings .
Witnes JOHN STOW.

Daniell Brewer hath sould vnto Joseph Weld three Accres of Fresh meadow by estimation abutting vpon Stony Riuer South and vpon the meadow and vpland of the said Joseph Weld East North and West Sixe pounds and tenn shillings in hand payed p'uided if ther be n[ot] three Accres to repay back againe for what is wanting after For * * shillings and three shillings and Fower pence an Accre and if ther be more then to gine more according to the value Dated the fift day of May 1640.
Witnes JOHN STOW senior.

The marke of ꝺ B DANIEL BREWER.

[4.] James Astwood, hath sould vnto Joseph Weld Three Accres of Fresh meadow more or lesse abutting vpon Stony Riuer South and vpon the vpland and meadow of the said Joseph East and North and to the Common West and also three Accres more or lesse of Vpland abutting vpon the Lands of the said Joseph West vpon Joshua Hewes North vpon Robert Scaner East and vpon the highway South for the some of Nine pounds to him in hand payed Dated the Nine and Twentyeth day of August 1640.
Witnes JOSHUA HEWES   (autograph) JAMES ASTWOOD
        JOHN STOW

Robert Masson hath sould vnto Lambert Jennery of Dedham Three Accres of land more or lesse lying to the highway East to the Lands of Mr Thomas Weld North and West and to the Lands of William Dennison South and also eleuen Accres more or lesse lying at the great hill going to Muddy Riuer towards the South of the highway towards the west of the land of Robert Prentice towards the East of the lands of [Blank] Roberts and towards the land of Arthor Gary els North Dated the 24th of Nouember 1640
Witnes JOHN STOW senior   p me ROBERT MASON
        JOHN STOW

[5.] Joseph Weld hath giuen in exchange Sixe Acres of Fresh meadow abutting to the meadow of [Blank] cheyney East to Joshua Hewes West and to the Comonds North and South Vnto Joshua Hewes * * * eight and Twenty Acres of Vpland abutting vpon the Lands of Phillip Elliott South vpon the Lands of Robert

Seauer North west and vpon the highway Eastward for Forty shillings of money already payed   Dated the nine and twentyeth day of August, 1640.

Witnes JAMES ASTWOOD   JOSEPH WELD
       JOHN STOW   JOSHUA HEWES

Mr Thomas Weld hath bought of Lambert Jennery of Dedham thr[ee] acres of Land more or lesse late the Lands of Robert Masson about * * * to the highway towards the East and to the lands of William De * * towards the south, and to the land of the said Mr Weld west and * as by the marks and bounds it doth and may appeare.   Dated the 24th day of Nouember. 1640.

Witnes ROBERT MASON   The mark of ℇ LAMBERT JENNERY
       JOHN STOW senior
       JOHN STOW

Samuell Chapin hath bought of James How a howse and * * Accres of Land more or lesse lying therevnto abutting to Thom[as] Bell one the west and p't South to Daniel Brewer one the * * and one Edward Bridg North and p't South as by the marks and bounds it doth and may appeare.   Dated the first of Aprill 1641

Witnes HENRY ARCHER.   JAMES HOW
       JOHN STOW senior.

Phebe Disborough in the absence of her husband by his assignment hath sould vuto James Morgan two howses and Fower p'clls of land for the some of thirty poundes to her in hand payed the bowses and howse lott abutteth to the highway against John Ruggles vpon the south of the way to the Landes of Robert Prentice North sixe Aceres one the other side of a way bounds as the howse plott S[outh] and North to John Ruggles and Robert Prentice Sixe accres m * * abutts to John Ruggles North and Griffin Craft South and Fi * * accres of marsh being a Creek round about It adioyning to Joshua Hewes and Thomas Lambe.   Dated the 26th of May 1641.

Witnes JOHN STOW   PHEBE DISBOROWE
       HENRY ARCHER

[6.]   It is agreed the eight of the First moneth 1644 in the p'sents of us whose names are vuder written that William Denison his heires and assignes shall for euer mainteine a sufficient fence from the place where the gate now hangeth which leades into the litle Marsh at Smilt Brooke to the ditch of John Johnson which is for euer to be mainteined for a fence betweene the land we * * John Johnson bought of John Pettit and the said William Denison.

                                   ISAAC HEATH
                                   JOSHUA HEWES
                                   THOMAS LAMBE

This agreement was iugrost in a noate vnder the handes of those three men aboue written the day and yeare abouesaid which noate remaines in the hands of John Johnson.

[**7.**] Mr Elliott 8 goats, 5 kidds
John Johnson 6 goats, 4 kids
Isaac Morrell 4 goats. 3 kids
Mrs Sheafe 14 goats. 10 kids
Edward Bugbie 6 goats 7 kids
John Burchly 2 goats. 2 kids
Edward Sheffild 2 goats. 1 kide
Wm Chandler 1 goat. 1 kid.
1640:

Elder Heath 12 goats. 7 kids
Wm Denison 2 goats. 3 kids
John Stow 20 goats. 8 kids
John Levins 8 goats. 8 kids
Thomas Waterman 7 goats. 6
   kids
Thomas Freman 3 goats.
Richard Peacock 1 goate 1 kid
Dorothy   1 goat. 1 kid

We whose names are vnder written haue appointed John Burdwell to   *   *12^d apeece for Goats and kids out of which we did appoint him to pay   *   *   * Burt for his boy for the full tyme that he did keepe the Goats.

                                    ISSAC H[EATH]
                                    JOHN STO[W]

A note of the estates and persons of the Inhabitants of Rocksbury

accres.	halfe ac		person & estate
3 -.	00 —	0	Edward Pason	1 – 00 .. 00 .. 00
6 ..	2 ...	0	John Tatman	2 – 06 – 00 .. 00
7	00	0	John Stonnard	2 – 00 .. 09 .. 00
6	00	0	Martin Stebbin	2 – 00 .. 00 .. 00
7	00	0	Giles Pason	2 – 10 .. 03 .. 04
6	2	0	Lawrence Wittamore	2 – 02 .. 06 .. 08
10	00	0	Richard Peacocke	3 ; 08 .. 00 .. 00
11	00	0	Edward Bugbie	3 .. 17 .. 00 .. 00
11	00	0	John Levins	3 .. 17 .. 00 .. 00
×	2	0	Gowin Anderson	3 .. 01 .. 00 .. 00
×	0	0	Christopher Peake	3 .. 06 .. 08 .. 00
×	2	0	John Ruggles	3 .. 04 .. 13 .. 00
12	2	0	Richard Peper	4 .. 03 .. 00 .. 00
12	0	0	Edward Rigges	4 .. 00 .. 00 .. 00
15	0	0	William Webb	4 .. 02 .. 00 .. 00
12	0	0	Edward Bridge	4 .. 02 .. 00 .. 00
12	0	0	Thomas Ruggles	4 .. 01 .. 15 .. 00
14	0	0	Robert Seaver	4 .. 17 .. 06 .. 00
12	0	0	Thomas Griggs	4 .. 00 .. 00 .. 00
12	0	0	John Hall	4 .. 00 .. 00 .. 00
12	0	0	John Trumble	4 .. 00 .. 00 .. 00
17	2	0	John Burwell	5 .. 17 .. 10 .. 00
15	0	0	Abraham Howe	5 .. 01 .. 00 .. 00
5	0	0	John Mathew	5 .. 01 .. 00 .. 00
15	2	0	John Bowles	5 .. 07 .. 10 .. 00
15 .	2 .	0	Isaac Johnson	5 .. 02 .. 00 .. 00 ℒ
16 .	2 .	0	Ralph Hemmenway	5 .. 09 .. 14 .. 08
15 .	0 .	0	John Corteis	5 .. 00 .. 00 .. 00
16 .	15 .	0	Arther Gary	5 .. 02 .. 00 .. 00
18 .	0 .	0	Thomas Waterman	6 .. 01 .. 16 .. 08
× .	0 .	0	Thomas Pigge	6 .. 17 .. 00 .. 00

accres.	halfe ac		person & estate
X .	0 . 0	Samuell Fi[nch] .	6 .. 14 .. 05 .. 00
22 .	0 . 0	Widdow Iggulden	7 .. 06 .. X .. X
22 .	0 . 0	Abraham Newell	7 .. 07 .. X .. X
22 .	0 . 0	Wm Chandler .	7 .. 06 .. X .. X
21 .	2 . 0	Robert Gamlien .	7 .. 03 .. X .. X
21 .	0 . 0	John Perry	7 X X X
21 .	0 . 0	Francis Smith .	7 X X X
24 .	2 . 0	John Pettit .	8 X X X
24 .	2 . 0	Wm Cheiney .	8 X X X
24 .	0 . 0	Samuell Chapin .	8 X X X
25 .	2 . 0	William Perkins .	8 X X X
25 .	2 . 0	Robert Williams .	8 X X X
26 .	0 . 0	John Crane .	8 X X X
27 .	2 . 0	Daniell Brewer .	9 X X X
28 .	0 . 0	James Astwood .	9 X X X
27 .	0 . 0	Edward Porter .	9 X X X
28 .	2 . m0	John Miller .	9 X X X
27 .	0 . 0	John Roberts .	9 X X X
30 .	0 . 0	Griffin Craft .	10 X X X
37 .	0 . 0	John Watson .	12 X X X
37 .	0 . 0	Thomas Lamb .	12 X 07 X
39 .	0 . 0	Mr John Elliott .	13 X10 X
39 .	0 . 0	William Curties .	13 X X X
[8.]			
X .	0 . 0	Thomas Bell	13 .. 18 .. 02 .. 00
X .	0 . 0	George Holmes .	13 .. 10 .. 00 .. 00
X .	0 . 0	Samuell Hagborne	14 .. 17 .. 00 .. 00
X .	0 . 0	William Parke .	15 .. 1 .. 10 .. 00
[X]6	0 . 0	John Johnson	15 .. 12 .. 06 .. 08 ℓ
[X]00	0 . 0	John Gore .	15 .. 16 .. 00 .. 00
2[X] 4	0 . 0	Isaac Morrell .	17 .. 00 .. 00 .. 00
242 .	0 . 0	George Alcock .	20 .. 03 .. 00 .. 00
256 .	0 . 0	Elder Heath	21 .. 18 .. 03 .. 04
[X]	0 . 0	John Stow .	21 .. 02 .. 17 .. 04
X7	0 . 0	Wm Denison .	24 .. 07 .. 06 .. 08 ↙
[X] 78	0 . 0	Joseph Weld .	23 .. 03 .. 15 .. 00
[X] 88	0 . 0	Joshua Hewes .	24 .. 00 .. 00 .. 00
3[X] 5	0 . 0	Phillip Elliott .	25 .. 07 .. 13 .. 04
333 .	0 . 0	Mr Thomas Weld .	26 .. 01 .. 13 .. 00
356 .	0 . 0	Mr Thomas Dudley .	10 .. 00 .. 00

[9.] The Accompt of Joshua Hewes Counstable chosen in the third moneth 1642 for two yeares expired and his accompt giuen in the first of the 3d mo: 1644. is as followeth.

A Rate bearing date the first of Nouember. 1642. out of which 62 poundes was assigned to be payable for our part for Rocksbury of 1000ls payable towards the discharging the Country charges which rate amounted vuto. — —

<table>
<tr><td></td><td align="right">ls</td><td>s</td><td></td></tr>
</table>

	ls	s	
Imp'mis paied to Mr William Tynge Tres^u	02 .. 10 .. 00
Itm paied to Mr William Perkins	02 .. 13 .. 06
Itm. p^d to John Scarbrow; for 1 p of wheeles in p't	00 .. 15 .. 00
Itm p^d to John Johnson	02 .. 00 .. 00

[**10.**] Blank.

[**11.**] This 20 day of 11 mo. 1657 the owners of the thousand ackrs at dedham agreed to put the sam into .10. lots. the partys all consenting thereto and agreed as followeth — Willi: Park .10.   110 ackr *

Name				lots	acres
Ed Passon	.	.	.	.41.	}
Robert Williams	.	.	.	.25.	.6.
Ed. Redgs	.	.	.	.10.	
Rafe Hiningway	.	.	.	.16.2^t	——— 092.2^t
Heath. P. Isak	.	.	.	.39.	}
Arth Gery	.	.	.	.39.	.7.
Robert Sener	.	.	.	.14.2^t	
Robri Pepper	.	.	.	.07.	——— 099.2
Sam Finch	.	.	.	.49.2^t	}
John Maho	.	.	.	.21.	.2.
John Rudgls	.	.	.	.09.2^t	
John Bouls	.	.	.	.15.2^t	——— 95.2^t
Robrt. Printes	.	.	.	.60.	}
Bro. Smith and Gard	.	.	.30.	.1.	
John Leuns	.	.	.	.11.	——— 101.
John Watson	.	.	.	.40.2^t	}
Abr^a Newell	.	.	.	.22.	
Ch. Peak	.	.	.	.10.	.3.
John Tatman	.	.	.	.06.2^t	
John Pery	.	.	.	.21.	——— 100.0
John Pierpont	.	.	.	.83.	}
Rich. Peacoke	.	.	.	.10.	.5.
John Trumbll	.	.	.	.12.	——— 105.
Hugh Clerk	.	.	.	.39.	}
Nat. Brewer	.	.	.	.27.	
Pedgs	.	.	.	.12.	
Sam Rudgls	.	.	.	.12.	
John Rudgls	.	.	.	.08.	8.
Willi. Chaulr	.	.	.	.22.	——— 120.
Willi. Cheny	.	.	.	.24.2^t	}
Ed. Budgby	.	.	.	.12.	
Tho. Lamb	.	.	.	.37.	9.
John Scarborow	.	.	.	.25.	——— 98.2^t
Abra. How	.	.	.	.15.	}
Tho. Pedg	.	.	.	.20.	
Cap. Johnson	.	.	.	.15.	.4.
Mr Ellyot	.	.	.	.39.	——— .89.

the same day it was Agreed by all these partys that the land shalbe suruaid at a just Chardg of the whole and the partys Chossen to see the same done and to lay it ought into 10. parts are. Robert Williams. sergeant John Rudgls with the help of such as they shall desire and agre with all to doe it: it was agred by all the sayd Partys that they that are desired may chose any one man of these owurs in any of the 10 parts to pay for the whole chardge of the p'reters.

the sayd lots to hede vpon the line next dorchester and. soe to run vuto the line next Cambrdg. the first lott to begine next the last dyuisyon of Roxbury lots and the last next deadham it was allsoe agred by the sayd partys that if there should not be land anufe for etch man all accordin [* * *] there proporchons to bee equally amongst all accordinge to the number of partys,

[12.] Blank.

[13.] At a Countie Court holden at Boston 31 July 1666.
Roxbury presentment was called and it being alledged that the Treasurer of the Countie and other the Committee had let out ther Bridges; The Court enjoyned that it be done by the next Court on penalty of five Pounds.
A true Copie taken out of the Court book of Records thence drawn and examined.

Attest JOSEPH WEBB Cler:

At a Countie Court held at Boston 26th January 1668
The Countie Bridge at Muddy River being presented as defective the Court ordered that Deacon Wm Park and John White be a Committee to order the substantial erecting of a Bridge there and they are herby impowered to impress meet workmen for the carrying on end that worke and bringing the charge therof to the next Court who will order the charges therof to be satisfied by the Treasurer of the Countie &c: and fees:
A true Copie taken out of the Court Booke of Records thence drawn and examined

Attestr

JOSEPH WEBB Cler:

These are true Copies of what was transcribed by Joseph Webb Cler out of the Records, and entered in this Book by order of the select men

p JNº GORE Town Cler:

[14.] Blank.

[15.] A Record of an Agreement betwen Thomas Cheney and Giles Payson, Tobias Davis

This wrighting testifieth a mutuall agreement betwen Thomas Cheney and Deacon Giles Payson with the helpe and concurence of the select men and feoffese of the schoole of Roxbury concerning a high way leading throw the land of Giles Payson and so leadmg into the Land of the said Thomas Cheney at the Great lo[t]

The agreement and conclusion of the foresaid diferdence with a great dale of loue and condesendancy (is as followeth) the said Deacon Payson doth freely giue throw his land, where the dirty barrs are where formerly proprietys vse to goe in at one Rood broad next to Ralph Himenways fence begining th * one Rood wide one the Right hand of a Rock sone after you a come into the barrs and there being a small parcell of land one the right hand sone after you are in at the bares this land the said Cheney is to bye of the said Payson and to allow him after three poun[ds] one acer and to pay it in mony.

Furdermore the said Payson is to fence out one halfe of this hye * begining his part at the first entring in at the barrs and * * * euen to make and soficiently maintaine the same and the said Thomas Cheney is to make and maintaine the other halfe fence betwen the High way and the land of the said Paysons and to * * * the fence soficient and for ever to maintaine it so and for the f setlement of this way Ensigne Dauis doth also agree to gui * * throw his land for the runing vp this way to the land of the said Cheneys the one making one halfe of the fence and the other the other halfe of the fence and for euer to make soficient and for euer to maintaine the same to the faithfull performance of the foresaid premises we haue herevnto set our hands this 10 : 11 72

Wittnes herevnto   GILES PAYSON
WILLIAM PARK   THOMAS CHENEY
ISAAC JOHNSON   TOBIAS DAVIS
GRIFFIN CRAFTS.

Ensigne Davis Giles Payson and Thomas Cheney hath acknowledged this agreement to be thare Act and Deed 21: 6 1677 before me

J DUDLEY Assist

[16.]   Blank.

[17.]   We whose names are under written being chosen by Mʳ William Denison and Stephen Williams, both of Roxbury in New England, in the Countie of Suffolk, to setle the bounds of a certaine parcel of land lately in controversie between the aforesaid Denison and Williams which sᵈ land lies in the Town of Roxbury aforesaid, and is bounded on Braintry Road West South on the land of Richard Hall South, on the land of Samuel Payson decesed East and on the land of Deacon Samuel Williams North : and to put an end to all difference contests and quarrells about said land or the bounds of it, or anything that apertaines to it Do conclude, determine, setle and award all matters concerning the foresaid land and bounds of it as followeth : By Braintry road a heap of stones, from thence by a line to a Walnut-tree neer to an old stump on the brow of the hill, from thence to a Walnut tree in the Valley and so to a heap of stones with a stake in the midle of it, and so from thence to a wallnut tree and from thence to another wallnut tree and so straight to a gray oak, and from thence to the North side of the edge of a rock leading to a heap of stones, by the high-way leading to Dorchester Brooke ; which Land is bounded

on a high way layd out this same day by the select men of the
Town of Roxbury aforesaid which is two rods wide; to the South-
ward of said line now setled for the land of foresaid Williams,
The said way to begin by Dorchester brook way and runn close by
the line of said Stephen Williams as the line now runns up to the
Road leading from Roxbury to Braintry: And the aforesaid M^r
William Denison to have all the land on the South side of foresaid
way unto the land of Richard Hall, and is bounded on Braintry
Road West, and on the land of Samuel Payson east: Further we
agree and determine that the aforesaid Denison and Williams shall
equally divide the wood of the foresaid way between them: Further wee determine agree and conclude, that this our award shall
be a finall issue and everlasting end of all quarrels and controver-
sies, lawsutes claymes and demands about the said land or the
bounds of it, or any wood formerly cut of from it, by said Denison
or Williams, or any imployed by them, And also of all differences
about the above said premises between the beires executors or ad-
ministrators of the abovesaid Denison and Williams, upon the penalty of forfeting fifty pounds money which they bound themselves
by a Bond bearing date the Eleventh of May 1697 to stand to the
award of the abovsaid arbitrators to be levied on the person or
estates of them that shall refuse to sit down satisfied with this
award: Witness our hands this seventeenth day of May one thousand six hundred ninety and Seven, and the nineth yeare of his
Majesties reigne:

> TIMOTHY STEVENS
> SAMUEL RUGGLES
> EDWARD DORR
> SAMUEL SCARBROUGH
> BENJAMIN GAMBLIN
> JOSEPH WELD
> ISAAC MORRISS

We whose names are underwritten being the persons within mentioned that have committed the setling of the land and bounds to
be arbitrated, and the controversie to be decided between us unto
the within named Arbitrators do hereby testifie our consent to the
within written award: witness our hands this seventeenth of May
1697.

> WILLIAM DENISON
> STEPHEN WILLIAMS

Witness
> JOSIAH HOLLAND
> the mark of
> PRUDENCE $\mathcal{S}$' PAYSON

[18.] Blank.

[19.] Know all men by these presents That Ephraim Lyon of
Roxbury in the County Of Suffolk and Province of the Massachusets
Bay in New England yeoman, for and In consideration of Stephen
Avery of the Same town yeoman, his makeing up And Continuing
a good suffiscient and Lawfull fence for all time to come After the

date hereof, of Seventene Poles In Length from the great Country
Road Leading to Dedham near unto and Adjoyning the lands of
said Avery on the South-westerly side of the strip or Piece of
Land hereafter given and granted, and Maintaining the said suffis-
cient fence, and For this Consideration onley the said Ephraim
Lyon hath given, and granted, Disposed of, and doth hereby give
Grant Sell and Dispose to the said Stephen Avery his Heirs, and
Assigns, A Strip or pcice of Land lying in Roxbury aforesaid being
Butted and bounded as follows, Against The said road North-
westerly, and there Measureing fourteen feet and no more and on
The Land of said Lyon, Southwesterly and There Measureing
Seaventeen Rodds or Poles, This being the length and where the
fence Is to be made and maintained as Aforesaid and Coming to a
point in Shape of a wedge North-easterly on Land Of said Avery. —
  To Have and to Hold to the said Avery his heirs and Assigns
said Piece of Land forever on the Condition Above Free and Clear
from all troubles, Inconvenience, or Mollestation, whatever In tes-
timony whereof the said Ephraim Lyon hath hereto set his hand and
Seal this 24th of Aprill 1722 and in the Eighth year of King George.
His Reign.   Signed, Sealed, and Delivered,
  In Presence of Benjamin Smith, & Isaack Bacon and a seal
                                        Ephraim Lyon
Memorandum.
On the Same Day and Year Abovementioned, The said Stephen
Avery for and on his part Doth Covenant, promiss, and Agree with
the Said Ephraim Lyon his Heirs, Executors, &c: That he will
fully performe and Accomplish What he the said Avery his Heirs,
and Assigns, are to do by the Abovementioned Instrument.
In Witness whereof said Stephen Avery has Set to his hand and
seal the 24th of April 1722.
Signed Sealed and Delivered
In presence of us   Stephen Avery & a seal O
Benjamin Smith
Isaack Bacon

[20.]   Roxbury January 23, 1722/3
Memorañd.
Whereas John Stone is Presented By the Grand Jury of the County
of Suffolk for Incroaching on a Town Highway leading Through
the Pond plain in Roxbury as by The said Presentment appears
and upon An Agrement between the said Stone and Captain Edward Bridge who Owns the Land on the other Side of the way Opposite to Stone, and has ingaged to leave Out as much Land of the
other Side as Hath been taken in by Stone, so as to Bring the way
to itts Due wedth According to Record: Wee therefore the Select
men Of Roxbury are well satisfyed in this Agrement and being
well Contented that The said way should have its Wedth from The
said Stons Wall, The Land being as Sutable for a way. —
  Therefore Desire The Honourable Justices In Court that the said
Presentment may cease.   W^M Dudley
                                  J^N Bowles
                                  Edward Dorr
                                  Stephen Williams.
                                  John Mayo.

BOOK OF POSSESSIONS.

	The Page.	Present Pagination.
John Mays	49	70
John Stebbins	50	71
Mr. George Alcock	¹[51]	72
Edward Porter	[52]	73
Robert Prentice	[53]	74
John Totman Mr. Henry Dingham . . .	[54]	75
Edward Riggs	[55]	76
Abraham How	[56]	77
William Cheiny	[57]	78
Christopher Peak	[58]	79
John Griggs, Joseph Griggs	[59]	80
John Dane	[60]	81
Robert Gamblin	[61]	82
Philip Torey	[62]	83
Samuel Finch		
Isaac Heath	[63]	84
Isaac Johnsou	[64]	85
Griffen Crafts	[65]	86
William Healy	[66]	87
Nathaniel Stow	[66]	87
John Gorton	[67]	88
Daniel Aynsworth. Peter ²Gardner . .	[68]	89
The Heirs of John Graves. Mary Graves .	[69]	90
William Potter Richard Chamberlain . .	[70]	91
George Brand	[71]	92
Richard Sutton Nathaniell Wilson . .	[72]	93
Thomas Meekins Hugh Thomas . .	[73]	94
Joseph Wise John Mayo	[74]	95
x John Hanchet John Polly . . .	[75]	96
Tobias Davis Edmund Parker . . .	[76]	97
Edward Morris William Lyon . . .	[77]	98
John Peiropoynt	78	99
William Gary	[79]	100
Thomas ³Brewer Abraham Newel junr . .	[80]	101
Nathaniel Brewer	[81]	102
Peleg Heath	[82]	103
Samuell Williams	[83]	104
John Newel William Davis . . .	[84]	105
William Lynckhorne John Mayes junr .	[85]	106
Henry Bowen Thomas Bacon . . .	[86]	107
	[87]	108

[22.] Blank.

[23.] *1. Mr Thomas Dudley Esquire. his dwelling house
with a little brewhouse standing neere the brooke, allso two
orchyards with yards and barnes, and other out houses, with fiue

---

¹ The outer margin of the page is gone, but the deeds were evidently numbered con
secutively as here restored. — W. H. W.

² The record reads " Widow Gardner." — W. H. W.

³ The record reads " Thomas Baker." — W. H. W.

aceres of earrable land more or lesse on the backside thereof with a skirt of meadow adioyning to it being halfe an acere more or lesse. and about foure score and ten accres of errable and meadow ground neere muddy riuer. Isaac Morrill on the south Mr Thomas Weld on the southweast, and the riuer on the other side. and sixteene accres of upland and meadow more or lesse abutting west upon the lower calues pasture land, being sold conditionaly unto William Parkes. and in the second alotment of the last deuission one hundred twenty eight aceres and a halfe and twenty pole, it being the seauenteenth lott in the last diuission lying betweene Robert Burnope and William Denison —

[24.] *2. Mrs Dudley and the beires of Mr Samuell Hagborne, being the landes of her former husband the said Mr Samuell Hagborne, one dwelling house and barn, one orchyard, and eight accres of medow and tilladge on the south east side theireof, and the street west. and fifty and six aceres more or lesse being upland and marsh upon Smelt brooke and the marsh of John Burwell east, and upon the marsh late the land of John Stow northwest, and by a highway leading to grauilly poynt west, and is further bounded with three aceres of marsh ditched in by John Johnson, and with two aceres of marsh of Thomas Lambes on the east and south, and seauen aceres more or lesse of arrable land in the calfes pasture betweene Isaac Heath and William Parke, and the end there of upon the highway leading to Dorchester. and forty and fiue aceres more or lesse upon the land of John Johnson North, upon Francis Smith south, and betweene two highwayes; Allso in the second alottment of the last diuission the fourteenth lott. betweene Joshua Hewes and Abraham Howe, one hundred and eighteene aceres and a halfe and one hundred seuenty seauen aceres in the foure thousand accres.

[25.] *3. Mr John Eliot his dwelling house orchyard and barne the high streete being upon the west and south of it, and the houselott two accres and a halfe more or lesse, the training place being at the east end thereof. and a great lott being one and twenty accres, upon the great pond North, upon Phillip Elliot west upon Isaac Heath east and upon the highway south, and nineteene accres more or lesse upon Edward Bugby, and upon a wooddy swamp late John Stowes south, and so betweene two highwayes. and six accres of fresh meadow at the west end of the greate meadow and nine accres of salt marsh more or lesse lying betweene Isaack Heath, and William Denison. and in the second alottment of the last deuission being the twelfe lott lying betweene Isaack Heath and Joshua Hewes. fifty fiue aceres and a quarter. and in the thousand accres at Deddam thirty and nine accres. and in the Nookes next Dorchester bought of Phillip Meadowes being the tenth lott, lying betweene John Gorton and Mr Henry Dingham, thirteene aceres and Twenty pole. and seauen aceres of woodland more or lesse lately the land of Robert Pepper abutting uppon the land of Phillip Eliot and Jeames Astwood east, upon the highway to John Totmans house North, up [** Isaac Johnson south, and upon

[26.]   *4. Isaack Heath his dwelliug house. barne, orchyard and house lott three acc es more or lesse upon the highway leading to the meeting house east, and South. upon Joseph Weld North, and upon Jasper Raulins west. and foureteene accres of salt marsh more or lesse, upon the west of the marsh of william Parke, upon the east of the marsh of Mr John Eliot, upon the North of the channell leading towards Pine Iland, and upon the south of William Denison and his owne land being more six aceres of upland in the calnes pasture, abutting thereon upon the North, and the highway leading to Dorchester south, upon the land of the heirs of Samuell Hagborne west, upon the lands of William Denison east, Allso six aceres of salt marsh in grauelly poynt, and foure aceres of upland at stony riner upon the east, and upon the highway leading to the great pond west, and fower and twenty accres not far from Gamblins end, upon the south of a highway leading to the great lotts, upon the North of the land of the heires of George Alcock, and upon the west of the heirs of George Holmes. and sixteene accres at the great pond upon the North, upon the south of a highway, upon Mr. John Elliot west. and six accres more or lesse lately bought of Mr William Perkins lying in the calnes pasture, upon William Denison west, upon a lane to the salt marsh east upon Mr. John Elliot and William Denison North, and upon a lane leading to the house of Richard Goade south, and in the second alottment of the last deuission being the eleventh lott, lying betweene John Stow and Mr John Elliot ninety foure accres three quarters and thirty pole. and in the fower thousand aceres two hundred fifty and six accres. and three roodes of swamp-land lately the land of John Stow, lying on the east of Isaac Morrill, upon the west of land lately John Stannards, and upon the highway North. and foure accres more or lesse lately the land of Richard Pepper, lying in the upper calnespasture inclosed with the lands lately John Stows, William Parkes, Edward Pason, and Robert Williams, as it doth and may appeare by the markes and bounds thereof.

[27.]   *5. Phillip Eliot his house, Barne and home lott three accres more or lesse, upon stoney riner east, and so betweene the lands of Jeames Astwood and the heires of John Graues. and twelue accres more or lesse upon Stoney riner south, upon the highway leading to the great pond North, upon Edward Denison west, and upon Robert Seaner east, with a highway leading to it through the land of John Bowles. and thirty-three accres more or lesse, upon the great pond North upon Mr John Elliot east, upon a highway south, and upon the head of Thomas Ruggles heires west, and nine accres more or lesse, upon Daniell Ainsworth and John Ruggles senior towards the south, and upon William Curteis, and William Cheiney east, and upon the heires of William Web north, and upon Isaack Johnson west. and six accres of salt marsh in Grauelly poynt, upon Elder Isaack Heath and William Cheiney and three accres and a halfe in beare marsh, being the halfe of seauen aceres late Edward Porters, upon William Heath west, and William Curtis east. and in the second alotment, next William Curtis the foure and twentyeth lot, being the last lott there, ninety six accres three quarters and thirty pole, and in the foure thousand accres three hundred thirty and three accres.

[28.] *6. William Parke his dwelling house, and barne, together with yards, orchyards, and eight accres of errable land more or lesse adioyning unto the yards and orchyards, abutting upon William Cheineys orchard north upon the land of the heires of John Levens west, upon the land lately of John Stow, now of Edward Pason south, and upon the land lately John Woodies but now Edward Pasons south, upon the highway leading to Dorchester east, and upon the lands of Joshua Foote Edward Pason and Francis Smith northeast. and twenty fiue accres more or lesse of earrable land and meadow in the lower Calues pasture, the meadow being part of that which William Parke bought of Mr Thomas Dudley adioyning unto the land of the heires of Mr. Samuell Hagborne on the south and west, and Isaack Heath meadow on the south, and a creeke parting this meadow from Isaack Heaths meadow on the east, and a creeke parting this meadow from a parcell of meadow lately William Parkes but now Edward Pasons on the east side, and the meadow of the sayd Pason on the north and s › all along the land of the said Pason unto the highway leading to Dorchester, and Edward Pason is to make and maintaine for ever a sufficient fence against the land of the sayd Parkes through out betweene them. and nine accres of woodland more or lesse adioyning unto the house lott of John Gorton, and the land lately the land of John Turner North unto the highway leading from the dead swamp unto the towne east, and the land of John Burwell south, and the highway west. and ninety foure accres three quarters and thirty pole in the second alottment of the last deuision being the sixt lott lying betweene the land lately John Scarburroughs and Samuell Finch; and one hundred fourscore and one accres in the foure thousand accres, and thirteene aceres more or lesse in Springfeild, lately the land of Thomas Lamb, upon the highway to muddy riner south, upon stoney riuer north. and upon Captaine Prichard east, and upon the land lately of Joshua Hewes west. and one acere and a roode of meadow more or lesse upon the land of the beires of Thomas Pigg south, upon the highway to the tide mill east; and north east upon the land of Nickolas Clap. and nine aceres of upland and meadow more or lesse lately the land of Isaack Morrill, adioyning to the land of Captaine Hugh Prichard, east, west, and north, lying beyond the great meadowes, called by the name of Hallison, and ten accres of salt marsh more or lesse lately the land of John Johnson, and now by lease for certaine years to come in the occupation of the sayd Johnson.[1] and twenty five accres and a halfe lately the land of John Pieropoynt in the woods neare the great lotts lately the land of John Stow and sixteene accres of upland and salt marsh more or lesse, by the salt pan sold to Edward Pason conditionally. and the training place and all the land within the fence theirunto belonging being seauen accres more or lesse and allso one accre more without the

---

[1] halfe the twenty five accres is Edward Pasons

fence lately the land of Mr Thomas Weld. And halfe of sixteene accres of woodland lately the land of Richard Sutton, but bought by him of John Johnson.

Note on a slip of paper — part of the same and of the orchyard scrupled by Deacon Parke

[29.] *7. Isaack Morrill his two houses, two forges, one barne with out housing and two orchyards, and a swamp at the east end of it together with yards belonging to the houses upon the h'ghway west, the land running northward upon a straite line untill it cometh to range even with north side of the shop of Tobias Dauis upon the highway and the orchyard and land of Tobias Dauis North. and foure accres more or lesse upon pine hill south, and a swamp of the heires of John Stowe east. and six and twenty accres called by the name of foxeholes, upon Abraham Newell and Edward Bugby south and upon a Rocky highway west, upon pine-hill north and upon a highway leading to the great lotts east. and fifteene accres more or lesse called smithfeild, upon Mr Thomas Dudley his marsh towards the east, upon the heires of George Alcocke South. upon a way leading to the marsh of Mr Thomas Dudley about twenty foote broad west and north, and one accre and a halfe in the lower calues pasture more or lesse being part upland and part marsh called small gaines upon the land of Ralph Hemmingway South. upon the way leading into the marsh North, upon Francis Smith west, and upon the heires of John Levins east. and nine accres of salt marsh more or lesse upon Thomas Lamb Southwest, upon Daniell Bruer and Thomas Baker northeast, upon a creek called smelt-brooke Southeast, and a highway north-west. and in the second alottment of the last deuission betweene Mr Thomas Weld and John Scarbrow being their the fourth lott lyeth one hundred and thirteene accres one quarter and ten pole and two hundred and foure accres in the foure thousand accres and six accres more or lesse upon pine hill bought of William Denison, upon the land of Isaack Morrill South. upon the beires of John Stannard eastward, upon John Burwell North. upon Joseph Wise westward; and foure accres more or lesse upon the great hill bought of Griffen Craft upon the land of Griffen Craft west, upon John Ruggles senior south, upon William Lion North, and upon the pasture ground east. and fiue accres of the fresh meadow more or lesse bought of John Pieropoynt lying in the great meades upon John Stow west, and upon a ditch between Phillip Toory and It, east: with two rodds of upland at each end. And two accres of fresh meadow more or lesse in the great meade, lately the land of John Scarbrow, abuting upon the land of Isaack Morrill on the west, upon the common east and north, and upon the meadow of Phillip Torry south. And two accres and a halfe of land more or lesse lately the land of Robert Williams lying upon blackneck upon the north of the way to Dorchester tidemill betweene the lands of the beires of Thomas Pigg and the land of the beires of George Holmes.

[30.] *8. John Johnson his house barne, and hous lott on the back side of his orchyard and buildings lying together with liberty to inclose the swamp and brooke before the same, not anoying any highway, conteining in all eight accres more or lesse, upon Thomas Lambs heires towards the west, and upon william Denison towards the south. and three accres of marsh betweene the home lott and the marsh of the heirs of Samuell Hagborne, upon Thomas Lamb towards the north, and west, and william Denison east. and twenty aceres more or lesse of mowing ground upon the marsh of Mʳ Thomas Weld, and the land of Thomas Lamb on the east and so compassed with muddy riuer and stoney riner, and ten accres of woodland more or lesse lying betweene the great lotts and the lands of the beires of Samuell Hagborne, and so turning up betweene the lott lately bought of George Bowers and a way leading to Rocky swamp. and foure accres more or lesse lying betweene the way leading to Rocky swamp Northweast and upon the schoole land upon the south and east; and in the last deuission, in the first and third alottments of that deuission being the fourth lott their one hundred ten[1] accres and one quarter. and one and fifty accres and halfe bought of Edward Porter and John Pettit lying in the thousand accres at Deddam. and six accres more or lesse bought of Jeames Morgan, upon stoney riuer west. and upon a highway leading to the great pond east. and sixteene accres and a halfe more or lesse bought of Richard Goad lying at rocky swamp, abutting upon the land of Edward Pason west, and upon the land of Edward Bridges east. and an accre and a quarter more or lesse, lately the land of Thomas Lamb, upon the home lott and Meadow of John Johnson North-west. upon the highway leading to the watermill southeast. and upon the home lott of the beires of Thomas Lamb North. and three aceres of woodland more or lesse lately the land of John Stebbins, lying at Rocky swamp. And fower aceres of fresh meadow more or lesse lately bought of John Parepoynt lying in the great meades betweene the lands of Isaack Morrill and William Cheiney. And thirteene aceres and twenty rod of land wood and pasture bought of Thomas Gardner in the nookes next Dorchester, betweene the lands of Henry Farnham and the lands of the heires of Thomas Stannard.

[31.] *9. Mʳ John Gore, his house barne and home lott foure accres more or lesse, upon stoney riuer east, upon Griffen Craft South, upon a highway leading to the landing place or tide mill west; and upon' the land sometimes Edward Whites North. and upon the hill on the other side of the way called the night pasture eight aceres more or lesse betweene Mʳ Hugh Prichard and Griffen Craft, and so runneth westward unto two or three marked trees which are seauen or eight rodds eastward of John Roberts his fence. and tenn accres running from the highway that leades downe to muddy riuer bridge ouer the hill downe to Arther Garyes lott, lying betweene John Roberts and Robert Prentice. and upon the other side of muddy riner highway : twenty accres more or lesse of upland and marsh, upon muddy riner northwest, and upon the

---

[1] the nearest halfe of this hundred and ten accres is sold by John Johnson to Griffin Craft.

beires of Joseph Weld north. and foure and twenty accres more
or lesse neare the great pond upon Quenetticot highway northward, upon John Booles, and Robert Scaner east, upon Isaack
Morrills land called Squirrills delight north, and upon Boston
bounds west. and a fresh meade conteining eleuen accres more or
lesse, with six accres of upland more or lesse (as it was formerly
fenced in) round about it, which upland was perchased of the towne
of Roxbury for fifty shillings : upon Joshua Hewes his meade on the
north, upon the farme of the heires of Joseph Weld south east, a
hill lying betweene them and in the first and third alottment of
the last deuission lying betwene John Bowles, and Thomas Gardner is in all sixty and seauen accres one quarter and twenty poles.
and the lott of Edward White, by the lott of John Gore on the
south, sold to widdow Morrick, and by her to John Gore, with a
wood lott of tenn accres and a halfe, lying betweene the lotts of
Arthur Gary and Lewis Joanes in the Nookes ; and a lott sometimes Joseph Welds, and by him giuen to his daughter Hanna,
and by her husband sold to John Gore, lying by muddy riuer on
the east, and hauing the land of Mr Thomas weld on the North,
and John Gores owne land on the south, and three lotts lying by
the forementioned lott of John Gores at the fresh meadow, and
reaching to Dorchester bounds, perchased of Thomas Gardner
whose lott is fourteene accres ; of Edward Porter, whose lott is
twenty nine accres, lying in the first and third deuission ; and of
Richard Woody seni : whose lott is fifteene accres more or lesse.
And in the fower thousand accres one hundred eighty and eight,
accres.

[**32.**] *10. Mr Anthony Stodderd his house barne and out
housing with his Garden and orchard with two aceres of land more
or lesse upon the west theirof, and upon Isaack Heath South, and
upon William Denison north. and fifteene accres of meadow and
upland upon Mr Thomas Weld west, upon the highway leading
into the marshes east, upon Thomas Lamb South, and upon the
marshes north.

[**33.**] *11. Mr Thomas Weld his dwelling house, barne, and
other out houses with yards gardens orchyards and two aceres of
land more or lesse on the east side theirof, and upon the high streete
west, and eight accres more or lesse of upland and marsh enclosed.
hauing Smelt brooke on the north, and the highway to Boston
towards the south ; and fifteene accres of meadow and marsh, in
the neck enclosed lying betweene the land of John Johnson and
Mr Anthony Stodder, hauing the highway leading into John
Johnsons meadow upon the southwest of it, and fourteene accres
of upland and marsh more or lesse, upon the highway to muddy
riuer upon the south, and Stoney riner North, upon Captaine Hugh
Prichard west and upon Mr Joshua Foote east. and ten accres of
vpland and marsh more or lesse upon Muddy riuer west, upon a
highway leading into Mr Thomas Dudleys land east upon M^r
Dudley North and upon the land of Mr John Gore South ; and in
the second alottment of the last diuission being the third lott lying

betweene, John Roberts and Isaack Morrill, one hundred twenty two acres and a halfe. and in the foure thousand accres, three hundred thirty three accres, and twenty fiue accres more or lesse, bought of Henry Archer, upon the Assignes of John Stow north east, and upon Christopher Peake north upon Abraham How southeast, upon the line of the first deuission southwest and west, and upon the lotts of Robert Gamblin, Daniell Brewer and Thomas Bell northwest.

[34.] *12. Captaine Hugh Prichard, his house, barne with the outhouses, and fifty accres of marsh and upland butting upon the east side of a highway leading from Roxsbury to Muddy riuer, and so round by Stoney riuer to the landing place; and eight accres of upland upon the hill lying betweene Samuel Finch and Mr John Gore, conteining about eleven or twelue pole in breadth. and six aceres more or lesse bought of M^r william Perkins upon the meeting house hill and a highway betweene South, upon Samuell Finch and the heires of Thomas Ruggles west, and upon stoney riuer north, and the heires of Thomas Lamb east. and seauen accres of upland and marsh more or lesse, bought of Mr William Perkins, upon Stoney riuer north, upon the way leading to Muddy river south upon Edward Denison west upon Mr Thomas Weld east. and ten accres and a halfe of upland and meadow bought of John Johnson, upon a highway leading from Stoney riuer to the landing place east, and upon the highway to muddy riuer south, upon William Parke west, and upon stoney riner north. and in the last divission lying in the first and third Alottments of the said diusion being the thirtyeth lott, lying betweene Robert Seauer, and Robert Gamblin is in the two parts, one hundred and threescore accres one quarter and twenty rodds.[1] and twelue accres within the thousand aceres next Deddam. And ten accres of woodland more or lesse butting upon the land latly william Lewisses, lying South of the great hill, and east of the great lot lately of William Lewis.

[35.] *13. Mr Thomas Bell his house and barne, and lott, foure and twenty accres more or lesse butting upon the highway north, and west, upon Daniell Brewer south, and east upon the swamp of Robert Gamblin; and fourteene accres more or lesse, to the North of Daniell Brewers meadow, and to the west of his upland, and to the south of Christopher Peake, and to the east of Joshua Hewes. and one accre more or lesse of meadow one the southeast of the riner, and upon Christopher Peake northwest. and four accres more or lesse, upon the south of stoney riuer, and northwest upon the common, and upon Edward Bridg east. and two aceres and a quarter of salt marsh, upon Richard Pepper in Grauelly poynt north, upon Edward Porter and Christopher Peake east, and upon John Stowes asignes and Jeames Astwood south. and one house and foure accres of land more or lesse, compassed with the highway, Christopher Peake his house lott, and stoney riuer, and

---

[1] [fower accres of the 160 accres sold to Isaack Morrill.]

Robert Gamblin. and in the diuision of the Nookes, being the
twentieth lott betweene Widdow Gardner and Ioseph Wise being
with the sayd house bought of John Mathew eighteene aceres one
quarter and twenty rodds. and in the first and third parts of the
last deuision being the foure and twentyeth lott lying betweene
Robert Williams, and the heires of George Holmes is fourescore
and eleuen aceres and three quarters and twenty rodds. and in the
foure thousand aceres one hundred three score and six accres and
six aceres more or less bought of Hugh Thomas upon a highway
leading to Rocky swamp east, upon Daniell Bruer southwest, upon
his owne land northwest, and upon Edward Bridg north east. and
a fourth part of sixteene accres of salt marsh some times the land
of Mr Nickolas Parker, below the salt p[an] butting upon a creeke
parting Boston and Roxsbury north, upon Edward Pason south,
upon Abraham Newell east upon the highway from the towne to
the landing place at the salt pan west.

[36.] *14. Mr Daniell Weld A dwelling house, with a
barne, yard, orchyard and garden, with a parcell of land conteining three quarters of an accre more or lesse, adioyning to the
sayd house and barne, upon the high streete west, upon the
training place east, upon Richard Woody Junior south, and upon
Mr Thomas Weld North, all of the said parcells of housing and
land being bought of Mr Richard Peacocke.

[37.] *15. Edward Denison fiue accres of land more or
lesse, butting upon Philip Eliott east, upon stoney riuer south
upon Jeames Astwood west, and upon the highway to the great
pond North. and in the first and third alottments of the last deuision the twentyeth lott lying betweene Jeames Astwood and
Isaack Johnson is fifty fiue accres and one quarter, and giuen to
him by his Father, and perchased by him of his brother George
Denison A dwelling house Bakehouse, Barne and other buildings
with the orchard in the swamp before the house east : and an
orchard and home lott on the west side thereof being three accres
more or lesse, butting upon John Johnson north, upon Joseph
Weld south, and upon Thomas Lambs beires west. And three
accres more or lesse of marsh and upland, upon Mr Thomas Weld
east, upon John Johnson and a way that leades to it west, (the
way lying by or through John Johnsons yard either for cart foote
or drift) upon the highway to Boston south, and upon smelt
brooke north. and twenty fower accres of land more or less, upon
the great pond southeast upon Boston bounds northwest, upon Mr
Gore North, upon William Curtiss South. And twelue accres
more or lesse of Marsh and upland, upon the highway to Muddy
riner South upon Stoney riuer north, upon the beires of Mr
George Alcocke west, and upon Mr Hugh Prichard east. and three
accres of upland and marsh more or lesse, upon the heires of Samuell Shearman east, upon Mr Thomas Weld and the highway to
Boston west, and south, and upon smelt brooke north. And
seauen accres more or lesse upon Thomas Lambs beires north,
upon the land sometimes John Johnsons south, upon a highway

west, and east being neare dead swamp. And nine aceres more
or lesse in the calues pasture upon Elder Heath south, and north,
upon Mr John Eliot east, and upon a highway leading into the
marshes west. And fiue accres more or lesse of marsh upon John
Levens heires west upon Joshua Foote east, upon the highway
leading into the Marshes north, and upon black-neck south. And
twelue aceres of marsh more or lesse, upon Mr John Eliot North
upon the land lately Thomas Robisons south, upon Isaack Heath
west, and upon the land belonging to pine Ilaud east. And a
peece of marsh and upland called pine Ilaud being fower accres
more or lesse upon the riuer that leades to Dorchester tide-mill
South east, north and west compassed with a creeke, and upon
the marsh lately Thomas Robisons south. And six aceres of land
more or lesse bought of Richard Pepper upon the great-pond south
and west, and upon the highway north. And in the second part of
the last diuision the eighteenth lott lying betweene Mr Thomas
Dudley and Edward Bridg threescore accres and one quarter.
And the fifteenth lott bought of Nathaniell Manuring lying in the
Nookes betweene John Staunards heires and George Denison
seauen accres and three-quarters.

[38.] *16. John Weld (his brother Edmund being to haue
his part of it according to the last will of ther father Captaine
Joseph Weld) A dwelling house, barne, yaids and orchyard upon
the land of Robert Seauer south, north and west upon the highway
to bare marsh and upon the brooke east; and foure score accres of
upland and meadow, upon stoney riuer south, upon the way aforesayd North upon Joshua Hewes and a highway east. and three
accres bought of John Graue more or lesse loyning to the oxe pasture upon the way leading to Deddam north, upon a way to the
land of Phillip Elliott east, and upon John Polleys bought, of
Joshua Hewes west. and six accres more or lesse of salt marsh,
lately the land of Samuel Shearman, upon Mr Thomas Weld and
the land of the heires of Mr Joseph Weld south, upon John
Watson north upon the riuer west, and upon a highway leading
into the marshes east. and in the last diuision the second part
their of being the two and twentyeth lott lying betweene John
Burwell and William Curtiss one hundred twenty eight accres and
a halfe, and twenty rodds. and fifty accres more or lesse (which is
wholy John Welds) bought of William Healy being in the first
alottment of the last deuision lying betweene the beires of John
Levens and Robert Williams, being the foureteene, fiueteenth, and
sixteenth lotts besides fiue aceres of it which was bought by the
said William Healy of Samuell Finch. And twenty fower aceres
of land bought of Thomas Robbison of Boston lying in the first
and third alottments of the last deuision in Roxbury, being the
seauenteenth lott there.

[39.] *17. Robert Seaver his house and lot one acere more or
lesse Butting upon John Bowels west, upon the highway and the
riuer east, north, and south, and two accres and a halfe more or
lesse, upon Phillip Elliot South and east, upon John Bowles north,

and ten aceres more or lesse upon John Bowles north, and upon a high way south, and upon muddy riner northwest. and foure accres and a halfe more or lesse upon muddy riner northwest, upon a highway east, upon William Lewis south, and upon William Heaths heares north. and foure and twenty accres and a halfe lying in the first and third alottments of the last deuision, being the nine and twentyeth lott betweene Griffen Craft and Mr Hugh Prichard. and fourteene accres with in the thousand accres at Deddam. and foure accres of salt marsh more or lesse lying in the Iland lately Captaine Hugh Prichards, abutting upon the land of William Curtiss east upon Daniell Ainsworth and George Brand north and upon the riuer south and west. and three accres more or lesse abutting upon the land of Robert Pepper North, upon William Curtisse east, upon John Ruggles Junior south, and upon the highway towards the great pond Northwest.

[40.] *18. Edward pason, his house and barne, and two aceres and three roodes of land more or lesse butting upon William Parke south, upon Joshua Hewes eastward, upon Francis Smith west upon the towne clay pitts north: and sixteene accres[1] more or lesse upon Georg Holmes his heires east, and upon Gamblinns end south, and west. and fiue roodes bought of Robert Williams, upon John Stow his assignes and Richard Peppers land lately, west. upon Giles Pason northeast. and the second lott in the third alottment in the last diuision betweene Edward Bugby and John Watson fiueteene accres and a quarter and ten rods. and fifteene aceres more or lesse of salt marsh and upland, lately bought of William Parkes conditionally, and seauen accres of upland, and about foure accres of upland and salt marsh, part of the meadow lately bought by William Parke of Mr Thomas Dudley ; and about scauen accres of swamp and upland, and about foure aceres of land, lately the land of Thomas Gardner, with a barne, and orchyard, all this land was lately the land of William Parke, adioyning alltogether, bounded on the ditch from the place called the salt pan on the north, and a creeke on the east, and a creeke betweene the meadow of William Parkes lately the meadow of Mr Thomas Dudley southwest, and a ditch made by the sayd Pason south, and a fence running up unto the highway leading to Dorchester from the towne, and a highway leading all along unto the salt pan west and North. and three aceres more or lesse of salt marsh and upland, lately the land of William Parkes, adioyning upon the land of the beires of George Alcocke west, and a creeke betweene Boston and Roxbury on the north, and the landing place northeast, and the highway leading from the towne to the salt pan on the south. and tenn accres more or lesse lately the land of John Stow in the upper calues pasture, adioyning unto the land lately John Levens northeast, and the land of William Parke north east. upon Isaack Heath, southeast, and the highway leading to dead swamp from the towne west. and ten accres more or lesse lying in the great lotts, lately the land of John Johnson, abutting upon the land of John Johnson

---

[1] fower accres of this sixteene more or lesse is sold to Edward Bridg.

north east, upon Daniell Bruer south west, upon the land lately John Stannards south east. and foure accres lately the land of Thomas Robison more or lesse. lying by the eight acere lotts, the land lately John Levens south, upon John Stebbin west, and upon Giles Pason east.

[41.] *19. The beires of Thomas Lamb, his dwelling house. barne, and house lot with other grounds as upland and marsh lying together, (through which lyeth a cart way reserued for the use of the towne for euer) eighteene aceres and three roodes more or lesse upon the land of Mr Hugh Prichard and the meeting house hill north west, upon the home lotts of Isaack Heath, Mr Anthoney Stodder. and John Johnson east, and with Stoney riner on the north, and so along their unto the land of Mr Thomas Weld, Mr Anthoncy Stodder and the heires of Samuell Hagborne on the northeast. and nineteene accres and three roodes more or lesse, upon the south east of the dead swamp, the other end upon a highway leading to the fresh meadow upon Robert Williams east, and upon William Denison west. and nine accres of salt marsh upon Boston bounds east, upon the heires of Samuell Hagborne South, upon Isaack Morrill north, and upon a highway west. and in the first and third part of the last diuision being the twenty sixt lott betweene George Holmes his heires, and Daniell Brewer in both the parts is threescore and ten accres, one quarter and thirty pole, and in the thousand accres next Deddam, thirty and seauen accres.

[42.] *20. The heires of John Leuens, A house, barne, and house lott seauen accres more or lesse; upon William Cheincy, William Parke and land lately Martin Stebbinns north, and east, — upon John Stowes asignes southwest, and a way leading into diuers lotts west. and foureteene accres heading upon the great lotts, upon the beires of Thomas Pigg east, upon John Stow his asignes west, and so betweene the fence of the great lotts and a swamp being the land of Abraham How. and one accre of salt marsh in black neck, between Isaack Morrill and William Denison. and a fresh marsh without the hogg yard on the left hand lying in the last diuision lott of Isaack Morrill. and in the first and third alottments of the last diuision, being the thirteenth lott betweene Giles Pason and lately the lott of William Web, foure and twenty accres and a halfe; and in the thousand aceres neare Deddam eleven accres. and an accre and three roodes of land more or lesse, lying east upon the land lately John Stows and west upon the land of William Parke, upon his owne land south and upon the land lately John Stows North.

[43.] *21. Mr Joshua Foote, his house, barne, with out houses, with garden yards and house lot at the east side their of foure accres more or lesse, butting upon Mr Thomas Weld east and south, and upon the heires of Samuel Hagborne North. and twelue accres more or lesse inclosed, upon the highway to muddy riner south, and upon stoney riuer north, upon William parke east, and Mr Thomas Weld west. and fifteene accres more or lesse, upon

Francis Smith east, upon Abraham Newell west, and both ends betwixt two highwayes. and three accres more or lesse in the upper calues pasture, upon the highway northward, upon William Parke east and south, and upon Edward Pason west; and fifteene accres of salt marsh upon Thomas Robbisons land (lately) north, and a creeke compassing it on the east and south; and fourcteene accres upon the north of the way that leadeth to the fresh meadowes, upon Abraham How and Thomas Bell south, the end upon Christopher Peake east, and upon Daniell Brewer west. and foure accres of fresh meadow more or lesse adioyning to the meadow of Richard Goad. and fiue accres of salt marsh, upon the end of the twelue accres abouesaid, compassed with the creeke bought of Jeames Morgan and Richard Pepper; and foure accres more or less within Boston gate. and in the thousand accres neare Deddam twelue acercs. and in the second alotments in the last diuison the foure-teenth lott, betweene Mr John Eliot and Samuell Hagborne, one hundred and eighteene accres. and in the foure thousand accres two hundred nynty and fower accres.

[44.] *22.   John Perry his heires, their house and lott two accres more or lesse, butting upon the highway west, upon William Heath east upon John Graues his heires South. and upon a lane leading to William Heath his house north. and six accres more or lesse lying by the way to Muddy riner south and east, and upon Jona'han Graues west, and upon william Heath north. and fower accres more or lesse, upon the highway leading towards the great pond south, and upon a highway leading to muddy riner north, and upon Arthur Gary east. and upon William Heath west. and fiue accres of salt marsh and upland, upon muddy riner west, and betweene the lands of the heires of William Heath south and north. and in the diuision of the Nookes next Boston the ninth lott lying betweene the heires of Thomas Grigs and John Totman eighteene accres one quarter and twenty rodds. and in the thousand accres neare to Deddam one and twenty accres.

[45.] *23.   Abraham Newell his house, barne, and lott, nine accres and a halfe more or lesse abutting upon Edward Porter west. and south, upon Edward Bugby east. and upon Isaack Morrill north. and ten accres upon Richard Peppers asignes north and upon Mr Joshua Foote south, and so betweene two highwayes east and west. and fourcteene accres one end their of upon the great pond, and so betweene John Burwell and a highway to Quenetticot;[1] and three accres at beare marsh betweene Isaack Johnson west, and John Ruggles east, and stoney riuer south. and in the first and third alottment in the last diuision being the eleventh lott lying betweene Ralph Hemmingway and Giles Pason forty-two accres three quarters and twenty rodd and in the thousand accres at Deddam twenty and two accres. and two accres of salt marsh more or lesse lying below the salt pan, sometimes the land of

---

[1] the three accres, is to be three accres more or lesse as it is now bounded and staked out.

Nickolas Parker ; and six accres of salt marsh more or lesse, lately
the land of Edward Pason, being halfe the marsh giuen to Edward
Pason by the towne, lying next to the creeke that leads to pine
Ilaud, and compassed with creekes, all but a ditch made betweene
the former meadow and this meadow, and twenty six aceres of
woodland and broken up more or lesse lately the land of Richard
Woody senior, and Richard Woddy Junior, adioyning south of
Edward Porter, Mr John Alcocke west, John Watsons land north
and a highway (leading from Abraham Newells house to the towne)
east. and six aceres of land lately the land of Edward Porter, adioyning upon the land of the said Porter westward and upon a
highway leading to the towne great lotts eastward.

[46.] *24. Daniell Bruer his house and orchyard and yard
about it etc.
and six accres of swamp upon the lotts of Edward Bridg and
Thomas Bell north, and south and upon the highway east. and six
accres upon the highway west, upon Thomas Bell north, and upon
Robert Gamblin south. and sixteene accres more or lesse upon
Robert Gamblin southwest, and upon Thomas Bell northwest. and
one accre of fresh meadow more or lesse upon Thomas Bell southeast, and upon William Curteis Northwest. and three accres of salt
marsh more or lesse, lying upon the creeke North east, and upon
Isaac Morrill southwest. and in the first and third alottments in the
last diuision being the seauen and twentieth lott, lying betweene
the heires of Thomas Lamb and Griffen Craft, fifty-three accres and
a halfe and ten rodds.' and six accres of salt marsh more or lesse
lying at Grauelly poynt, bounded upon Elder Isaack Heath, Isaack
Morrill and William Cheiney Northward, and south and southwest
and upon the land of John Peiropoynt east. and an acere of upland
and meadow more or lesse, bounded upon John Ruggles Junior
east, upon John Weld west, upon stoney Riuer southeast and upon ✗
John Polly Northwest. and seauen accres of land lately bought of
John Stannard butting upon the schoole land east, upon John
Johnson south, upon Edward Pason and Thomas Waterman North
and upon the highway to rocky swamp west.

[47.] *25. Francis Smith his house buildings and lott,
three accres and a halfe more or lesse, butting upon Edward Pason
and the Calfe pasture east, upon William Parke west and upon
the highway north. and one accre and a halfe in the calfe pasture
upon Isaack Morrill east, and upon the heires of George Holmes
west. and a wood lott of ten accres more or lesse upon the heires
of Samuell Hagborne south, and upon Joshua Foote north. and in
the first and third alottments in the last diuision lying betweene
the land lately Thomas Robinsons and Jeames Asıwood being the
eighteenth lott theirin is one and twenty accres, one quarter, and
thirty rodd and in the thousand accres neare Deddam one and
twenty aceres.

[48.] *26. John Bowles ten accres of land more or lesse
upon a highway south, and east, upon Robert Seaner North, and

upon Mr John Gore west. and three accres of salt marsh more or lesse upon Mr Thomas Bell west, and north, and upon a creeke south, and in the first and third allotments, in the last diuision being the three and thirtieth lott, lying betweene the lott lately of Mr William Firkins and Mr John Gore, is three and thirty accres and a halfe and thirty rodd and in the thousand accres neere Deddam fifteen accres. and seauen aceres of woodland lately the land of William Curtis lying neare to the house of Daniell Ainsworth abutting upon the land of Mr John Elliot South, upon Robert Peper North, upon John Peiropoynt east, and upon William Curtis west.

[**49.**] *27. George Holmes his beires, their dwelling house barne and lott, fiue accres more or lesse. Butting on the way at Dorchester brooke South, and upon the beires of Thomas Pigg west. and two aceres of salt marsh more or lesse adioyning to it west and south, and to Robert Williams east. and three accres more or lesse in the neck upon Nickolas Clap east upon Nickolas Butler west. and eight accres more or lesse upon the beires of Mr William Firkins South, upon the heires of Thomas Pigge west, and upon Robert Williams east. and twelve aceres more or lesse upon Elder Isaack Heath east, upon Gamblins end west and south, and three accres in the Necke bought of Richard Goad, upon Nickolas Clap west, and upon Ralph Hemmingway east. and in the first and third alotments in the last diuision being the five and twentyeth lott lying betweene Thomas Bell and the beires of Thomas Lamb fifty-six accres and a halfe and fiue and twenty rodds, and in the foure thousand accres one hundred sixty and two accres.

[**50.**] *28. Mr Jeames Astwood his house barne and lott foure acres more or lesse upon Phillip Elliot north, upon Isaack Johnson south upon the highway east, and upon the heires of John Graues west. and three accres and a halfe upon Edward Denison South, upon George Brand North, upon Stoney Riner west and upon a highway east. and ten accres more or lesse upon the great pond east, upon a highway west, upon John Watson south, and upon George Brand north. and in the first and third alotments in the last deuision being the nineteenth lott lying betweene Francis Smith and Edward Denison is foure and twenty accres and a halfe. and three accres and a halfe more or lesse upon the great hill beyond, the pond, abutting upon the pond east, upon John Ruggles Junior north, and west, and upon Edward Bugby south.[1] and ten accres of land more or lesse bought of william Cheiney, abutting upon Daniell Ainsworth east, upon the highway North, upon Mr John Elliot west, and upon Phillip Elliot south. This housing and land was sold by William Parkes to John Hanchet who was chosen by the Court to be Administrator of the estate; and Authorized their unto by the Generall Court

[**51.**] *29. John Ruggles senior his house out houses and lott three aceres more or lesse butting upon Griffen Crafts north.

---

[1] This tenn accres is sold by John Hanchet to Daniell Ainsworth.

and upon stoney riuer east. and six accres more or lesse upon the
hill, butting upon the heires of Thomas Griggs south, upon Griffen
Crafts north, and upon Samuell Finch west. and six aceres in the
night pasture, upon Nathaniell Willson south, upon Griffen Crafts
North, and upon a highway east. and three accres more or lesse at
Beale marsh with two rodds of upland at the end of it, upon
stoney riner south, upon Robert Gamblin east; and one accre of
salt marsh more or lesse, upon the heires of Samuell Shearman,
and a creeke betweene John Watson and it, North and east. and
in the first and third alotments in the last deuission being part of
it out of the lot of Samuell Chapin which with his lyeth betweene
John Graues his heires and Thomas Griggs the other parte and the
lott of the beires of John Graue being the seauenth and eight lott
theirin is twenty and eight accres more or lesse. and in the thousand
accres at Deddam nine accres and a halfe. and fiue accres of earrable land more or lesse bought of Samuell Finch bounded by the
heires of John Graue towards the south, upon Robert Prentice,
east, upon William Healy west, and upon the land of the said
John Ruggles North. and one acere and a halfe of meddow being
the halfe part of three accres more or lesse, upon the land of
Edward Porter south, and south east, and upon the land of William
Lewis north and northwest, and one end upon the great riuer, and
twelue accres and a quarter bought of Edward Culuer lying in the
first deuission late the lot of Ralph Hemingway being the tenth lot
in that deuission lying betweene the lot of the heires of John Graues
and Abraham Newells lott, the one end of it butting upon the
meadow of Mr John Gore.

[52.] *30. John Ruggles Junior the sonn of Thomas Ruggles deceased; his dwelling house with outhousing, orchyard and
backside being about three accres more or lesse, upon Samuell
Ruggles west, upon John Pieropoynt south, upon the high way
North, and upon William Lion east. and two aceres of salt marsh
in the Ilaud lately Captaine Hugh Prichards, abutting upon the
riner east and south upon William Curtiss west, and upon Edward
Bridg, Isaac Johnson and John Mayes north. and fifteene accres
more or lesse lately the land of William Curtiss called hurtlebury
hill, abutting upon John Totman west, upon William Curtiss south,
upon William Curtis and Robert Scauer east, and upon a highway
north. and in the thousand accres neare Deddam eight accres, and
two[1] accres of meadow and upland more or lesse lately the land of
William Curtiss abutting upon Stoney riuer south, and upon Daniell
Ainsworth north. and one[1] acere lately the land of Daniell Ainsworth, abutting upon Daniel Ainswoorth east with a highway leading to it betweene the brooke and the fence of John Weld and
betweene Edmund Parker and Isaack Johnson. and halfe of foure
accres more or lesse, lately the land of Philip Elliot being part
meadow and part upland abutting upon stoney riner south and
upon John Weld north, and two[2] accres and three[2] Roodes lately

---

[1] The two accres and the one accre is sold to Daniel Ainsworth.
[2] This land is now Thomas Bacons.

the land of Arthur Gary abutting upon Arthur Gary east, upon William Lion south, and upon Robert Pepper North. And eighteene acres of land more or lesse bought of Jeames Morgan, being the twelfe lott. lying in the third deuission betweene the beires of John Leuins and Abraham Newell se:

[**53.**] *31. Samuell Ruggles, two accres and three roodes more or lesse upon the pond hill lately the land of William Lion, abutting upon the land of William Gary east and north, and upon Abraham Newell Junior west. and upon the land lately Lorrence Whittamoores south. and a quarter of the orchyard adioyning to the house of William Lion, abutting upon the sayd house and the orchyard of William Lion north, and east, and upon Samuell Finch west, and upon the highway south; and an accre of errable land giuen to him by his father Thomas Ruggles deceased being in the home lott, abutting upon John Ruggles east, upon John Pieropoynt west and south, and upon the highway north. and three aceres and three roodes of land giuen to him by his sayd Father, lying beyond the great pond, abutting upon the land of Arthur Gary north, upon the beires of John Perry south, and upon William Lion west and east, and in the thousand accres neare Deddam twelue accres giuen to him by his father; and the halfe of foure accres more or lesse, of upland and meadow lately the land of Phillip El-liot abutting upon stoney riuer south, and upon the land of John Weld north.

Widdow Ruggles lately the wife of Thomas Ruggles deceased, foure accres of land more or lesse lying neare muddy Riuer giuen unto her by her sayd husband abutting upon Robert Prentiss east, upon the land of the heires of Thomas Griggs south and west, and upon the highway north. and an accre and a halfe lying in the home lott giuen her by her afooresayd husband, abutting upon the land of John Dane east, upon John Pieropoynt south, and upon her sonne John Ruggles west, and North.

[**54.**] *32. Ralph Hemmingway his house, barne, Garden, and lott two accres and a halfe more or lesse, butting upon the highway south, and west, and upon the beires of Thomas Pigge east. and three accres and a halfe more or lesse lying in black-neck upon the heires of Thomas Pigge northwest; and one accre more or less in the calues pasture upon the highway east, upon the beires of Thomas Pigge north, and upon Giles Pason south and west; and one accre and a halfe more or lesse of salt marsh running west from a Creeke loyning to Edward Riggs. and eight aceres more or lesse, running southwest upon William Cheiney, and upon Giles Pason south. and a fresh meadow betweene the sayd Ralph and Giles Pason; the said Ralphs part being two accres more or lesse bounded upon the north by the riner, and incompassed by the land of Mr Thomas Weld on the other sides. and twenty foure accres and a halfe more or lesse exchanged with John Roberts for so much of his lott lying in the second alottment in the last diuision being the second lott their lying betweene Richard Wooddy and Mr Thomas Weld. and sixteene accres in the thousand accres neare Deddam.

[55.] *33. Robert Williams his house, barne, and lott fiue accres more or lesse, butting upon Edward Riggs and Giles Pason southwest, upon Giles Pason northeast, upon the highway south, and upon Edward Pason west, and seauen accres of land more or lesse upon Thomas Lamb south, upon John Burwell north, and betweene two highwayes. and twelue accres more or lesse, upon Richard Goad south, upon the heirs of George Holmes west and upon Dorchester marshes east. and twenty accres more or lesse bought of Mr William Pirkins upon the west of the way leading to the fresh meadow loyning to the said twelue accres and so upon Richard Peacocke and John Johnson[1] and in the first and third alottment in the last diuission being the three and twentyeth lott lying betweene Jacob Sheafe his assignes and Thomas Bell thirty and two accres. and in the thousand accres neare Deddam twenty and fiue accres. and nine accres more or lesse bought of Thomas Gardner lying in the great lotts, abutting upon Isaack Heath senior northwest, and upon Tobias, Dauis and the schole land southeast and one accre and a halfe of salt marsh, upon widdow Holmes west, and upon Edward Riggs east. and three roodes bought of Edward Riggs, butting upon Ralph Hemmenway east, and upon Edward Riggs west, and upon the heires of George Holmes north. and foure accres in the fresh meadow bought of John Johnson, butting upon the land of the heires of John Stannard westward, and upon the land of Giles Pason, and William Lion eastward. and one acre of fresh meadow bought of Edward Riggs butting upon Edward Riggs. southwest, and upon the beires of Thomas Pigge northeast. and one acere more of fresh meadow bought of William Cheiney lying without the ditch, butting upon the land of William Cheiney north, and Richard Sutton and upon Dorchester highway south east and a dwelling house, barne, and orchard with the land the housing stands upon, and adioyning to it, being about an accre more or lesse, lying upon the west side of a highway and so butting upon Edward Riggs and Giles Pason towards the north. and the home lott and swamp within the fence belonging to the house affoursayd being eight aceres more or lesse together with six aceres more or lesse lying without the fence, butting west upon a highway leading into the woods, and upon Dorchester brooke south east, And two accres and a halfe more or lesse of marsh being part of ten accres bought of Edward Pason, and now sold by William Lyon to Robert Williams now lying below the salt pan.

[56.] *34. John Watson his house barne and lott eleven accres more or lesse butting upon the assignes of John Stow west, upon Richard Woody south, upon a highway east. and upon John Dane north. and foureteene accres of land more or lesse, upon Jeames Astwood south, upon Thomas Baker or his assignes north, upon the great pond one end of it, and the other end upon the highway, six accres of this foureteene John Prentiss is to inioy after the decease of the sayd John Watson and foure accres of

[1] halfe of the sixteene accres in the first alottment of the thirty and two acres is sold to William Lyon.

meadow more or lesse in the great meade with two rodds of upland at each end lying betweene Edward Riggs and Mr John Elliot. and four accres more or less of salt marsh upon Mr Stodder south-west, and so betweene the creeke and the marsh of Isaack Morrill Northeast. and in the third alottment of the last deuission being the third lott lying betweene Edward Pason and John Johnson twenty six accres three quarters and fiue rodds. and in the thousand aceres neare Dedham thirty and three aceres, and six accres of land bought of Robert Pepper butting upon the land lately of William Curtiss east, upon Isaack Johnson south, upon William Healy west, and upon Robert Pepper North.

[57.] *35. Edward Bridge his house, barne and lot, with a swamp eight aceres more or lesse, butting upon the beires of George Holmes towards the east, upon the highway towards the north, and upon Thomas Bell towards the south. and six accres more or lesse upon the highway at the great lotts south east, upon Edward Pason North, and upon Thomas Bell and Jerimy Elsworth towards the southwest. and twelue accres more or lesse upon Henry Archer towards the south, upon the riuer towards the west, and upon Robert Gamblin toward the north. and fiue accres of meadow more or lesse at Rocky Swamp lying along upon the riner towards the west. and foure accres more or lesse at beare marsh, upon Isaack Morrill or his assignes towards the North, and running up by or to the brooke towards the south. and in the second alottment in the last diuision being the nineteenth lott lying betweene the heires of William Denison and the beires of Thomas Pigge twenty accres and one quarter. and foure accres of salt marsh more or lesse lying in the Ilaud lately Captaine Hugh Prichards, butting upon Griffen Craft south, upon John Mayes North, upon stoney riuer east, and upon John Ruggles and Isaack Johnson west. and sixteen accres of land more or lesse bought of Edward Pason, butting upon the land of John Johnson west, upon the land of John Mayes senior south, upon the land of the sayd Edward Bridg east, and upon the common southeast.

[58.] *36. John Burwell his dwelling house barne yard, and orchyard, and two accres and a halfe of land more or lesse, upon a highway west, and upon the land of Isaack Morrill south, east, and North, and one accre in the calues pasture upon the highway towards the north, betweene the assignes of John Wooddy and the heires of Thomas Pigge, and one end upon John Stow his assignes. and foure accres and a halfe upon the highway to the great lotts west, and upon William Parke or his assignes North. and two accres and a halfe upon Daniell Brewer his house lott west. and upon a highway east. and fiue accres more or lesse with two rodds wide leading from the highway into it betweene Robert Pepper and the assignes of Thomas Baker and so leading to the pond betweene Christopher peake and Abraham Newell at which end the way to the pond is foure rodds wide. and nine accres of salt marsh, butting upon the marsh of the heires of Mr Samuell Hagborne, and so with a creeke, and in the second alottment in the last diuission being the one and twentyeth lott, lying betweene Thomas Piggs heires and the heires of Joseph Weld twenty accres and one quarter.

John Woody his heires, one house, and a garden plott at the east side their of one quarter of an accre more or lesse upon Mr John Elliott south, and upon Richard Woody north.

[59.] *37. Giles Pason his house barnes, and lott fiue accers more or lesse butting upon the highway towards the east, and south, upon the beires of Thomas Pigge North, and upon Ralph Hemingway west. and six accres and a halfe in the great lotts, upon the assignes of Thomas Gardner south, and one end upon Richard Peacocke, and one side upon the highway; and seauen aceres at the side of the lotts upon Dorchester bounds, betweene Edward Riggs, and the beires of Thomas Pigge. and one acere more or lesse of salt marsh lying betweene Edward Denison and Dorchester tide mill. and in the first and third alottment of the last diuision being the twelfe lott lying betweene Abraham Newell and the beires of John Levens, exchanged with John Roberts for thirty-three accres and a halfe and thirty rodds in his lott lying in the second diuission the second lott betweene Richard Wooddy and Mr Thomas Weld. and in the thousand accres neare Deddam seauen accres and a halfe. and three accres more or lesse in the great lotts, upon John Stebbins wes'ward, upon Ralph Hemingway eastward and upon the schoole land south. and sixteene accres more or lesse bought of John Butler lying at the dead swamp, butting upon the highway west, and upon the brooke. east. and two accres and a roode more or lesse in the fresh meadow upon Richard Sutton east, upon Robert Williams west, and upon William Lion south and foure accres more or lesse bought of Thomas Robison butting upon Edward Riggs and Richard Goad southward, upon Edward Pason westward and upon John Stebbins Northwest. And an acere and a halfe more or lesse bought of Richard Sutton, butting east upon Robert Williams, south upon Edward Riggs North upon Isaack Heath se, and west upon Richard Sutton.

[60.] *38. Thomas Pigge his heires, his house, Barne, and lott with a swamp three accres and a halfe more or lesse butting upon the heires of George Holmes east, upon Dorchester brooke south, and upon Ralph Hemmingway west, and three accres more or lesse upon Blackneck, upon George Holmes Northeast, upon Nickolas Butler northwest, and upon Ralph Hemmingway south-east. and one acere and a halfe in the calues pasture upon the highway east, upon Giles Pason, Ralph Hemmingway and Robert Williams south. upon John Burwell towards the North, and upon John Stows assignes west. and one acere and a halfe of salt marsh upon blackneck east, upon Giles Pason south, and upon Richard Goad North. and fiue aceres more or lesse, upon Dorchester brooke, east, betweene the lands of the assignes of Humphrey Johnson North, and south, and a highway west. and five accres more or lesse, upon the highway leading to the great

lotts South, upon Edward Riggs east, and upon Giles Pason west.
and eight accres more or lesse upon the beires of George Holmes
south, and upon the last alottments North. and two accres of fresh
meadow lying betweene Edward Riggs and the assignes of Richard
Pepper, with two Rodds of upland at the ends theirof. and in the
second alottments in the last diuission being the twentyeth lott
lying betweene Edward Bridg and John Burwell twenty fowre
accres and a halfe; and in the thousand aceres neare Deddam
twenty accres.

[**61.**] ***39.** Edward Bugby his house, barne and lott three
accres more or lesse upon the highway east. upon Abraham Newell south, and west, and upon Isaack Morrıll north. and three
accres more or lesse betweene two highwayes east, and west, and
upon Mr John Elliot south, and a part east. and eight aceres more
or lesse, at the great pond east and North, and upon Arthur Gary
south. and in the first and third alottments in the last diuission
being the first lott. Edward Pason the second is nineteene accres
three quarters and twenty rodd. and in the thousand accres at
Deddam twelue aceres. and bought of William Gillfoord lately Mr
John Elliots a house and an acere of land more or lesse butting
upon the highway west, and upon the land of Mr John Elliot, cast,
south, and north. and foure[1] accres more or lesse in the upper
calues pasture butting upon the highway west, upon John Gorton
south and upon William Cheiney east. and sixteene accres and a
halfe more or lesse lying in the Nookes, exchanged with my sonne
Richard Chamberlinn, butting upon the land of James Braddish
east, and upon Robert Harris northwest. and tenn accres more or
lesse, lying in the Nookes butting upon Boston bounds east, upon
Robert Harris north, and upon his owne land west. and eight
accres more or lesse of swamp bought of Richard Pepper, butting
upon the land of Abraham Newell north, upon the highway west,
and east, and upon Tobias Dauis south. and an accre and a halfe
of salt marsh more or lesse, upon Muddy riuer east, upon John
Johnson North, and upon John Weld west. and two accres of
marsh more or lesse, upon John Watson south, upon John Ruggles sen: west, upon John Weld east, and upon Thomas Waterman North.

[**62.**] ***40.** John Scarbrowe his heirs, his house out house
and lott thereto Northeast to the highway, and upon Isaack
Morrill and John Stow his assignes South and west being about
one accre more or lesse, and in the first and third alottments in
the last diuision being the two and twentyeth lott bought with the
house of Jacob Sheafe lying betweene Isaack Johnson and Robert
Williams nineteene accres three quarters and twenty Rodds; and
eight aceres in the end of the great meade next Dorchester upon
John Stows assignes on the side thereoff. and in the thousand
accres neare Deddam fiue and twenty accres.

---

[1] sold to John Newell.

[63.] *41. Robert Pepper, his house, Barne, and lott being two accres more or lesse butting upon Isaack Johnson east, upon the highway south, upon Jeams Astwood north, and upon John Graues his beires west. and fiue accres more or lesse upon John Burwell west, upon a highway east, upon Abraham Newell north and upon Jeames Morgan his assignes south. and six accres more or lesse upon the land lately William Curtisses east, upon William Heath west, upon a highway north, and upon Isaack Johnson south. and six accres more or lesse upon Isaac Johnson east, and upon Boston bounds west. and in the last diuission in the Nookes next Dorchester the fourth lott his owne, and the fift Robert Oynion, and the seauenth lot bought of William Dauis being two accres and a halfe which maketh in the whole foureteene accres, one quarter and thirty pole. and in the thousand accres next Deddam seauen accres. and foure accres more or lesse of salt marsh lying upon the Iland lately Captaine Hugh Prichards butting upon the land of Peleg Heath, Griffen Crafts and Edward Bridg, and two accres more upon the same Iland, bought of William Curtiss upon the land of Isaack Johnson west and upon Edward Bridg, and the great Creeke.

[64.] *43.[1] William Lewis his house, barne, and fiue accres of land more or lesse, butting upon William Heath south, upon the heires of John Graues west, and upon a highway North, and east. and thirty fiue accres more or lesse abutting upon Peleg Heath north, upon the beires of William Heath east, upon Arthur Gary south, and upon Mr Hugh Prichard west.

[65.] *44. William Curtiss his house, barne orchyard, and ten accres of land more or lesse, butting upon stoney riner south upon Robert Pepper north, upon John Ruggles and John Totman west, and upon George Brand east. and one accre of upland and meadow more or lesse upon Daniell Ainsworth east, upon stoney riuer south, upon William Gary west, and upon Nathaniell Brewer North. and three accres which he had in way of exchange betweene him and Jeames Morgan and Rodert Pepper the land lying in the lott of the sayd Robert be ng the fourth lott. and two accres and a roode more or lesse of salt marsh bought of John Ruggles Junior lying in the Iland lately Captaine Hugh Prichards butting upon the land of Robert Seaver west, upon John Ruggles east, and North, and upon the creeke south.

[66.] *45. Richard Peacocke two[2] accres and three roodes of errable land bought of William Parke one end of it lying upon Giles Pason, the other end upon a swamp and so betweene the as-signes of Humphrey Johnson, and the assignes of Thomas Gardner and ten accres more or lesse bounded betweene Robert Williams, William Parke, the assignes of Gowin Anderson and a high way leading to the fresh meade. and in the Nookes next Dorches-

[1] There is no No. 42 in the original. -- W. H. W.
[2] sold to Tobias Dauis

ter being the seaventeenth lott lying betweene George Denison and
John Stebbin fiveteene accres and three quarters, and in the thousand accres neare Deddam ten accres. and two aceres and a halfe
and twenty rodds bought of John Stebbins being the eighteenth lot
lying in the Nookes next to Dorchester.

[67.] *46. Arthur Gary his house Barne and lott. fiue accres
more or less an accre of it being exchanged with William Heath,
butting upon the beires of William Heath of John Perry, and of
John Graues, and one corner of it upon the highway southwest.
and foure accres and a halfe upon a lane leading to the meadow of
the heires of William Heath. and so compassed with the lands of
Mr John Gore, John Roberts, Robert Prentiss, and the beires of
Thomas Ruggles. and foure accres and three quarters neare the
great pond, compassed with the lands of Phillip Elliott, the beires
of Thomas Ruggles, Edward Bugby, and the lotts in the last denis-
sion. and in the Nookes next Boston being the twelfe lott, lying
betweene William Lewis, and the Assignes of Edward White,
eighteene accres, one quarter and twenty rode and one accre of
salt marsh upon Edward Porter the Assignes of Richard Pepper,
and Thomas Griggs, and so compassed with the sea. and in the
thousand accres neare Deddam fifteene accres. and two accres of
salt marsh more or lesse bought of Richard Pepper abutting upon
John Griggs next the sea, and upon Mr Thomas Bell south,
and upon Edward Porter west, and twenty seauen aceres and
a halfe and ten pole bought of Richard Burnopp lying in the
second deuission the sixteenth lott being betweene the lott of
Abraham How and Mr Thomas Dudley. and two accres and
three roodes more or lesse as it lyeth with in fence layd out, the
ends thereof upon the hill behind the great pond as it is staked out
or marked betweene William Lion, one end at a water ditch of
little pond their and the other end at the great pond, and so lying
the sides their of betweene Edward Bugbyes lott, and a lott or
Daniell Fullers. and in the thousand accres neare Dedam twenty
foure accres. William Heath his heires and assignes for ever are
bound as appeares by writing and witnesse to make and maintaine
for ever that part of the fence which did belong to Arthur Gary in
the swamp betweene his ground that he bought of John Graues
about forty rodds more or lesse, for the which the sayd Arthur
Gary bath fully payd and satisfied the sayd William Heath. Is
appeares allso by an agreement betweene the sayd William Heath
and Arthur Gary, that Arthur Gary is to haue a highway from the
house of the sayd Arthur to the highway leading to muddy riuer
which highway he perchassed of and satisfied the sayd William
Heath for.

[68.] *47. Richard Woody senior, one house and barne
adioyning to the house and barne of Richard Peacocke upon the
north ; and errable land one accre and a halfe more or lesse at the
east side theire of. upon Mr Elliott south, upon Mr Daniell Weld
North and upon the training place east and in the middle deuision
next Dorchester forty accres and one roode.

[69.] *48 Richard Goad his house, barne and home lott
three accres more or lesse, upon two highwayes west, and north,
and upon Ralph Hemmingway south. and foure accres more or lesse,
upon Edward Riggs north. and upon Robert Williams south. and
one accre and a halfe of salt marsh more or lesse, upon the west of
the beires of George Holmes, and two accres of fresh meadow in a
little meadow whereof the assignes of Joshua Hews haue the
ressidue. and thirteene accres and a halfe bought of John Johnson
being the sixt lott in the Nookes, and lying next Dorchester.
betweene John Mayes, and John Gorton.

[70.] *49. John Mayes senior eighteene accres of land
lying next stoney Riuer over against the farme of the beires of
Joseph Weld the farther end theirof poynting southwest and the
hether end northeast. and in the Nookes next Dorchester being the
seauenth lott lying betweene Edward Riggs, and the assignes of
Gowin Anderson eleven accres three quarters and ten rodds; and
sixteene Rodd of land where upon his house did stand, upon
Thomas Bell south, and southwest, upon Robert Gamblin east, and
upon the highway northward. and one accre in the lott of Christopher
Peake.[1]
John Mayes A house and fowerteene rods of ground more or
lesse lying in a triangle abutting upon Robert Gamblin east, upon
the highway northwest, and upon Thomas Bells orchard southwest,
And an accre of land more or lesse bought of Joshua Hewes,
abutting upon Stoney riuer east, and the highway ouer Stoney
riuer south west. And two aceres more or lesse of salt marsh lying
in the Iland lately Captaine Hugh Prichards abutting upon Edward
Bridg southwest. upon the land lately William Lyons northeast,
and upon John Ruggles Junior south-east. And six accres more
or lesse lately bought of Edward Bridg abutting upon Thomas
Meekins east upon Thomas Weld west. and upon the common
south. And eighteene accres bought of Thomas Bumstead abutting
upon Edward Bridg east, and west, and south, upon the common
Weast.

[71.] *50. John Stebbins his house, and about three
quarters of one accre of land more or lesse, butting upon the highway eastward, and so compassed with the land of Isaack Morrill.
And in the Nookes next Dorchester being the eighteenth lott. lying
betweene Richard Peacock and widdow Gardner two acces and a
halfe and twenty rodds which land is sold to Richard Peacocke. and
three accres in the great lotts more or lesse, butting upon the
heires of John Levins east, and upon Edward Passon North, and
upon the beires of Thomas Pigg west. and foure aceres and a halfe
of land more or lesse lying in the great lotts, and butting upon a
swamp of William Cheiney south, upon Giles Pason west, upon
Edward Pason east, and upon the land of Thomas Waterman
North. and six accres or land more or lesse, bought of Deacon
William Parkes, butting upon William Cheiney and Edward Bug-

bye west. upon Edward Pason south, and upon the highway east
And two aceres and a roode more or lesse of meadow in the fresh
meades bought of William Lyon abuttinge upon Giles Pason south
upon Richard Suton and Samuell Williams west, upon Robert
Williams and Samuell Williams east, and upon the common north.

[72.] *51. Mr George Alcocke his heires their house barne
and out house with fiue accres of land more or lesse thierunto,
butting upon the heires of Mr Thomas Dudley Esq. : North, upon
John Dane South, upon a highway east and upon the meeting
house common west.   And forty accres more or lesse upon Richard Woody east, upon Edward Porter towards the south upon John
Stow, his assignes toward the west, and upon a highway towards
the north.   and fourteene accres more or lesse of upland and
meadow upon William Denison south. upon Isaack Morrill North
upon the highway west, and upon stoney riuer east. and twenty
accres of upland and marsh, upon the highway to Boston toward
the west, upon Boston Marshes towards the North upon a way
leading to Dorchester, and upon the landing place marshes towards
the east and upon Mr Thomas weld south And in the first and
third alottment in the last diuision being the sixt lott lying betweene William Cheiney and Samuell Chapen his assignes, sixty
foure aceres one quarter and ten rode.   And in the foure thousand
accres two hundred forty and two accres.

[73.] *52. Edward Porter his house and land their unto
adioyning Thirty accres more or lesse butting upon the lands of
Richard Woody [Blank] upon George Alcocke his heircs North,
and west, and upon Isaack Heath and others southward and upon
Abraham Newell and a highway eastward.   And two accres of
salt marsh to the north of the oysterbank, upon the marshes of
Thomas Bell Richard Pepper, and Christopher Peake east, and
upon Samuell Finch west and one eight part of a neck of land
being salt marsh lately the land of Edward Pason, but now the
other parts in the hands of Abraham Newell, Thomas Meekins,
and Willian Lyon, bounded by a ditch upon the land lately the
land of Nicholas Parker toward the towne.

[74.] *53. Robert Prentise his house and orchyard and lott
two accres more or lesse butting upon stoney riuer towards the
southeast, and a way towards the north. and six accres more or
lesse upon the other side of the highway upon Samuell Finch
north. upon Robert Pepper east, and upon the heires of William
Heath west, and eight accres more or lesse neere Muddy riuer
upon Mr John Gore north and upon the heires of Thomas Griggs
and the beires of Thomas Ruggles South, and in the thousand
accres neare Deddam being in exchange with Samuell Finch is
forty eight accres and a halfe and two accres of land more or
lesse upon the great hill butting south upon my owne six acere
lott, North upon John Griggs, east upon Hugh Thomas, and west
upon John Ruggles senior.

[75.] *54. John Totman his house and lott theirunto adioyning nine accres and a halfe more or lesse upon a highway leading from his house to the great pond South, and Northeast upon William Curtiss and John Ruggles Junior. and in the Nookes next Boston being the tenth lott lying betweene John Perry his beires, and William Lewis ten accres and a halfe : And in the thousand aceres neare Deddam six accres and a halfe. And one accre of fresh meadow lately the meadow of Samuell Finch lying neare John Welds house. And one accre of salt marsh, lately William Curtisses upon William Gary west, upon Samuell Finch north, and upon the Sea east.

Mr Henry Dingham his beires in the diuision of the Nookes next Dorchester the eleuenth lot lying betweene Phillip Meadows And George Bowers ten accres and a halfe.

[76.] *55. Edward Riggs his house barne and home lott, fiue accres more or lesse butting upon the highway southward one end upon the land lately William Parkes northward, one side upon Robert Williams eastward and the other side upon John Turner westward. And three accres upon the end of the great lotts northward, and upon a way betweene Roxsbury and Dorchester southward upon Nickolas Butler eastward, and upon Giles Pason westward, and seauen accres upon the sayd highway southward, and upon Richard Goad northward, one end upon Thomas Robison or his assignes eastward, and the other end upon the highway to the great meade westward. And one accre in the fresh meade with two rodds of upland at each end, lying betweene John Watson, and Robert Williams. And three roodes of salt marsh in blackneeck, upon Robert Williams northwest and southeast, and upon the creeke south, and upon Nickolas Clap east. and in the diuision of the Nookes being the sixt lott lying betweene the beires of John Stone and the lott of John Mayes being thirteene accres and twenty rodds. And in the thousand accres neare Deddam ten accres.

[77.] *56. Abraham How his house and lott nine accres and a halfe butting upon a highway, and upon the beires of Jeames Howe southeast. And twelue aceres upon the heires of John Stow Northwest, and to the last Deuided lands southeast, and upon Henry Archer or his assignes with a way to passe through the same, to and from his ground east. And in the second alottment of the last diuision being the fifteenth lott their in lying betweene Samuell Hagbornes heires, and Robert Burnope or his assignes foure and twenty accres and a halfe ; And in the thousand accres at Deddam fifteene aceres.

[78.] *57. William Cheiney his house barne Garden and land theirto about two accres and a halfe butting upon William Parkes south and east and upon the highway north and west ; And sixteene accres in the great lotts more or lesse betweene the lands of John Johnson towards the west, and the schoole lands towards the east. And ten accres of swampe neare the great lotts lying betweene Giles Pason, and Ralph Hemingway, and the heires of Samuell Hagborne. And six accres of salt marsh in Grauelly poynt   And six aceres of fresh meadow in the great meade, upon John Stow his heires east, and Richard Sutton west, with two rodds wide of upland at both ends and so upon the commons. And seauen accres more or lesse of errable land upon Richard Sutton north, John Gorton west, and upon John Turner south. And in the first and third allottment of the last deuission being the fift lott lying betweene John Johnson and the heires of George Alcocke three score and sixteene accres and a halfe and ten rod. And foure and twenty aceres and a halfe within the thousand accres neare Deddam. And twenty accres of land more or lesse lying in the great lotts bounded on the way to the fresh meadow in the east the land of the heires of John Levens on the south, the schoole land and Richard Peacockes north west, and upon Giles Pason and the highway northerly. And three accres and a halfe of meadow lying in the fresh meades butting east upon my owne fresh meade and upon John Peiropoynt west. And an accre of land commonly called the wolfe trapp bought of Humphrey Johnson lying on the north of the land of John Gorton, and west upon the highway. And halfe of sixteene accres of woodland lately the land of Richard Sutton, but bought by him of John Johnson.

[79.] *58. Christopher Peake his house and lott theirto elleuen accres more or lesse upon Abraham Howe east, and upon Thomas Bell north. And two accres of salt marsh in Grauelly poynt upon Isaack Heath south upon Thomas Bell north. And seauen accres and a halfe upon Joshua Hewes west, upon Henry Archer or his assignes south, upon Robert Gamblin north, and upon a great hill east. And in the last diuision the second parte of the three alottments being the eight lott theirin lying betweene Samuell Finch and the heires of William Heath twenty accres and one quarter. And in the thousand accres neare Deddam ten accres. And ten accres bought of Jeames Morgan lying west upon the highway to the pond, upon John Watson north, south upon John Burrill, and east upon the pond. And three accres of salt marsh more or lesse, lying north upon John Weld, east upon Edward Bugby, west upon Thomas Waterman. And an accre of meadow neare John Totmans house, and north of the riuer. And two accres in bare-marsh lying south of Samuell Finch, west upon the riuer, and east upon the highway to Beare-marsh.

[80.] *59. John Griggs his Dwelling house,[1] and one accre of land, bought of Griffen Craft upon the south side of his lott, and upon the northside of John Ruggles se ·   And one accre and a halfe neare unto it, upon the assignes of Jeames Morgan south and east, upon Griffen Craft and a way west, and upon John Ruggles south. And two accres on the great hill bought of Jeames Morgan, upon Robert Pepper south, and upon John Ruggles north.

---

[1] John Griggs is to maintaine all the fence betweene his accre and Griffen Craft.

And in the first and third alottment of the last deuision being in the seauenth lott betweene the heires of George Alcocke and John Ruggles se. nine accres late Samuell Chapen his lott. And in the thousand accres neare Deddam twelue accres. And eighteene accres more or lesse lying in the Nookes next Boston betweene the lotts of John Johnson Samuell Finch, and the heires of John Perry. And one accre more or lesse upon the north side of the great hill next the pasture, Griffen Craft being on the south. And two accres of salt marsh more or lesse lying at Grauelly poynt abutting upon Arthur Gary west, and William Gary south and Mr Thomas Bell east and upon the sea North.

Joseph Griggs fower accres and a halfe upon Robert Prentice east, and upon the marsh of the heires of William Heath west. And two peeces of marsh lying at muddy riner bridge the riner running betweene, in all one accre more or lesse bought of Robert Prentice.

[81.] *60. John Dane his house and lott with a swamp before the house, butting upon the way leading to the house of John Watson east, in all fiue accres and a halfe more or lesse, upon John Watsons swamp south, upon the heires of Thomas Ruggles west, and upon the heires of George Alcocke north. And in the nookes next Dorchester being the second lott lying betweene Phillip Tory and the assignes of Joseph Patching ten accres and a halfe, And in the thousand accres neare Deddam
all the lands with the house aboue mentioned were latly belonging to the heires of William Chandler. And in the Nookes next Dorchester late the land of Joseph Patching being the third lott lying betweene William Chandlers heires, and Lewis Jones ten accres and a halfe. And bought of Thomas Beckwith being formerly the land of Lewis Jones thirteene accres and twenty rodds lying in the Nookes next Dorchester being the fourth lott lying betweene the land of Joseph Patching and John Stone his assignes. And two accres more or less bought of Edmund Parker lately the land of William Webb, butting east and south upon John Watson, upon John Pieropoynt west, and upon John Dane North.

[82.] *61. Robert Gamlin his housses and lott, three accres and a halfe more or lesse butting upon Thomas Bell south upon the highway east, upon stoney riuer west upon the assignes of John Stannard north. And six aceres more or lesse, upon Daniell Brewer east, upon a highway south and upon a lane west. And three roodes more or lesse being part of a swamp compased with the land of Edward Bridg, Thomas Bell, and a highway. And fourteene aceres more or lesse upon Daniell Brewer north, and upon Edward Bridg South. And two accres of meadow at Beare marsh lying betweene the land of the beires of William Heath, and John Ruggles. And one accre of salt marsh more or lesse, compassed with a creeke and so upon Isaack Heath and others upon Grauely Poynt. And in the first and third allottment in the last diuision being the one and thirtyeth lott betweene Mr Hugh Prichard and

M^r william Pirkins twenty seauen accres and ten rodd. And in the thousand accres neare Deddam one and twenty accres and a halfe. And foure accres and a halfe of salt marsh lying by Grauelly poynt lately the land of John Pieropoynt lying north upon Christopher Peake, and west upon William Curtiss. And foure accres more or lesse of upland, upon Stoney riuer west, upon Phillip Eliot North, and upon Nathaniell Brewer east.

Phillip Tory in the Nookes next Dorchester being the first lott fiue accres and one quarter. And halfe an accre of salt marsh more or lesse, lying in a Nooke neare Grauelly poynt at the end of Thomas Halyes lott.

[83.] *62. Samuell Finch his house with other buildings, and house-lott two accres more or lesse upon the highway south upon the assignes of Jeames Morgan west, upon Mr Hugh Prichard north, and upon the beires of Thomas Ruggles east. and one accre and a halfe and ten pole more or lesse of salt marsh upon the north of the riner leading to muddy riner, and towards the east of the marsh of John Johnson, and Isaack Johnson west. And an accre and a halfe of salt marsh, upon the southwest of Edward Porter and upon William Lewis northeast. And five accres and a halfe, upon Mr Hugh Prichard northeast, and upon the southwest of the highway. and fiue accres of fresh meadow more or lesse at the heather end of Beare-marsh. And in the second allottment in the last diuision the seauenth lott lying between William Parke and Christopher Peake threescore and nine accres and three quarters. And in the thousand accres neare Deddam being his owne lott, and Mr John Millers which he bought of Mr Miller in both lotts fifty and eight aceres, and is now exchanged with Robert Prentice for his lott in the Nookes, the sixt lott lying betweene Robert Onion and William Dauis being eleuen accres three quarters and ten rodd. And the halfe of six accres of land butting upon Edward Bugby east. upon the schoole land and William Curtiss north and Northwest, And upon Robert Pepper southwest. And three accres more or lesse of salt marsh bought of John Hanchett lying neare Grauelly Poynt, butting upon the sea west, upon John Totman and William Gary south, and upon Robert Gamblin north and Northwest.

[84.] *63. Isaack Heath his dwelling house with all the housing about it together with the home lott and the orchyards with all the meadow about home being in all foure aceres more or less butting east upon Stoney riuer, north upon Robert Prentise, west upon the highway upon the hill, and south upon Phillip Eliot and the heires of John Perry. And six aceres of land more or lesse butting upon the highway to the pond south, upon his owne land north upon the beires of John Perry east and upon William Potter west. and eleuen accres of land more or lesse upon the great hill, butting east upon the high way, north upon Robert Prentise, west upon the heires of John Graue, and south upon the heires of John Perry. And foure accres of meadow with the upland ioyning to it he the same more or lesse lying next muddy riuer bridg abbutting upon the highway north, upon muddy riner west, upon the heires of Thomas Griggs east, and upon the beires of John Perry south. and an acere and a halfe of land more or lesse, abbutting upon the highway east, upon Robert Seauer south, upon Peleg Heath North and west. And the halfe of foure accres of land more or lesse, abbutting upon the land of Pelegg Heath cast, upon William Lewis west. upon the highway north, and upon Arthur Gary south. And the halfe of forty two aceres three quarters and twenty pole, being in the second allottment of the last diuision the ninth lott betweene Christophcr Peake and the assignes of John Stow. And in the thousand accres neare Deddam twenty six accres.

[85.] *64. Isaack Johnson one house Barne out house and lott two accres more or lesse butting upon the highway east and south upon Robert Pepper west, and upon Jeames Astwood North. And nine aceres more or lesse upon the great pond Southeast, upon Deddam highwav east, and betweene Isaack Heath and Jeames Astwoods lotts North and west. And seauen accres more or lesse, lying betweene the highway and Robert Burnops lott on the north, and the lotts of William Healy, Robert Pepper, the beires of William Webb and Phillip Eliot on the south, one end upon Deddam highway west, and the other end upon Phillip Eliot east.[1] And in the first and third allottment of the last diuision the one and twentyeth lott lying betweene Edward Denison and Jacob Sheafe twenty seauen aceres and a halfe and ten rodds. And in the thousand accres neare Deddam fifteene accres. And twelue accres and a quarter more or lesse bought of Edward Culuer in the third alottment of the last diuision being the tenth lott lying betweene the lott of Abraham Newell se: and the heires of John Graues which was the land of John Roberts which he exchanged with Ralph Hemmingway. And eleuen accres more or lesse bought of Thomas Waterman and Margret his wife lately the land of John Stannard abbutting upon Stoney riuer northwest, and upon the land of the heires of Daniell Brewer and John Burwell southeast, and the lott of the beires of George Alcocke north east and the lott of Robert Gamblin south. And halfe of foure accres more or lesse of meadow in Beare marsh, the foure accres being bought ioyntly by William Dauis and Isaack Johnson of Isaack Morrill, butting upon Edward Bridg towards the southwest or west, upon the brooke running from the dry cattle house south, and to be as broad at one end as at the other with two rodds of upland, and upon the land of Abraham Newell east. And two accres more or lesse of salt marsh lying in the Iland lately Captaine Hugh Prichards, abutting upon stoney riner east, and the marsh of John Ruggles Juni south, on Edward Bridg west, and on William Curtis North.

[86.] *65. Griffen Craft his house and lot three accres with six accres more or lesse at the end theirof. And six accres more

---

[1] seauen accres of the fiıst alotment at the hethermost end is sold to William Lion.

or lesse at the great hill against the house of Nathaniell Willson,
lying next to John Ruggles upon the North.   And three accres of
salt marsh more or lesse at muddy riuer beyond the bridg butting
upon Peter Olliuer east.   And twenty accres ioyning to it upon
Isaack Morrill south, and upon part of a highway.   And in the
first and third allottments of the last diuision being the eight and
twentieth lott betweene Daniell Brewer and Robert Seauer forty
two[1] accres one quarter and twenty rodds.   And in the thousand
aceres neare Deddam thirty accres.   And halfe a quarter of the
Ilaud of Marsh that was Mr Hugh Prichards bounded upon Robert
Pepper north, upon Edward Bridg south, and east, and upon
Muddy riuer west.   And sixteene aceres more or lesse called
squirrills delight bounded by his owne land on the north, upon the
way leading to Mr Hibbins farme west, upon Mr John Gores land
South west and upon William Lewis Pelegg Heath and Robert
Seauer southeast.   And two accres of swamp more or lesse lying
at the west end of Edward Morris his lott being part of Edward
Morris his lott lying upon the east of Griffen Craft Robert
Seauers land lying north and south of it.   And three roodes of
swamp more or lesse bought of Pelegg Heath neare muddy riner,
upon Robert Seauer north. upon his owne land east, and upon the
land lately belonging to William Lewis south.

[87.] *66.   William Healy his dwelling house and orchyard
with the mill lott being three accres more or lesse abbutting upon
the highway south, upon Mr Hugh Prichards land north, and upon
the highway to the landing place west.   And the old mill house
with the appertenances lately Mr Hugh Prichards butting upon
Stoney riner south, and on the other sides upon the highway.
And eleuen accres more or lesse bought of Thomas Robbinson
lying neare the great pond upon Isaack Johnson North, and upon
Robert Pepper east.   And a barne with two yards.   And twelue
accres of upland more or lesse lying upon the great hill, upon Mr
John Gore west, upon Samuell Finch east, upon a way leading to
William Heath meadow south, and upon the highway leading to
muddy riuer north. and the one halfe of seauen accres more or lesse
of upland and meadow which lyeth upon the west side of muddy
riuer within the fence of Peter Oliuer upon the west side, the south
end upon Mr Prichard and the north end upon muddy riner bridg.
And twenty seauen accres and a halfe and ten rodds lying in the
first and third allottment the sixteenth lott.   And in the thousand
accres neare Deddam twenty seauen accres bought of John
Roberts, And twenty six accres and three quarters the fifteenth
allottment lying betweenc William Webb and Richard Goad   And
in the thousand accres neare Deddam twelue accres.   And twenty
three aceres and thirty rodd in the first and third allotment bought
of William Webb.   William Healy hath sold forty of these last
accres unto John Weld.

Nathaniell Stow late of Ipswich, in the second allottment in the
last diuision bought of John Scarbrowe being the lift lott lying

---

[1] The nearest halfe of the forty two accres is sold by Griffen Crafts to John Johnson

betweene Isaack Morrill and William Parke thirty foure accres and a halfe, and twenty rodds.

[**88.**] *67. John Gorton his house, and six accres of land more or lesse called the wolfe trapp, butting upon William Parke south, upon William Cheiney east, and upon a highway west And in the Nookes next Dorchester being the ninth lott lying betweene Gowin Anderson his assignes and Phillip Meadowes his assignes thirteene accres and twenty rodds. And in the last diuision in the Nookes next Dorchester bought of Henry Farnham fiue accres and one quarter being the fift lott lying betweene Lewis Jones and Edward Riggs. And an accre of salt marsh more or lesse bought of Edward Pason butting southwest upon Edward Pasons land and euery other way being compassed with creekes.

[**89.**] *68. Daniell Aynsworth one house and twelue accres of land more or lesse bounded upon William Cheiney southwest, upon William Curtiss south and west and upon a highway north. And bought of William Curtiss two accres of meadow more or lesse butting upon the riner east upon his owne land north and west and upon William Curtiss south. And thirteene accres and twenty rodds more or lesse bought of William Lewis butting upon ⨯ John Polly south, upon Arthur Gary east upon Phillip Eliot north, and upon John Totman west. And two accres (doubtful) of marsh more or lesse bought of William Lion, and halfe of it sold to George Brand lying in the Ilaud lately Captaine Hugh Prichards butting upon the land of Robert Seauer south, upon John Mayes north, upon John Ruggles east, and upon the creeke west. And fiue accres of land more or lesse bought of Phillip Eliot butting upon stoney riner east, upon Robert Gamblin North and upon John Ruggles Juni: south.

Widdow Gardner in the last diuision of the Nookes next Dorchester being the nineteenth lott lying betweene John Stebbin. and the assignes of John Mathews seauen accres three quarters and twenty rodds.

[**90.**] *69. The heires of John Graues after his wifes decease now the wife of William Potter, one house, one barne and one orchard or Garden with foure accres of upland and three accres of meadow more or lesse ioyning theirunto, abbutting upon Arthur Gary towards the north and upon the highway towards the south upon seuerall yards or orchyards towards the east and upon the heires of William Heath west. And on the other side of the heires of William Heath two accres more or lesse, And thirty three accres and a halfe and thirty rodd in the first and third allottments of the last diuision the ninth lott lying betweene John Ruggles and Ralph Hemmingway.

Mary Graues foure accres of Arable land lying in the hill lotts abutting upon Samuell Finch north, upon a highway south, upon the beires of William Heath and John Hanchett east, and upon Arthur Gary west.

[91.] *70. William Potter foure accres lying at the salt pann which he bought of Samuell Graues. And six accres bought of William Graues abutting betweene two high wayes upon the south and north sides their of, upon the heires of William Heath east, and upon William Lewis north. And in the thousand accres neare Deddam bought of William Curtiss sixty two accres.

Richard Chamberlin an house and halfe an accre of land more or lesse adioyning to it abutting east upon the highway, and north and west upon Mr John Eliot, and upon Tobias Dauis on the south side of it.

[92.] *71. George Brand A dwelling house and halfe an accre of land more or lesse adioyning to it with a barne butting on one side upon stoney riner and every way els upon the common ; and two accres bought of Isaack Johnson butting upon stoney riner south, upon the highway north, lying betweene the land of Jeames Astwood and William Curtiss. And an accre of meadow more or lesse, butting upon stoney riuer east, upon Daniell Aynswoorth west, upon John Ruggles Ju. south, and upon William Gary north. And three aceres and three roodes of land more or lesse, upon the hill beyond the great pond bought of William Curtiss, butting upon the land of Edward Denison north, upon Pelegg Heath south, and upon William Gary west. And an accre of salt marsh lying in the Ilaud lately Captaine Hugh Prichards bought of Daniell Aynswoorth and he of William Lion abutting upon Robert Seauer south, upon John Mayes North, and upon the creeke west.[1]

[93.] *72. Richard Sutton sixteene accres of land more or lesse lately the land of Henry Farnham being the twelfe lott, abbutting upon the eight accre lots west. And foure accres and a halfe of fresh meadow bought of Edward Pason abutting east upon William Cheiney, and west upon Giles Pason and William Lyon. And ten accres lately the land of William Webb lying beyond the eight accre lotts, next Richard Peacockes ten aceres, and adioyning upon the twenty accres lately Mr Pirkins but now Robert Williams.

Nathaniell Willson his dwelling house and halfe an accre of land be the same more or lesse adioyning there unto lying west and south upon Peter Oliuers land, upon the highway north, and upon the meadow of William Healy east.

[94.] *73. Thomas Meekins six accres of land more or lesse which was George Brands abutting east upon the common, upon Thomas Weld west, upon William Lyon north, and upon

---

[1] Note. — Pinned on page [or deed] 71
Goodman Denison I wold pray you to take that eighton ackers of land mor or lese which is vpon my transcript and to put it vpon George Brand and John Bridge transcript by the order of John Rugles
Edmond Morry
Beniamin Child   G. Bran page 71

William Parkes south. And the fourth part of twelue accres of salt marsh more or lesse lying below the salt pan, incompassed with the sea and creekes only upon the west it butts upon the land where of Thomas Bell hath a quarter.

Hugh Thomas one house and home lott being three accres more or lesse abutting west upon Stoney riner, north upon the highway leading to the riuer, south upon Robert Prentise, and west upon the highway aboue. And foure accres and a halfe more or lesse in the night pasture, abutting west upon the highway, North upon John Ruggles se. and south upon Griffen Craft and Isaack Morrill. And three accres of broken up land more or lesse lying upon the hill, abutting upon John Ruggles north, upon Robert Prentise south upon the highway east, and upon Robert Prentise and John Griggs west.

[95.] *74. Joseph Wise A dwelling house malt house and other housing with the land it stands upon, and about three roodes of land more or lesse about it, bought of William Denison, abutting North upon John Burwell, west upon the highway leading to John Watsons, east and south upon the land of Isaack Morrill. and sixteene accres and three roodes in the Nookes next Rockyswamp being the nineteenth lott.

John Mayo foure accres of land more or lesse bought of Isaack Heath abutting upon the land of Edward Denison north upon William Gary east, upon Abraham Newell and John Mayes south, and upon Boston bounds west. And in the thousand accres neare Deddam giuen unto him by his father one and twenty accres and a halfe. And sixteene aceres of land more or lesse bought of John Johnson; And three aceres of land more or lesse bought of John Johnson lately the land of John Stebbinns adoiyning to the sixteene accres lying at Rocky swamp and so abutting upon Edward Pason west, and upon the land of Edward Bridg east. and fower accres of meadow more or lesse bought of John Johnson lately the land of Phillip Torry, butting upon Isaack Morrill west, upon Phillip Torry North. and upon the woodland east, and south. and two accres of land upon the pondhill bought of Isaack Heath, abutting upon William Denison north upon William Gary east, upon Phillip Curtiss south, and upon his owne land bought of Isaack Heath west.

[96] *75. John Hanchet A dwelling house barne and orchard being an accre of land more or lesse, abutting upon the highway south, and west, and upon Samuell Finch east. And six[1] aceres more or lesse of salt marsh lying below the salt pan, adioyning to the marsh of Thomas Meekinns and Abraham Newell, two of the six accres being bought of Robert Pepper, and fower accres of Humfrey Johnson.

---

[1] two accres of this six accres is sold to John Mayo.

John Polly A dwelling house and barne with other housing, and a great lott containing eighteene accres more or lesse abutting one end upon a highway leading to Beare marsh south, one end upon a highway west, and upon John Welds land south, east, and north.   And six accres of meadow more or lesse abutting upon the meadow of M[r] John Gore north east and upon the side of Baere hill.

[97.] *76.   Tobias Dauis bought of John Peiropoynt, A dwelling house and other out housing together with an orchyard and all the fence their unto belonging abbutting upon the land of Isaack Morrill west, upon the land of Phillip Tory south, and upon the highway east.   And ten accres of land more or lesse, abutting upon the land of M[r] John Eliot North, upon Edward Bugby south, and upon the highwayes east and west.   And a part of the orchard of his father Isaack Morrills against the sayd Tobias Dauis his shopp and fence, haning six apple trees upon it, giuen unto him by his sayd father Isaack Morrill.   And six or seauen accres of land more or lesse about the eight acere lotts upon the beires of Thomas Pigg south east, and upon the land of Abraham How northwest prouided he intrench not upon any mans land formerly granted to any.

Edmund Parker his lott fiue accres more or lesse lately the land of Edward Culuer, abutting upon the land of John Polly towards the south, upon John Weld east, upon the highway west, and upon Isaack Johnson north, with a conuenient highway to and fro the sayd lott.

[98.]   *77.   Edward Morris nine[1] accres more or lesse of woodland bought of John Ruggles Junior being in the first deuision of the last allottment the twelfe lott lying betweene John Leuens and Abraham Newell.   And eight[1] accres and a halfe of land more or less bought of Robert Pepper late the land of Jeames Morgan abutting upon the land of John Ruggles Junior on the one side, and upon Abraham Newells on the other side, and one end of it butting upon M[r] John Gores meadow   And three accres and a halfe more or lesse in Beare marsh bought of John Bowles butting upon the heires of William Heath towards the south and upon William Curtiss north.

William Lion The house he now dwells in with the orchard and yard conteining by estimation three roodes more or lesse he paying unto his Mother in law thirty shillings p yeare as by lease to his sayd mother in law bearing date the sixteenth of Febru: 1647. Allso Samuell Ruggles is to haue part of the lands, its now staked out, this apeares by a deed from John Ruggles for halfe the sayd house and land but for Samuell Ruggles part it doth not appeare any sale to him.   And one acere and a halfe of land neare the

---

[1] The eighteene accres sold to John Rugles Ju: and by him to George Brand and John Bridg.

meeting house lately the land of Gowen Anderson.[1] And fiue aceres more or lesse being part of eight accres lately the land of Samuell Ruggles, abutting upon Samuell Ruggles east, upon John Ruggles north, and upon John Griggs south. And one acere and three roodes more or lesse lying neare the meeting house, butting upon the widdow Ruggles land southwest, upon John Ruggles west, upon the highway noith. the sayd William Lyon is to maintaine a sufficient fence for euer betweene the land of the sayd John Ruggles, and this land; sold by the sayd John Ruggles unto the sayd William Lyon. And foure accres of land more or lesse, late the land of Phillipp Eliot part of his lott called the pond plaine, abutting upon the same land of the sayd Phillip Eliot towards the east and south, upon Samuell Rugles towards the west and upon Arthur Gary North-west. And a house and three accres of land, more or lesse, butting upon William Dauis north, upon the highway to John Welds east, upon Henry Bowen south, and upon William Dauis west.

[99.] *78. John Peiropoynt Eleuen accres and a halfe upon the meeting house hill, one end upon the highway, and so betweene the land of John Ruggles, Richard Woody Abraham Newell and M[r] Alcocke. And sixty accres more or lesse lying in the last diuission being the tenth lott, lving betweene the lotts of the heires of William Heath, and Isaack Heath. And in the thousand accres neare Deddam eighty-three accres certaine, and foure accres, and a halfe more claimed which as yet remaines doubtfull. And in the foure thousand accres giuen by the Court to Roxbury two hundred fifty and three accres : These two last percells of land he inioyeth as beire to John Stow his Father in law lately deceased. And fiue accres and a halfe of land more or lesse bought of William Curtiss neare the pond plaine, abbutting upon the land of John Bowles south, upon Robert Pepper west, upon a highway north. and upon the land of M[r] John Eliot east.

[100.] *79. William Gary his house, barne, orchyard and yard, with three accres of land more or lesse bought of John Bowles abutting upon the highway to Deddam northwest, upon Phillip Eliott and Robert Seaver south, and upon Stoney riuer east. And fiue accres more or lesse upon the pond hill, lately the land of Thomas Curtiss butting upon John Mayos land west, upon John and Samuell Ruggles south, upon George Brand east, and upon Edward Denison North. And three accres and fifty rodds of errable land upon the pond hill, lately William Lyons abutting upon the schoole land south, upon Arthur Gary east, upon Peleg Heath north and upon Samuell Ruggles west. And seauen accres wanting twenty rodds of woodland lately Robert Peppers lying upon the common neare the pond hill, abutting upon Boston bounds west, upon Samuell Finch south, upon John Ruggles east, and upon William Curtiss North. And one acere of fresh meadow more or lesse neare Stoney riner lately the land of William Cur-

---

[1] And an accre more or lesse of the fiue accres is sold to Thomas Bacon

tiss, abutting upon Robert Gamblin west, upon George Brand south, and upon Stoney riuer east. And one accre of salt marsh lately the meadow of William Curtiss lying neare Grauely poynt abutting upon John Totman east, upon Samuell Finch north, upon Robert Gamblin west, and upon the great Creeke south. And one accre of salt marsh more or lesse lately the meadow of Arthur Gary lying at Grauelly poynt abutting upon John Bowles east, upon John Griggs north, upon Arthur Gary west, and upon Thomas Bell south.

[101.] *80. Thomas Baker his house and the ground upon which it stands together with his garden and a parcell of land adioyning being in all about halfe an accre more or lesse, abutting upon the land of Thomas Hally east and south, upon the highway north, and upon the land belonging to the mill west.

Abraham Newell Junior, bought of Phillip Curtisse fower accres of land more or lesse, butting upon John Mayes north, upon John Mayo east, upon the schoole land west, and upon Samuell Ruggles south. And halfe of two accres more or lesse bought of Daniell Ainswoorth, upon Robert Seauer west, upon John Mayes east, upon Stoney riuer North, and upon John Ruggles Junior south. And a dwelling house, and a barne with the land it stands upon, and adioyning to it, being fiue accres more or lesse, lately bought of Edmund Parker, butting east and south upon John Weld, north upon the land of Isaack Johnson, and west upon the highway leading to beare-marsh. And two accres of salt marsh lately bought of Peleg Heath, lying in the Ilaud lately Captaine Hugh Prichards, butting upon the land of Robert Pepper south, upon Peleg Heath west, and upon Stoney and Muddy riuers North and east.

[102.] *81. Nathaniel Brewer in the thousand acres neare Deddam twenty seauen accres and a halfe ; And three accres more or lesse of planting ground bought of William Curtisse abutting south upon Robert Gamblin, east upon Daniell Ainswoorth and south east upon William Curtiss his meadow, this last for the present is doubtfull, but now the doubt is removed.

[103.] *82. Peleg Heath, fiue accres more or lesse of meadow in Muddy riuer marsh, with foure accres of upland more or lesse ioyning unto it which was bought by his Father William Heath of Mr Gore lying along by Muddy riuer on the north, and upon the land of William Lewis on the west and south, and upon the land of the heires of John Perry on the east, with a highway to the said land from the highway that goes by the dwelling house of William Lewis, by the land of William Lewis and Captaine Prichard on the one side, and the land of William Potter, William Healy, Arthur Gary and the heires of Thomas Ruggles on the other side. And six accres of upland more or lesse bought by the said William Heath of John Scarbrough which was Bowers land, abutting upon the highway that goeth up to the great pond by the house of William Lewis on the east, and upon the lands of Isaack Heath on the south, and upon the lands of Griffen Crafts on the west, and upon the land of William Lewis on the north. And fower acres of land more or lesse lying neare Arthur Garyes house abutting upon the lands of the heires of John Graues on the east and west, and upon the great highway that leades towards Deddam on the south, and upon the land of Arthur Gary on the north, and a highway to it by the dwelling house of Arthur Gary. And fiue accres of land more or lesse with a barne, upon the highway that leades to the house and upon the land of William Lewis on the north, and upon the lands of Isaack Heath on the west, upon the land of Arthur Gary on the south, and upon the lane to Arthur Garyes house on the east. And fower accres of marsh more or lesse lying in the lland that was Mr Prichards lying on the north corner of the Ilaud by the riuer called Stoney riuer, and upon the land of Robert Pepper on the south, with an eight part of the cart way bought of John Johnson and of the new creeke, and a cart-way to the sayd land through the land of Robert Pepper, and of Edward Bridg and the land of Griffen Craft. And two accres of upland lying upon the pond hill, bought of Daniell Fuller, butting upon the land of Arthur Gary on the east, and upon the land of William Gary on the south, and upon the land of Samuell Ruggles on the west, and upon the land of George Brand on the north. And fower accres of meadow more or lesse in bare marsh, abutting upon the land of Phillip Eliot and John Bowles on the north, and upon Stoney riuer on the east, and upon the land of Robert Gamblin on the south, and upon the highway that goeth to the dry cattle house on the west. with two rodds wide upon the upland on the west end of the sayd meadow. And one and twenty accres of land more or lesse lying in the commons being the one halfe of his father William Heaths part in the last alotment. And a third part of his fathers land in the thousand accres neare Deddam.

[104.] 83. We whose names are under written being chosen by the towne upon the twenty ninth of January fifty fower to examine the transcript which Edward Denison was to write out according to the coppies deliuered to him, hauing examined the sayd transcript upon the fowerteenth of Februa: fifty fower, and we find that he hath performed exactly according to the coppies commited to his charge what he was betrusted with to write for the towne: as far as we are able to discerne.

Witnesse our hands

JOHN JOHNSON
WILLIAM PARK
(autographs) GRIFFIN CRAFT
EDWARD RIG

Samuell Williams, A dwelling house, with halfe the barne, and out houses together with his orchyard and backside being an accre of land more or lesse butting upon Edward Riggs east and south, and upon the highway goeing into the woods northwest. And halfe an accre more or lesse bought of Richard Sutton in the great

meade lying at the south end of Richard Suttons meadow, John
Stebbins upon the east side of it. and his oune land on the west
side ; And halfe an accre of fresh meadow, in the great meades at
the south end of his father Robert Williams his meadow from the
furthest ditch to the railes.   And an accre more or lesse of fresh
meadow in the great meades, upon Richard Sutton east and upon
John Johnson and Isaack Morrill northeast, Samuell Williams
being to make and maintaine all the fence at the head of his accre
of meadow for ever. and eleuen accres in the eight accre lotts giuen
him by his father Williams and is butted and bounded in his fathers
transcript and halfe of the lott against his dwelling house giuen
him by his sayd father and bounded in his fathers transcript.
And fiue roodes of salt marsh giuen him by his father Parkes butting upon the heires of Thomas Pigg south, upon the highway to
the tidemill east, and northeast upon the land of Nickolas Clapp.
And the halfe of the lott that lyeth at the end of the great lotts
which was bought by his father Parkes of John Peiropoynt, and
by him the whole lott was giuen to his sonn Williams, the halfe
of which lott is exchanged by Samuell with his father Williams
for tenn accres of his twenty accres lott lying at the foote of the
eight accre lotts as appeares in his father Williams transcript.
And fiue accres of salt marsh, butting upon pine Ilaud south,
upon Boston lands north, and upon the flatts east.   And two
accres of fresh meadow lately the land of Giles Pason, lying in
the meadow together with Ralph Hemingway and Thomas Andrews
And fower accres of land lying against the highway to dead swamp
west upon the heires of Thomas Lamb north, and upon John Burwell south.

[105.] *84.   John Newell, A dwelling house with halfe an
accre of land about it more or lesse abutting upon the highway
east upon John Stebbin south, upon Isaack Morrill west, and upon
Thomas Waterman north.   And fower accres of land more or lesse
in the upper calues pasture, bought of Edward Bugby, butting upon
the highway west, upon John Gorton south, and upon William
Cheiney east.   And in the first alottment in the last deuision being
the third lott, lying betweene Edward Pason and John Johnson
twenty six accres three roodes and fiue rodd.   And in the deuision
of the Nookes next Dorchester being the sixteenth lott lying betweene Nathaniell Manuring (now sold to William Denison) and
Richard Peacock fifteene accres and three quarters.   And one accre
late the land of John Stebbin, upon the land of John Stebbin south,
and upon the highwayes to the great lotts, and to Dorchester
brooke, east, west, and north.

William Dauis his house, and three accres of land more or lesse,
butting upon John Mayes and upon William Linckhorne north ;
south upon William Lyon ; east upon the highway to John Welds
farme, and west upon his oune land.   And the halfe of three accres
more or lesse, the three accres being bought by him and Mr Bowen
ioyntly of Isaack Johnson lying in halfe way meadow, butting the
south side upon Phillip Eliot, and euery other way upon Robert
Pepper.

[106.] *85. William Linckhorne, his house and fower accres of land more or lesse bought of William Peacocke, abutting north upon Deddam highway, east upon John Mayes, south, and west upon William Dauis.

John Mayes Ju. his house and fower accres of land more or lesse, butting upon the highway to Deddam North, and upon a highway to John Welds east, upon William Dauis south, and upon William Linckhorne west.

[107.] *86. Henry Bowen, five accres of land more or lesse, bought of John Rugles Junior, abutting upon William Lyon north, upon John Weld and the highway east, upon his owne land, south, and upon the land of William Dauis west.

Thomas Bacon, fower accres of land more or lesse beyond the pond abutting upon William Lyon and Samuell Ruggles south, upon William Lyon east, upon Samuell Finch west, and upon Arthur Gary north.

[108.] Blank.

[109.] Blank.

WOODSTOCK LANDS.

[110.] Entered In the Book on Transcript of the lands of Roxbury 26 February 169⅚

This list Containes an acco^t of the first Range of lots in the Town's half of Woodstock land as they were drawn at a Town Meeting appointed for that end 26 April 1695, and surveyed and layd out by M John Butcher and the Committee chosen by the Inhabitants proprietors of the same the s^d Range containeing thirty four lots in number all of which ly upon the right hand of the path which leadeth to Woodstock the first lot of which s^d first Range abutteth upon s^d path or highway and is bounded by the lines or highway which divides between the land of the first goers or first setlers of Woodstock and the stayers, or other inhabitants of Roxbury as by a Plat of the same under the hand of the Mr. John Butcher may be more cleerly and perticularly appeeres, deciphered on the other sides.

No.		Acres.
1	John Gore	3 1¾
2	Pals Grave Alcock	05–
3	Joseph Lyon	30–
4	Palsgrave Allcock	05–
5	& Samuel Ruggles 5 acres } Serg^t John Ruggles 42½ acres }	47½
6	Roger Adams	25–
7	Lt. Samuel Ruggles	42¼

No.		Acres.
8	Samuel Weld	30–
	A highway two rods wide.	
9	Isaac Newel jun^r	17$\frac{1}{2}$
10	Maj^r Wait Winthrop.	67$\frac{1}{2}$
11	William Heath.	44$\frac{1}{4}$
12	John Gore	10$\frac{1}{2}$
13	Lt Samuel Ruggles	18
14	Moses Drapers heires	19
15	Mr Danforths beires.	10
16	George & James Griggs	33$\frac{1}{4}$
17^1	Edward Dorr.	18$\frac{1}{2}$
18^1	Jacob Pepper	30$\frac{3}{4}$
	A highway 5 rods wide.	
19^1	Samuel Williams jun^r	36$\frac{3}{4}$
	Exchanged with J^r: Mayo; No: 93:	
20^1	Joseph Mayo	55
21	The heires of Mr. John Bowles. . . .	65
22	Mr. William Denison	46$\frac{3}{4}$
23	Edward Bridge	30
24	James Draper jun^r	29$\frac{3}{4}$
	in his fathers right.	
25	Thomas Cheiney	31$\frac{3}{4}$
26	John Weld	25
27	John Bennet of Boston	05
28	John Davis (Smith)	37$\frac{1}{2}$
29	the heires of Joshua Lamb	30–
30	Mr. Thomas Ruggles	52$\frac{1}{2}$
	Highway 2 Rodd	
31	Joseph Newel or his heires	20–
32	Samuel Perry	30
33	John Holms	22$\frac{1}{2}$
	in right of John Newel	
34	James Frissel sen^r	27$\frac{1}{2}$

[111.] Blank.

[112.] This list Containes the number and quantity of the second Range of Lots as they were layed out by the aforesaid Surveyor and Committee, the first lot whereof being the 35 lot is bounded Southwardly by a high Way lying between the land of the first setlers of Woodstock land and the other Inhabitants of Roxbury according as s^d Lotts are deciphered in the Plat therof on the other side.

No.		Acres.
35	The beires of Isaac Curtiss	26–
36	Samuel Williams jun^r	41$\frac{3}{4}$
	in right of his unkle Stephen Williams	
37	Jacob Parker	25–

---

^{1} these lotts lye Double and the High way gos between. 17 : 19 & 18 : 20.

No.		Acres.
38	Henry Bowin : the medow rescr^d for a se. division	73$\frac{3}{4}$
39	Roger Adams	50–
40	Benjamin Childe	30–
41	Abraham Newel sen^r his heires	28$\frac{1}{4}$
42	Isaac How	25–
43	Nathanael Brewer	47$\frac{1}{2}$
44	Joseph Dudley Esqr	34$\frac{1}{4}$
45	Samuel Scarbrough	26$\frac{3}{4}$
46	Benjamin Gamblin	34$\frac{1}{4}$
47	John Scot	18$\frac{1}{2}$
48	Jabes Totman	34$\frac{1}{4}$
	in the right of his father in Law Davis	
49	Peter Collimore	35
50	Daniel Draper	19$\frac{1}{4}$
51	Jacob Newel	23$\frac{3}{4}$
	Passed over by deed to James Bennet	
52	Robert Baker	12$\frac{1}{2}$
53	Jacob Parker	12$\frac{1}{2}$
54	Jonathan Davis	35
	otherwise Joseph Gord or his heirs	

A highway of four rods wide layd out between the 48th and 49 lot of this Range.

The under list Containes the number and quantity of each of the Lots of third range as they were layed out by the aforesaid Surveyor and Committe, the first lot of which range being the 55th in number begins at the aforesaid highway between the inhabitants of Roxbury and Woodstock.

No.		Acres.
55	[1]Thomas Mory	22$\frac{1}{2}$
	taken up by Jonathan Parker	
56	Edmund Chamberlaine	21–
57	John Bugbey	24$\frac{1}{4}$
58	Free Schole of Roxbury	20–
59	Roger Adams	20–
60	Roger Weld Glazier	19$\frac{1}{4}$
61	Roger Adams	30–
	a highway two rods wide	
62	Sheball Sever	40–
63	John Ruggles 2^d his beires	26$\frac{3}{4}$
64	James Bennet	18$\frac{1}{4}$
65	Phillip Curtiss his beires	10–
	The lott reserued for the mill	
66	Widow Elisabeth Craft :	55–
67	Ralph Brodhurst	20–
68	Edmund Weld	44$\frac{1}{4}$
69	Benjamin Tucker	39$\frac{1}{4}$
70	John Davis sen^r	15–
71	Joshua Sever	37$\frac{1}{2}$
72	Isaac Newell sen	50–

---

[1] relinquished by Mory.

[**113.**] Number 14 Entred Moses Drapers Heirs and number 50 Entred Daniel Drapers being found Blanck Numbers were filled up as they now stand Entred by order of the Selectmen they being a Committee with some others Impowered by the town to hear that matter the 28th of June 1710

W^M DUDLEY Select man.
in presence and by order.

Major John Bowles Mr Edward Dorr and Samuel Williams being a Committee chosen and impowered by a vote of the proprietors of Woodstock north — half the 19th May 1713 to enquire and inspect any wrong entry in the Book in relation to any of these Lands meet this 20th Novemb^r 1716 and then Did Declare as their opinion and report that the 54th Lott entered Jonathan Davis 35; aceres ought to have been entred Joseph Gord or his heirs and accordingly ordred the Clerk to enter his name therein this was Done on examination and enquiry of the s^d Davis and two of the heirs of s^d Gord being present.

by order of s^d Committee
W. DUDLEY clerk.

[**114.**] The fourth Range wherof the 73^d lot is the first (and so all the other Ranges) begins at and is bounded Southwardly by the aforesaid highway lying between the land of Woodstock and Roxbury inhabitants:

No.		Acres.
73	Lt. Samuel Ruggles	21–
✗ 74	John Polley his heires	$37\frac{1}{2}$
75	Matthew Davis	$17\frac{1}{2}$
76	John Payson	$36\frac{3}{4}$
77	Roger Adams	$24\frac{1}{4}$
78	James Mosman	$17\frac{1}{2}$
⟍ 79	the heires of Jonathan Casse	$24\frac{1}{4}$
80	Nathanael Johnson	$47\frac{1}{2}$
	A highway four Rods wide.	
81	Samuel Payson	$47\frac{1}{2}$
82	Ebenezer Pierpont	20–
83	Jacob Parker	30–
84	Martha Armstrong	15–
85	Joshua Hemmenway	20–
86	widow Jane Davis	20–
87	Samuel Lyon	$21\frac{3}{4}$
88	Joseph Weld	$63\frac{1}{4}$

The fifth Range of lots wherof the 89th is the first is bounded by the aforesaid highway dividing between the land belonging to the inhabitants of Roxbury and the inhabitants of Woodstock southwardly the said lots being set forth in the Plat on the other side:

No.		Acres.
89	Edmund Weld	20–
90	Thomas Bacon	47½
91	Roger Adams	30–
92	John May	27½
93	John May	31¾
	Exchanged with Sam¹ Williams No. 19.	
94	Thomas Swan senʳ his heires	30¾
95	The beires of John Pierpont	71¾
96	Elisha May¹	15–
97	Sergₜ James Draper	26¾
	A highway two rods wide.	
98	Abraham Newel junʳ	15–
99	Samuel Williams junʳ	27½
	In right of his Grandfather Williams	
100	Lt. John White his heires . . . . -	06¾
101	Caleb Philips his heires	16¾
102	Isaac Morriss	30–
103	Jacob Parker	14¼
104	John Holbrooke	21¾

[**115.**] Blank.

[**116.**] The sixth Range of Lots begins with the 105th lott and bounded by the aforesaid highway divideing between the land of the inhabitants of Roxbury and Woodstock and are layd out by the aforesaid Surveyʳ and Committee as in the Plat on the other side is expressed.

No.		Acres.
105	Jacob Chamberlaine	23¼
106	Samuel Williams junʳ	85¾
	In right of his father Williams.	
107	Sergᵗ John Ruggles	47½
	S: Willᵐˢ.	
108	James Frissel junʳ	13¼
109	John Pike his heires	21¾
110	Edward Morris	20¾
111	Caleb Sever	51¾
	S Willᵐˢ.	
112	John Whitney	35–
113	Joseph Weld	40–
114	Jonathan Peake	44¼
	In right of Daniel Brewer	
115	Joseph Griggs	38¼
116	Samuel Williams junʳ	31¾
	In right of Mr. John Smith.	

The 7th Range beginning with 117th lott lying upon the aforesaid high way is as followeth : and deciphered in the plat on the other side : But said highway not being passable in that place by rea-

---

¹ Opposite in margin, S. Will. — W. H. W.

son of a swamp the highway is turned to the other side of the 117th lot and to be four rods wide and said 114th lot to run home to Woodstock line.

No.		Acres.
117	Peter Gardner .	35¾
	a highway of 4 Rods	
118	William Cheiney his heires	26¾
119	Roger Adams .	50–
120	John Davis sen^r	52½
121	Capt. Timothy Stevens	70–
122	John Searles	12½

[**117.**] Blank.

[**118.**] This list Containes the eighth Range of Lots layd out by the aforesaid surveyor and Committee beginning at and abutting upon the aforesaid high way by Woodstock line and lying as in the Plat on the other side.

No.		Acres.
123	William Pecock heirs	14¼
124	John Grosvenors heires	36¾
125	John Griggs jun^r	34¼
126	Jonathan Parker	62½
127	Samuel Knight his heires .	23¼
128	William Davis .	17½
	purchased of Edward Ainsworth	
129	Caleb Lamb's heires .	15¾
130	Samuel Gove his heires	39¼
131	John Baker	28¼
132	John Lyon sen^r	29¼
133	Thomas Bishop	30–
134	Samuel Payson	32½

The nineth Range of lots begins also at the aforesaid highway and is layd out by said Surveyor and Committee as in this list is mentioned and in the Plat on the other side deciphered.

No.		Acres.
135	Jonathan Peake	39¼
136	Roger Adams .	40–
137	John Holbrooke	18¼
138	Widow Hawley wth Cleaves	09–
139	Capt. Samuel Ruggles	12½
140	John Sever	05–
141	`Widow Abigail Johnson .	02½
142	Abigail & Mehetabel Heath	07½

All the lots above mentioned in the severall Ranges thereof were entered by order of the selectmen of Roxbury the twenty sixth day of February in the year of our Lord one thousand six hundred ninety $\frac{five}{six}$

By me

JOHN GORE

Town Cler

[119.] Blank.

[120.] Entred in the Book or Transcript of the Lands of Roxbury 22 Sept. 1715.

This List contains an accompt of the first Range of Lotts of the Towns half of of Woodstock in the Second Division as they were Drawn at a proprietors meeting appointed and assemble dfor that end the 19ᵗʰ July 1713 and Surveyed and Laid out by Mʳ Ebeneser Woodward with the Committee chosen by the proprietors for that end. The said Range contains twenty one Lotts in number and is 164 perch wide and begins at the north bounds of the Town, where the Line betwixt the second and third range laid out by Mʳ Butcher intersects the said North bounds according to the vote of the proprietors and runs Southward untill it meets the third range before Laid out by said Mʳ Butcher. all these Lotts are 160. rodds in Length and the 4 rodds more is for a high way at the west end of all these Lotts Conformable to the said Mʳ Butchers work.

No.				Accrs.	Allowance for Quality. Accrs.	Whole Quantity. Accrs.
1.	Serjᵗ James Draper	.	.	36.¼		36.¼
2.	Capt. Joshua Lamb	.	.	37.½		37.½
3.	Serjᵗ James Draper	.	.	33.¼		33.¼
4.	John Scott	.	.	23.		23.
5.	John Davis Smith .	.	.	46.¾		46.¾
	High way four rodds wide					
6.	Deacon Samᵐ Scarboro .	.	.	33.¼		33.¼
7.	Jacob Parker	.	.	31.¼	7.¾	39.
8.	Edmund Weld	.	.	25.	13.½	38.½
9.	Widow Johnson	.	.	2.¾	2.¾	5.½
10.	William Peacock .	.	.	17.¾	12.	29.¾
11.	Samuel Williams .	.	.	39.¾	25.½	65.¼
12.	Phillip Curtice, heirs	.	.	12.½	6.	18.½
13.	John Weld	.	.	24.¼	13.	37.¼
14.	John Bugbee .	.	.	30.¼	5.¾	36.
15.	James Frisell junʳ .	.	.	16.½	¾	71.¼
16.	James Mosman	.	.	21.¾	½	22.¼
17.	John Pason	.	.	46.	1.¾	47.¾
18.	Jonᵃ Parker for Mory	.	.	28.	¼	28.¼
19.	John Holmes .	.	.	28.	¼	28.¼
20.	Joseph Lyon .	.	.	37.½		37½
21.	Isaac Morrise	.	.	37.½		37.½

Highway of 6 rodds wide between this Last Lott and the last lott in the third range in the first Division.

[121.] Blank.

[122.] This List contains the number and Quantity of the Second Range of Lotts as they were laid out by the aforesaid Surveyour and Committee in this Second Division the first lott being the 22 lott and is bounded Southerly on the last Lott in the fourth range in the first Division as it is perticularly Decyphered in the platt under the hand of the said Surveyour.   these Lotts are 160. rodds. long and a 4 rodd highway at the west end of them.

No.					Acres.	Allowance for Quality. Acres.	Whole Quantity. Acre.
22.	Benjamen Child	.	.	.	37.$\frac{1}{2}$	3.$\frac{1}{2}$	41.
23.	John Gore	.	.	.	39.$\frac{3}{4}$	7.	46.$\frac{3}{4}$
24.	Jacob Parker	.	.	.	17.$\frac{3}{4}$	6.$\frac{1}{4}$	24.
25.	William Denison	.	.	.	58.$\frac{1}{4}$	9.$\frac{3}{4}$	68.
26.	Sert John Davis	.	.	.	18.$\frac{3}{4}$	2.$\frac{1}{4}$	21.
27.	Samuel Ruggles	.	.	.	53.	$\frac{1}{4}$	53.$\frac{1}{4}$
28.	John Griggs junr	.	.	.	42.$\frac{3}{4}$	$\frac{1}{4}$	43.
29.	Samuel Gores heirs		.	.	49.		49.
30.	John Witney	.	.	.	43.$\frac{3}{4}$		43.$\frac{3}{4}$
31.	Heury Bowen	.	.	.	92.$\frac{1}{4}$	21.$\frac{1}{4}$	113.$\frac{1}{2}$

A peice of Common or undivideble land to the north line 298 acrees

This list contains the number and Quantity of the third range of Lotts in this Second Division as they were laid out by the said Surveyour and Committee the first lott being the 32 lott and is bounded northerly on the north bounds of the town as is partienlarly Decyphered in the platt, these lotts are 160 rodds long and a 4 rodd's highway at the west end of them.

No.					Acres.	Allowance for Quality. Acres.	Whole Quantity. Acres.
32	Benjamin Tucker	.	.	.	49	6 ·	55
33	Moses Drapers beirs	.	.	.	23$\frac{3}{4}$	6$\frac{3}{4}$	30$\frac{1}{2}$
34	Edward Morrise	.	.	.	27	18	44

there is a four rodd highway allowed out of these 3 Lots by the side of the meadow

35	Daniel Draper	.	.	. .	24	1	25
36	Jonathan Peak	.	.	.	49	1	50
37	Martha Armstrong	.	.	.	18$\frac{3}{4}$	$\frac{1}{4}$	19
38	John Baker	.	.	. .	35$\frac{1}{4}$	4$\frac{3}{4}$	40
39	John Gore	.	.	. .	12$\frac{1}{2}$	3$\frac{1}{2}$	16
40	Roger Addams	.	.	. .	62$\frac{1}{2}$	4$\frac{1}{2}$	67
41	Joseph Griggs	.	.	.	47$\frac{3}{4}$	16$\frac{1}{4}$	64

A piece of Common or undividable Land of 202 acrees

42	Shobaal Seever	.	.	.	50	10$\frac{1}{2}$	60$\frac{1}{2}$
43	Thomas Cheny	.	.	.	39$\frac{1}{2}$		39$\frac{1}{2}$

A piece of common between this lott and the last lott in the fifth range in the first Division of 14 rodds wide containing 14 accres or thereabout

[123.]   A high way from the fourth range line of four rodd's wide is allowed through the wedth of Drapers Lott to come at the meadow his the said Drapers Lott lying length way by the side of the meadow called Mapple Island meadow.

by order of the Committee
W. DUDLEY

[**124.**] This list Contains the number and Quantity of the fourth range of Lotts in the Second Division as they were laid out by the said Surveyour and Committee the first Lott being the 44th Lott and is bounded southerly by the last lott in the Sixth Range of the first Division and Decyphered in the platt these Lotts are 172: perch in Length and 4 rodds for a high way at the westerly end of them.

No.		Acres	Allowance for Quality. Accres	Whole Quantity. Accres
44	Caleb Sever	$64\frac{1}{2}$	$5\frac{1}{4}$	$69\frac{3}{4}$
	now S. Williams			
45	Caleb Phillips heirs . . .	21	$1\frac{1}{2}$	$22\frac{1}{2}$
46	Thomas Ruggles . . .	$65\frac{1}{2}$	$4\frac{3}{4}$	$70\frac{1}{4}$
47	Nathl Johnson	$59\frac{1}{4}$	5	$64\frac{1}{4}$
48	Joseph Dudley: Esq: . .	$167\frac{3}{4}$	$13\frac{1}{4}$	181
	A peice of Common or undivideble Land of			$107\frac{1}{2}$
49	Saml: º & J: Ruggles . . .	$59\frac{1}{4}$	$18\frac{1}{4}$	$77\frac{1}{2}$
50	Samuel Ruggles . . .	$23\frac{1}{2}$	2	$25\frac{1}{2}$
51	Abigail & Mehit: Heath: . .	$9\frac{1}{4}$	$\frac{3}{4}$	10
52	Jonathan Parker . . .	78	$9\frac{1}{2}$	$87\frac{1}{2}$
53	Saml: Ruggles	$26\frac{1}{4}$	$12\frac{3}{4}$	39
54	Saml: Knight, heirs . . .	29	29	58
55	Joshua Sever	$46\frac{3}{4}$	$3\frac{1}{4}$	50

[**125.**] Blank.

[**126.**] This List contains the number and Quantity of the Lotts in the fifth range of Lotrs in the Second Division as they were laid out by the said Surveyour and Committee the first Lott being 55th: or the allowance for the Quality of that Lott and is bounded by the North Line of the Town on the northward, and Decyphered by the Platt these Lotts are 170 rodds in Length and a high way of four rodds wide at the easterly end of them which makes that way between this and the fourth range 8 rodds wide and also there is a four rodd High way allowed at the westerly end of these Lotts which makes this range includeing the said two high ways 178 perch in Length.

No.		Acres	Allowance. Acres	Whole Quantity. Acres
55	Joshua Sever		$28\frac{1}{4}$	$78\frac{1}{4}$
56	William Davis	$21\frac{3}{4}$	$20\frac{3}{4}$	$42\frac{1}{2}$
57	George & James Griggs . .	$41\frac{1}{2}$	111	$155\frac{1}{2}$

Muddy Brook Pond is contained in this Lott and is almost half of the Lott there is a way of 4 rodds wide round the pond allowed out of this Lott also

58	Free School	25	30	55
59[1]	Jonath Davis	$43\frac{3}{4}$	4	$47\frac{3}{4}$
60	Edmund Weld	$55\frac{1}{4}$	$4\frac{1}{4}$	$59\frac{1}{2}$
61	Peter Cullimore	$43\frac{3}{4}$	$8\frac{1}{4}$	52

[1] Goad x

No.		Acres	Allowance. Acres	Whole Quantity. Acres
62	Nathl. Brewer	59¼	31¾	91
63	Isaac How	31¼	3¾	35
64	Roger Addams	25	1½	26½
65	Joseph Weld's	50	3	53
66	Samuel Ruggles	15½	¾	16¼
67	Isaac Newell jun^{r}	21¾	1¼	23
68	William Heath	55¼	3¼	58½
	Highway of 4 rodds wide			
69	Roger Addams	31¼	2¾	34
70	Samuell Williams	52	3¼	55¼
71	Samuel Pason	40½	2½	43
72	Eben^{r}. Pierpont	25	1½	26½
73	Edmund Chamberlain	26¼	1½	27¾
74	Caleb Lambs heirs	19½	1	20½
75	John Searle	15½	¾	16¼

The Lott of 124 acres and half for the publick use of the proprietors . . . which joins the last Lott in the Seventh range in the first Division.

[127.] Blank.

[128.] This List contains the number and Quantity of Lotts in the Sixth range of Lotts in the Second Division as they were laid out by the said Surveyour and Committee, being 160 rodds in Length and the first Lott is 76 and bounded Southerly on the Last lott in the eighth range in the first Division as platted by the said surveyour.

No.		Acres.	Allow: Acres.	Whole Quantity. Acers.
76	Jonth Case's heirs	30.¼	½	30.¾
77	Timothy Stevens	87.½		87.½
78	Edward Dorr	23.		23.
79	John Lyons heirs	36.½		36.½
	A highway of four rodds wide			
80	Joseph Newell's he[irs]	25.	0	25
81	John Holbrook	22.¾		22¾
82	Joshua Hemingway	25.	3	28
83	Saml. Williams	34.¼	4	38¼
84	Jacob Parker	37.½	12.½	50
85	Mathew Davis	21.¾	18¼	40
86	Widow Hawley & Cleaves	11.¼	8¾	20
	495 rodds of Common to the North Bounds.		495 acrees.	

This List contains the number and Quantity of Lotts in the Seventh range of Lotts in the Second Division as they were laid out by the said Surveyour and Committee beginning with the 87th Lott bounded by the Comon. these Lotts are 160 rodds in Length and at the east end a high way of four rodds wide which makes this range 164 rodds wide as platted by the said Surveyour &c. .the first lott beginns 616 rodds from the north bounds —

No.		Acres.	Allow. Acres.	Quantity. Acres.
87	Mr Danforth^s heirs . . .	$12\frac{1}{2}$	$7\frac{1}{2}$	20
88	Isaac Curtice	$32\frac{1}{2}$	$12\frac{1}{2}$	45
89	Abr^a Newell Senr . . .	$35\frac{1}{4}$	$10\frac{3}{4}$	46
90	Benj^a Gambling . . .	$42\frac{3}{4}$	$13\frac{1}{4}$	56
91	Abra: Newell jun^r . . .	$18\frac{3}{4}$	$5\frac{1}{4}$	24
	A high way of four rodds wide			
92	John Welds	$13\frac{1}{4}$	$4\frac{3}{4}$	36
93	John Sever	$6\frac{1}{4}$	$1\frac{3}{4}$	8
94	Jabez Totman	$42\frac{3}{4}$	$1\frac{1}{4}$	44
95	Elisha May	$18\frac{3}{4}$	$2\frac{1}{4}$	21
96	Saml Williams	107		107
97	Thomas Bacon	$59\frac{1}{4}$	$1\frac{3}{4}$	61
	A high way two rodds wide.			

[129.] Blank.

[130.] This List contains the number of Lotts and Quantity of acrees in the eighth range in the Second Division as they were laid out by the said Surveour and Committee beginning at the Dividing line between the goers and Stayers and there is a four rodds high way to the north ward of that Line, the first Lotts is the ninety eighth Lott all these Lotts are 160 rodds in Length and a four rodd high way on the east end of these Lotts.

No.		Acres	Allowance. Acr	Whole quantity Acc
98	Jonathan Peek . . .	$55\frac{1}{4}$	$\frac{3}{4}$	56
99	Thomas Bishop	$37\frac{1}{2}$	$7\frac{1}{2}$	45
100	Jacob Newell	29	6	35
101	John Ruggles second . .	$33\frac{1}{4}$	$15\frac{3}{4}$	49
102	John Pike's heirs . .	27	9	36
103	Peter Gardner . . .	$44\frac{1}{2}$	$10\frac{1}{2}$	55
104	Roger Adams . . .	$37\frac{1}{2}$	$\frac{1}{2}$	38
105	Jacob Chambelain . . .	29		29
106	Saml Lyons heirs . . .	27		27
107	*John Mayo	$39\frac{1}{2}$	$20\frac{1}{2}$	[1]50

this range falls short of the north bounds 856 perch that Land being unfitt for Division.

This Lott is changed with Saml Williams.

This list contains a Truc number and Quantity of Lotts in the nineth Range of Lotts as laid out by the Surveyour and Committee and beginns upon the Common Northward and goes up to the said Dividing Line being from the said line 303 rodds these lotts are

---

[1] Error in original; should be 60. — W. H. W.
[2] This is on p. 131. — W. H. W.

160 rodds in Length and have a four rodd high way at the east end of them which makes this range 164 perch wide.

No.		Acres	Allow. Acres	Whole Quantity
108	Mr John Bowles heirs . . .	81¼	10¾	92
109	Palsgrave Alcock . . .	6¼	3¾	10
110	James Frisell *Sen . . .	16½	9½	26
111	John Bennett	6¼	3¾	10
112	John May's	34¼	15¾	50

A high way of four rodds wide and ten acrees Southward as Common

113	Samuel Perry	37	5¼	42¼

Mem : 'Frisell's Lott should have been 34 acrees the remaining 17½ to be taken out of the common or undivided Land next his Lott of meadow in Pine Swamp meadow allowed to Mr Sumner in right of said Frisell which has accordingly been Laid out. —

[132.] This List contains the number & Quantity of the Lotts in the tenth range in the Second Division as laid out by the Surveyour and Committee, and begins with the 114th Lott which lyes next to the Dividing line northward these Lotts are 160 rodds in length untill it comes to the great Cedar Swamp and then the Lotts are shorter and all perticularly Decyphered in the platt, there is also a high way at the east end untill it comes to the Cedar swamp and the high way at the west end is included in the Lotts.

No.		Acr	Allow: Ac.	Acc.
114	John Davis	65½	2½	68
	A high way of four rodds wide			
115	Jacob Parker	15½	4½	20
116	Roger Addams	50	25	75
117	John Grosvenour . . .	45¾	9¼	55
118	Roger Addams	37½	18½	56
	A high way four Rodds wide			
119	Widow Jane Davis . . .	25	5½	30½
	16 rodd short at the east end			
120	Whites heirs'	8¼	¾	9
121	Joseph Mayo	68¾		68¾
	these two lotts and the last are but eighty rodds in Length.			
122	James Bennet	22¾		22¾

This List contains the number and Quantity of the Lotts in the 11th· range in the second division as laid out by the said Surveyour and the Committee and begins on the common northward vist. rodds from the North bounds it being not fit for Division these Lotts are 166 : rodds in Length there is a high way at the west end of these Lotts of four rodds wide which makes the range 164 : rodds wide all Decyphered by the platt.

No.		Acres.	Allow: Acres.	Whole Quantity. Acc.
123	Joseph Weld	79	1	80
124	Saml Williams	45¾	¼	46
	now exchanged with John Mayo			
125	John Pierpont	89½	20½	110
126	Robert Baker	15½	14½	30
127	Willm Cheeny	33¼	11¾	45
	A highway four rodds wide			
128	Widow Craifts	68½	13¼	82
	Now Nath Craifts			
129	Edward Bridge	37½	42	79½
130	Saml. Weld	37½	15	52½
131	Ser^t Jo^h: Ruggles . . .	59¼	19¾	79
132	Roger Addams	62½		62½
133	Jacob Pepper	38¼		38¼

[133.] Blank.

[134.] This List contains an accompt of the Lotts and ther Quantitys in the 12th Range in the second division as laid out by the Surveyour and the Committee all which ranges were laid out in May and June 1715 and the first Lot herein being 134th begins at the Dividing Line between the goers and Stayers and these Ltots are Seventy Six perch in Length and bounded on the east end by the said way in the eleventh range and the west bounds of the Town on the west.

No:		Acres Quat	Allow: Acres Quat	Whole Quantity Acres Quat
134	Thom Swans heirs . .	38½	8¾	47¼
135	Roger Addams . . .	30¼		30¼
136	Palsgrave Alcock . .	6¼	3	9¼
137	John Polley . . .	46¾		46¾
138	John Holbrook . . .	27	3¼	30¼
139	Isaac Newell . . .	62½		62½
140	Wait Winthrop Esqr . .	84	¼	84¼
141	Samuel Pason . . .	59¼	½	59¾
142	Ralph Bradhurst . .	25	3½	28½

All these Lotts above mentioned in the severall ranges thereof were entred by the advice and Direction of the Committee this twenty second of September 1715

by mee   W. Dudley

(autograph)   Clerk to the Proprietors

[135.] Blank.

[136.] Blank.

[137.] Roxbury 26 June 1716

whereas that Tract of Land now known by the name of the township of Woodstock was granted by the General

Court to the inhabitants of Roxbury and the said Town some time after gave one half of that grant to a number of persons inhabiteng on that part and reserved the other vist. the north half to themselves and whereas the said inhabitants of Roxbury and proprietors of the north half hold and enjoy their severall shares and proportions of the Land by the records of the Town, and whereas the proprietors by their votes in their severall meetings of the 9th: November 1714 and 14th: March 1715 have impowered Majr: John Bowles Mr Edward Dorr and Mr Samuel Williams to Dispose certain peices and parcells of meadow hereafter named to Receive the money arriseing upon the Disposition of those meadows and pay out the same or so much thereof as shall be expended in the Laying out the several Lotts lately proportioned amongst the several proprietors and whereas sundry proprietors have Desired shares of meadow and have engaged to pay for them immediately after they are laid out which is now Done, we therefore the said Committee and Subscribers being impowered as is above said Do allow of and Dispose of the 26 Lotts in the meadow commonly called and known by the name of Senexitt unto the Severall proprietors and purchasers here under written each Lott containing five acrees who have also paid the Severall Sums against their Lotts : the receipt whereof we Do acknoledge and every part and severall and Different parcells there of from the said purchasers we Do Declare we have received and them their heirs &c. aquitt and discharge.

Mens Names.	No of Lotts	Quantity	Sums of money p £ s d
Joseph Scarborough . . .	1	5	2 10 —
made over to Maturing Allard			
made over by sd. Scarbro to Saml Williams he having paid the sum			
Peter Cullimore . . .	2	5	2 10 —
in Right of Edward Dorr			
Peter Cullimore . . .	3	5	2 10 —
in right of John Totman			
Peter Cullimore . . .	4	5	3 10 —
Samuel Gore	5	5	3 15 —
Edward Bridge	6	5	1 10 —
in right of Eben Eastman			
Samuel Williams . . .	7	6	3 12 —
made over to Govr Dudley .	8	5	3 15 —

(margin: Senexitt meadow west side.)

[1] The Lot entered Jos: Scarborough and after Saml. Williams is now Maturing Allard ; he haveing paid the said sum of two pounds ten shillings.

[138.]   Blank.

[1] Entered on opposite page (136). —W. H. W.

[139.]

Mens names.	No. Lotts.	Quantity.	Sums of money p'd. £	s.	d.
John Bowles	1	5	3	15	—
Jacob Pepper	2	5	3	15	—
Edward Dorr	3	5	3	5	—
William Denison	4	5	3	5	
Edward Bridge	5	5	3	10	
Nathaniel Draper	6	5	3	15	
Thomas Checny	7	5	6	5	
John Welds	8	5	6	5	

Senexitt meadow East Side

Ensigne John Davis	9	5	2	10	—
Joseph Lyon jun^r	10	5	3	15	—
Edward Child in right of his brother Ephraim	11	5	6	5	—
Capt: Joshua Lamb	12	5	5	—	—
Capt: Joshua Lamb	13	5	1	5	—

These Lotts go through the said meadow

The owner of these Lotts not to hinder at any time the flowing and benefitting thereby of this meadow by makeing a Dam therefor.

And we the said Committee and Subscribers Do Dispose and allow the Meadow commonly called and known by the name of Pine Island Meadow to the persons and purchasers as is before Specifyed and recorded.

Mens Names	No. Lots.	Quantity.	Sums. Pd.		
Edward Sumner in right of James Frisell sen^r	1	5	3	10	—
Isaac Curtice	2	5	3	10	—
Isaac Newell	3	5	3	15	—
Samuel Williams in right of Eben^r Swan	4	5	1	5	—

is now said Swan's heirs the widow haveing Repaid the money.

And we the said Committee and Subscribers Do allow and Dispose the pcice of meadow commonly called and known by the name of Connecticutt or May's meadow to the persons and purchasers under written as is before specifyed and recorded.

	No.	Qua.	Sums. pd.		
Jacob Pepper in right of Capt. Ruggles his heirs by agreement.	1	5	10		—
Joseph Lyon	2	5	8	15	—
Benjamen Child's	3	4	7	—	—
Icabod Holmes	4	3	4	12	—

and to Serj^t John Mays with his Son John May's jun^r is allowed in said meadow — 10 acrees Lying within and to the eastward of the westward Line of the said John Mays jun^r Lott as it is now Run and laid out the sum they haveing paid therefore is.........£20.

[140.] Blank.

[**141.**] We the said Committee and subscribers Do allow grant and Dispose of the meadow commonly called and known by the name of Mapple Island Meadow the Severall Quantitys thereof as they are entred and recorded against their names they haueing paid the Sums entred against their names.

Mens names.	No Lotts.	Quan.	Sums paid £ s. d.
Joseph Dudley Esq	i	5	3 5 —
made over to Saml Williams			
John Holbrook	2	5	3 .. ..
Thomas Baker	3	5	3 .. ..
John Pikes heirs	4	5	3 15 ..
P^d by Thomas Baker			
Nathaniel Draper	5	5	3 .. ..
in right of John Lyons heirs			
	6	5	1 5 ..
	7	5	1 5 ..
Timothy Ruggles	8	5	1 5 ..
in right of John Pierpont			
Joseph Addams and Henry Smith heirs to their father . . . . . }	9	5	2 15 ..
Joseph Welds heirs	10	5	3 15 ..
	11	5	3 .. ..
George Bacons heirs	12	5	3 .. ..
Jacob Chamberlain	13	5	3 .. ..
Samuel Williams	14	5	3 .. ..

In witness to the said Committees Consent and intire Satisfaction to the above and before entrys of the Severall persons names number of Lotts Quantity of meadows and sums of money paid as is before entred and recorded the said Committee have signed these presents: this 20th November 1716.

EDWARD DORR

autographs   SAMUEL WILLIAMS

JOHN BOWLES

Entred as above by me

W. DUDLEY prop^rs Clerk.

[**142.**] Mem°: 17th May 1717
the Committee within mentioned mett & made up accounts of the money Bills and bonds which are in Mr Dorr the Treasurers hands and there is in money   10 .. 2 .. —
Bills and bonds   74 .. 4 .. 6

£84 .. 6 .. 6

Besides the Lotts undisposed of

[**143.**] Memorandum Roxbury 26th June 1716: by mistake John Holbrook's name is entred in the Lotts of meadow as if paid but he not being. present this Day nor any person paying for him and the Committee not allowing his name to be raised out this memorandum is made the Day and year above

Signed and entred by order } W. DUDLEY clerk.
of that Committee for sale }

Septem^r 4 1716 John Holbrook appeared and payd The money for his grant.

[144.] Blank.

[145.] By a warrant from the Honorable Isaac Addington and Paul Dudley Esqr under their Hands and Seals Directed to Mr William Dudley according to a Law of the province in that Case made and provided ordred a meeting of the Proprietors of Lands in Woodstock and notice being accordingly given fourteen Days before the Time in Roxbury and Woodstock They Did on Wednesday the Sixth of May 1713 meet accordingly and Chose William Dudley their Clark and voted:

1. That all the undivided Common Lands Lying in the old Town half fitt and usefull to be Divided be forthwith as soon as Conveniently may be Divided and apportioned to and amongst the severall proprietors according to their Severall proportions:

2. That Mr William Dudley Capt: Joshua Lamb and L^t: Edward Bridge be a Committee for the Division of the said Lands:

3. That the said Committee bring in proposalls for the Division and the good management of the said Lands to the proprietors the 19th: of May Instant at three of the Clock afternoon to which Time the meeting was by a vote adjourned:

Roxbury 6th May 1713 W. DUDLEY Clerk.

On the 8th: of May 1713 William Dudley personally appeared before Paul Dudley Esqr one of Her Majestys Justices of the Peace and was by him Sworne to the true and faithfull performance of the offices of proprietors Clerk according to the Choice that was made by the proprietors to the Lands in Woodstock. W. D.

[146.] At a meeting of the proprietors in Woodstock Lands held by adjournment the 19th May 1713 wherein it was voted as follows

1: That there be two Divisions or allotments made of the undivided Land if the same be fitt if not then one of upland another of swamp and meadows:

2: That the proprietors shall Draw Lotts:

3: That the Committee be impowered to allow Quantity for Quality in these Divisions:

4: That it be Left to the Committees Judgment where to begin in these Divisions:

5: That that there be a Distinct Division of Swamps and meadow and to every proprietor their respective proportions of each, and that this Division is under the same penaltys as the other:

6 : That the Committee is impowered to Lay out and Establish Roads and ways in Convenient places and least prejudiciall to any persons property:

7 : That Capt Saml: Ruggles M^r. Edward Dorr and John Holbrook be a Committee to assess and Levy the charges and Disbursments that shall arrise on these Divisions when they are known and adjusted on the severall proprietors according to their proportions and Receive the same according to the Rate or assesment and that they pay out the same according to the accompt of Charges when given in by the Committee that Divide the Land :

8 : That every proprietor and all the proprietors shall pay their Severall rates or proportions of the Charges to the said Committee appointed to Levy and Receive the same in Twenty days after the Same is Levyed and published on the penalty of Looseing their Severall shares or lotts in these Divisions not excludeing any person that shall be orphans, widows or absent by the providence of God ;

9 : That the Scool Lot he free of all charges :

10 : That the aforesaid assessors be a Committee to Enquire and inspect into any persons pretences to a right in any of these Lands or any wrong entry that may have been made :

11 : That this Day nine weeks after Lecture be the Day for the proprietors to Draw Lotts notice to be given :

[147.] 12 : That both these Committees be Sworne to shew neither favour or affection, in the Discharge of their Trusts but to Deal faithfully and uprightly according to their best skill and Judgement :

13 : That all the papers platts and Records in any wise respecting or Belonging to these Woodstock Lands be put into the Clerks hands for the Committees help and Direction :

14 : That all future meetings of the proprieters shall be by notification put up in publick places by the Clerk :

15 : That the Committee for the Division be allowed five shillings pr Diem a piece for themselves and Time and Trouble And be impowered to agree with a Surveyor :

16 : That the assessors shall have two shillings and six pence pr Diem when they are makeing the assesment :

17 : That no other Lott be allowed either in Swamp, Meadow or uplands for the Mill as in the past Division :

attestatur pr

W. DUDLEY: Clerk

July 21th: 1713

Voted that these Lotts Viz^t 142 in number : be the only Lotts to be Drawn for the three Divisions of Swamp meadows and upland. and that the proprietors Draw but this once for the three Divisions.

[148.] Novembr 9th : 1714.

At a meeting of the proprietors of Woodstock north half Summoned and warned according to agreement at Roxbury it was unanimously Voted, as follows

1 : Upon Consideration of the Dificulty and Damage of Laying out the meadows Distinct and in a perticular Division according to a former vote. it is therefore at this time voted that all the meadows and Swamps except what is hereafter excepted be laid out with the uplands and accounted as such in the after allotments and Division.

2 : That Senexitt meadow, Maple Island, Pine Swamp, and May's meadow be sold, the proprietors to have the first offer in order to the Defraying the charges of laying out the Lands and that no perticular proprietor shall buy above five accres of the above said meadows.

3 : That whereas Capt. Samuel Ruggles Mr Edwd. Dorr and John Holbrook were appointed assessors to Levy and Receive the Rate on the proprietors, it is now — Voted that the said three persons with the addition of Lt. Samuel Williams be the Committee for the Disposall of the aforesaid meadows who are accordingly fully Impowered and authorised to make Sale and ample Deeds thereof as is above voted.

4 : That where the line betwixt the second and third Range already laid out Intersects the north line of the Town Shall be the place where the first Range in this present Division Shall begin and that the other Ranges shall proceed westward in the same order as the former were butting one on the other.

5 : That against the Seventh Range 100 aceres of Land be allotted and Layed out for the publick use and benefitt of these proprietors in this half of the Town.

6 : That the Committee be impowered to agree with any persons for the Conveniency of a way from the Second Range to the Country Road and that they be impowered to allow Some undivided land next adjoining to the said persons across whose land the said way will go as a Recompence for the Damage Such way will cause.

7 : That Lt: Saml. Williams be one of the Committee in the Room and Steed of Capt: Lamb for time past and to Come.

[**149.**] 8th: That the Cedar Swamp be left Distinct and excepted from this present Division and be under Restrictions and Reservations from any persons cutting any Timber there without leave had from the Committee or persons appointed to Inspect and take Care of that Swamp, after which the meeting was ended.

Roxbury 1715.
At a meeting held at the old meeting house this 14th March it being by adjournment from the 14th December Last 1715 and Mr Denison being chosen Moderator it was voted

1. That what has been already Done in respect to the Severall Lotts lately Laid out is Sufficient and nothing further necessary at present to be Done as to those Lotts.   Voted

2. That Deacon Morrisse with the help of a Surveyor perfect the Line's of one range and two or three Lotts not Quite finished.
                                                            Voted.

3.   That Maj^r Bowles be of that Committee for the Disposall of the meadows in the Room of Captain Ruggles Dec̄d and M^r. John Holbrook he haveing absolutely refused to serve any Longer in that capacity   Voted

4.   That if any error or mistake in the Laying out of these last Lotts shall hereafter be found that any person injured shall have Due Satisfaction out of the remaining undivided Lands

After which the meeting ended.

Mem^o: the Committee for the Disposall of the meadows gave 30 Days notice by advertisements posted up in publick places that the purchasers should appear at the grey hound in Roxbury the 26th : of June 1716 : in order to pay the money promised for those meadows on which Day vis^t 26 June some Did appear and pay their money then the committee ordred one month more to be allowed vis^t to the 24th July to the remaining purchasers to pay their money or their engagement would be put in a course of Law at which time Some more came and others refused or neglected the committee then allowed Six weeks more in order that all might come and no person complain for want of time, until the 4th Sept. next these notifycation or copys are on file with the other papers

Attest to the truth above

W. DUDLEY

25 July 1716

[**150.**]   Roxbury, 26 March 1717

a meeting of Woodstock north half proprietors Legally called : it was voted that the money arriseing and remaining of the produce of the money, on the Sale of the medows be put out to interest and the best improvement by the Committee they rendring account thereof when and as often as called thereto by the propritors.

Voted that William Dudley be added to the said Committee for the Letting out and improvement of the money.

Voted that the whole records and Concernment of these Woodstock Lands be fairly recorded and transcribed into another Book of Records and kept Distinct to prevent any unforseen Casualty.

After which the meeting ended.

THE REV. JOHN ELIOT'S RECORD OF CHURCH MEMBERS, ROXBURY, MASS.

THE REV. JOHN ELIOT'S RECORD OF CHURCH MEMBERS, ROXBURY, MASS.

A recorde of such as adjoyned themselves vnto the fellowship of this Church of Christ at Roxborough: as also of such children as they had when they joyned, & of such as were borne vnto them vnder the holy Covenant of this Church who are most p͞perly the seede of this Church.

m͏ʳ William Pinchon, he was chosen an Assistant yearely so long as he lived among vs: his wife dyed soone after he landed at N. Eng: he brought 4 children to N.E. Ann, Mary. John, Margret. After some years he married m͏ʳⁱˢ Francis Samford, a grave matron of the church at Dorchester. When so many removed fr͞o these parts to Plant Conecicot riv͏ʳ he also w͏ᵗʰ othr company went thith͏ʳ, & planted at a place called Agawam. & was recom͞ended to the church at windsor on Conecticott, vntill such time as it should please God to p͞vide y͏ᵗ they might enter into church estate among themselves. his daughter Ann: was married to m͏ʳ Smith, so͞ne to m͏ʳ Samford by a former husband, he was a Godly, wise young man, & removed to Agawam w͏ᵗʰ his parents. His daughter mary was married to m͏ʳ Hollioke, the so͞ne of m͏ʳ Hollioke of Linn: m͏ʳ Pluchons ancient freind.

he came in the first company: 1630 he was one of the first foundation of the church at Rocksbrough.

Afterwards he wrote a Dialogue concerning Justification, w͏ᶜʰ was Printed anno 1650, stiled the meritorious price, a book full of error & weaken͏ˢ, & some heresies w͏ᶜʰ the Generall Court of y͏ᵉ Massachusetts Condemned to be burnt & appointed m͏ʳ John Norton then Teacher at Ipswich to confute y͏ᵉ errors contained therein.

M͏ʳ Thomas Welde

William Dennison, he brought 3 children to N.E. all sons; Daniel, Edward, & George: Daniel married at Newtowne, & was joyned to the church there he afterwards moved to the church at Ipswich.[1]

Thomas Lambe, he came into this land in the yeare 1630 he brought his wife & 2 Children Thomas & John: Samuel his 3͏ᵈ so͞n was borne about the 8ᵗʰ month of the same yeare 1630 & baptized in the church at Dorchester. Abel his 4ᵗʰ son was borne about the 6ᵗʰ month 1633. in Rocksbury. Decline his first daughter was borne in the 2͏ᵈ month 1637. Benjamin his 6͏ᵗ child was borne about the 8ᵗʰ month 1639 of w͏ᶜʰ child his wife died & the child lived but few hours.

---

[1] The rest of the paragraph has been cut out by some mutilator. See REGISTER, xxxiii., 238, and note.

He afterwards married Dorothy Harbitle a godly maide a sister of o^r church : Caleb his first borne by her, & his 7th child was borne about the midle of the 2^d month 1641.

Samuell Wakeman. he came to N.E. in the 9th month. 1631. he bur_ҍed his only child at sea : he was one of the first foundation of the church at Rocksbry Elizabeth his first borne here was borne about   in the yeare.

William Parke. he came to N.E. in the 12th month, 1630. a single man, & was one of the first in the church at Rocksbrough : he afterwards married Martha Holgrave, the daughter of   Holgrave of Salē. he married the month

Thomas Rawlins. he brought 5 children to this Land. Thomas. mary. Joane. Nathaniell. John. he came wth the first company : 1630

Robert Cole. he came wth the first company. 1630.

-- John Johnson

Robert Gamlin senio^r.

Robert Lyman. he came to N.E. in the 9^t month, 1631. he brought children : Phillis. Richard, a Sarah. —— John. he was an ancient christian, but weake, yet after some time of tryal & quickening he joyned to the church ; wⁿ the great removall was made to Conecticot he also went, & vnderwent much affliction, for goeing toward winter, his catle were lost in driving, & some never found againe ; & the winter being could & ill p̄vided, he was sick and melancholly, yet after he had some revivings through Gods mercy, and dyed in the yeare 1640.

Jehu Bur.

William Chase. he came wth the first company, 1630 he brought one child his soñ williā. a child of ill qualitys, & a sore affliction to his parents : he was much afflicted by the long & tedious affliction of his wife ; after his wives recovery she bare him a daughter, wch they named mary borne aboute the midle of the 3^d month. 1637. he did after y^t remove (intending) to Situate, but after went wth a company who maide a new plantation at yarmouth

Richard Bugby.

Gregorie Baxter.

Francis Smith.

John Perrie.

John Leavens he arrived at N.E. in the yeare 1632. his wife lay bedrid divers years. after she dyed he maried Rachel write a Godly maide a memb^r of o^r church : John. his first borne, wat borne the last of the second month año. 1640.

M^{ris} Margaret Welde the wife of m^r Thomas Weld.

Sarah Lyman. the wife of Richard Lyman.

Elizabeth Lambe the wife of Thomas Lambe.

Mr Richard Dumēer.

William Talmage.

John Carman. he came to N.E. in the yeare 1631. he broughs

no child^r — : his first borne John was borne the 8^t of the 5$_t$ month 1633. his daughter Abigail was borne on the 5^t month : 1635. his 3^d child Caleb was borne in the first of the first moneth : 1639.

Elizabeth Wakeman, the wife of Samuell wakeman.

—— Bur. the wife of Jehu Bur.

Thomas Woodforde. a man servant. he came to. N.E. in the yeare. 1632. & was joyned to the church about halfe a yeare after, he afterwards maryed mary Blott. & removed to Conecticott, & joyned to the church at Hartford.

Marjery Hammond a maide servant. she came to N.E. in the veare 1632 & about halfe a yeare after was joyned to the church : & after some years she was married to John Ruggls, of this church :

Mary Chase, the wife of William Chase. she had a paralitik humor wch fell into her back bone, so y^t she could not stir her body, but as she was lifted, and filled her wth great torture, & caused her back bone to goe out of joynt, & bunch out from the begining to the end of wch infirmity she lay 4 years & a halfe, & a great p̄t of the time a sad spectakle of m^{i}sery : But it pleasd God to raise her againe, & she bore children after it

John Coggshall.

Mary Coggshall, the wife of John Coggshall.

John Watson

Margret Dennison, the wife of Willi ̄a Dennison, It pleased God to work vpon her heart & change it in her ancient years, after she came to this Land ; & joyned to the church in the yeare. 1632.

Mary Cole, the wife of Robert Cole. God also wrought vpon her heart (as it was hoped after her coming to N.E but after her husbands excommunication, & falls she did too much favor his ways, yet not as to incur any just blame, she lived an aflicted life, by reason of his vnsetlednesse & removing frō place to place.

William Heath. he came to this Land. in the yeare. 1632. & soone after joyned to the church. he brought 5 children. Mary. Isaak. Mary. Peleg. Hañah.

Mary Heath the wife of Willi ̄a Heath.

William Curtis he came to this Land in the yeare. 1632. & soone after joyned to the church, he brought 4 children wth him. Thomas. Mary. John. Phillip. & his eldest soñ Willi ̄a, came the yeare before. he was a hopefull scholler, but God tooke him in the end of the yeare. 1634.

Sarah Curtis. the wife of Willi ̄a Curtis

Thomas Offit.

[Isabel] Offitt the wife of Thomas Offitt.

Isaak Morrell.

[Sarah] Morrel the wife of Isaak Morrel.

Daniel Brewer

[Joanna?] Brewer the wife of Daniel Brewer.

Griffith Crofts

[Alice?] Crofts, the wife of Griffith Crofts.

Mary Rawlins, the wife of Thomas Rawlins, she lived a godly life, & went through wth weaknesse of body, & after some years, when her husband was removed to sittuate, she dyed. about the yeare, 1639.

Thomas Gouldthwaight.

M[r] John Eliot; he came to. N.E. in the 9[t] month. 1631. he left his intended wife in England, to come the next yeare ; he adjoyned to the Church at Boston, & there exercized in the absens of m[r] wilson the Pastor of y[t] church, who was gone back to England, for his wife & family. the next sumer m[r] wilson returned, & by y[t] time the church at Boston was intended to call him to office ; his freinds w[r] come & settled at Rocksbrough, to whom he was fore ingaiged, y[t] if he were not called to office before they came. he was to join wth them, wherevpon the church at Rocksbrough called him to be Teacher, in the end of y[t] sumer & soone after he was ordained to y[t] office in the church. Also his wife came along wth the rest of his freinds the same time, & soone after theire coming, they were married. viz in the 8[t] month, 1632. Hañah. his first borne daughter, was borne. the 17 day of the 7[t] month año. 1633. John his first borne son, was borne in the 31 day of the 6[t] month. año 1636. Joseph his 2[d] soñe was borne in the 20th day of the 10th month. año : 1638. Samuel his 3[d] soñe. was borne the 22[d] day of the 4[t] month. año : 1641. Aaron his 4[t] sonne was borne the. 19. of the 12[t]. año 1643. Benjamin his 5[t] sonne was borne the 29 of the 11[t]. 1646.

M[ris] Ann Eliot the wife of m[r] John Eliot.

m[r] George Alcock, he came wth the first company año. 1630. he left his only son in England, his wife dyed soone after he came to this land, when the people of Rocksbrough joyned to the church at Dorchester (vntill such time as God should give them oportunity to be a church among themselves) he was by the church chosen to be a Deakon esp'c to regard the brethren at Rocksbrough : And after he adjoyned himselfe to this church at Rocksbrough, he was ordained a Deakon of this church : he maide two voyages to England vpon just calling therevnto ; wherein he had much experiens of Gods p'servation & blessing. he brought over his soñ John Alcock. he also brought over a wife by whom he had his 2[d] son Samuel borne in the year. he lived in a good and godly sort, & dyed in the end of the 10th month año. 1640. & left a good savor behind him ; the Pore of the church much bewailing his losse.

Valentine Prentise. he came to this land in the yeare. 1631. & joyned to the church in the yeare 1632. he brought but one child to the Land, his son John. & buryed anoth[r] at sea : he lived a godly life. & went through much affliction by bodyly infirmity. & died leaving a good sav' of Godlyness behind him.

Allice Prentise the wife of Valentine Prentise after her husbands death, she was married to John watson of this church.

Abraham Pratt.

Johannah Pratt, the wife of Abrahā Pratt.

m^{ris} Francis Pinchon the wife of m^r williā Pinchon ; she was a widdow, a matron of the church at Dorchester. w^r m^r Pinchon married her. she came w^{tn} the first company. año. 1630.

M^{ris} Mary Dumer, the wife of Mr Richard Dumer : she was a Godly woman but by the seduction of some of her acquaintances she led away into the new opinions in M^{ris} Hutchinsons time, & her husband removing to Nubery she there openly declared herselfe, & did also (together w^h oth^r indeavour) seduce her husband & p̄suaded him to returne to Boston ; where she being young w^h child, & ill ; Mr Clark (one of the same opinions) unskillfully gave her a vomit, w^h did in such mañer torture & torment her w^h the riseing of the moth^r & other vyolences of nature y^t she dyed in a most uncomfortable mañer ; But we believe God tooke her away in mercy, from worse evil, w^h she was falling unto & we doubt not but she is gone to heaven.

—— Talmage the wife of Willia Talmage. she was a g[r]aᴧe matron a godly woman, & after her husband was removed to Liñe, after a few years she dyed & left a gracious savor behind her.

Ann Shelly a maide servant she came to the Land in the yeare 1632, & was married to Foxall a godly broth^r of the church of Sittuate

Rebeckah Short a maide servant, she came in the yeare 1632, & was married to   Palmer a godly man of Charlestowne church.

Judith Bugby the wife of Richard Bugbie.

Florenc Carman the wife of John Carman.

Mary Blott a maide servant. she came in the yeare 1632, & was after married to Steward Woodfrod of this church, who after removed to Conecticott to Hartford church, where she lived in christian sort.

William Hills, a man servant, he came over in the yeare 1632. he married Phillice Lyman, the daughter of Richard Liman, he removed to Hartford on Conecticott, where he lived seuerall yeares, w^{h}out giving such good satisfaction to the conscienes of the saints.

Mary Gamlin a maide servant, daughter of Rob. Gamlin the Ed^r she came w^h her fath^r in the yeare 1632. she was a very gracious maiden ; she dyed in Mr Pinchons family of the *small pox* in the yeare 1633.

Robert Gamlin junio^r he arrived at N.E. the 20th of the 3^d month he brought only one child, w^h was the soñe of his wife by a former husband, his name is John Mayo, he was but a child.

Elizabeth his first borne was borne about the 24th of the 4th month : año dni : 1634.

Joseph borne the 16th of the 10th month año 1636

Benjamin borne the 20th of the 6th month : 1639.

Elizabeth Gamlin the wife of Robert Gamlin junio^r

Phillis Lyman the daughter of Richard Lyman, she came to the Land w^h her fath^r año 1631.   God wrought upon her heart in this Land, she grew deaf; w^h disease increasing was a great affliction to her, she was married to Williã Hills & lived w^h him at Hartford on Conecticot.

John Moody.   he came to the Land in the yeare 1633 : he had no children, he had two men servants, y^t were ungodly, especially one of them ; who in his passion would wish himselfe in hell ; & use desperate words. yet had a good measure of knowledg, these 2 srvãnts would goe to the oister bank in a boate, & did, against the counsell of theire governo^r where they lay all night ; & in the morning early when the tide was out they gath^ring oysters, did unskillfully leave theire boate afloat, In the verges of the chañell, & quickly the tide caryed it away so far into the chañell y^t they could not come neare it, w^h maide them cry out & hallow, but being very early & remote were not heard, till the water had risen very high upon them to the armehols as its thought, & then a man fro Rockbrough meeting house hill heard them cry & call, & he cryed & ran w^h all speed, & seing theire boate swam to it, & hastened to them, but they were both so drowned before any help could possibly come. a dreadfull example of God's displeasure against obstinate servãts.

Sarah Moody, the wife of John Moody.

John Walker

Elizabeth Hinds a maid servant, she came in the yeare 1633. she had some weaknesses, but upon the churches admonition repented. she was afterwards married to Alexander   of Boston wheth^r she was dismissed.

Elizabeth Ballard, a maide servant. she came in the yeare 1633 & was soone after her comeing joyned to the church ; she was afterwards married to Robert Sever of this church, where she led a godly conversation.

John Porter

Margret Porter the wife of John Porter.

William Cornewell

Joane Cornewell, the wife of Witlia Cornewell

Samuell Basse

Ann Basse the wife of Samuell Basse

Nicholas Parker he came to N.E. in the yeàre 1633. about the 7^t month : he brought two children, Mary, & Nicholas : Johañah his third child was borne the first of the 4^t month 1635
he removed frõ us to the church of Boston.

Ann Parker the wife of Nicholas Parker.

Phillip Sherman. he came into the Land in the yeare 1623. a single man, & after married Sarah Odding, the daughter o the wife of John Porter by a former husband. this man was of a melancholy temp, he lived honestly & comfortably among us severall years. upon a just calling went for England & returned againe w^h a blessing : But after his fath^r in Law John Porter was so caryed away w[h] these opinions of familisme & siszme he followed them & removed [h] them to the Iland, he behaved himselfe sinfully in these matters (as may appeare in the story) & was cast out of the church.

Margret Huntington widdow ; she came in the yeare 1633. her husband dyed by way of the small pox, she brought children with her.

Thomas Pigge

Mary Pigge the wife of Thomas Pigge.

Samuel Finch

Martha Parke, the wife of Williā Park.

John Tatman.

Thomas Willson he arrived in N. E. in the 4[t] month añno 1633. he brought 3 children Humfrey, Samuel, Joshua.

Deborah borne in the 6[t] month 1634.

Lidea borne in the 9[t] month 1636.

he had his house & all his substans consumed w[h] fire to his great impoverishing. himself being fro home.   he was a very weak man, yet was he out of affection to the Psōns of some, led aside into error, siszme, & very proud & contemptuous caryage for w[h] he was cast out of the church, & he went away w[h] m[r] wheeleright, But the L[d] awakened his heart, so y[t] after.   years he returned & repented, & was reconciled to the church ; and recommended to the church of Christ at

.. Margery Johnston the wife of John Johnson.

Ann Wilson the wife of Thomas Wilson.

Jasper Rawlings.

Jeane Rawlings the wife of Jasper Rawlings.

Joshua Hues.   he came into the Land a single man ; about the 7[t] month of the yeare 1633.   & joyned to the church aboute halfe a yeare after, his wife being the daughter of   Gouldstone came the next sumer & aboade at Watertowne, where she was adjoyned to the church ; & in the 8[t] month 1634 he married her ; & she was then recommended to our church : his first borne son Joshua Hewes was borne the 19 day of the 8th month 1639. but dyed the 19 day of the 10th month 1639. it dyed of convulsion fitts :

Isaak Johnson

Ralph Hinningway a man servant

Sarah Odding. she was daughter in law to John Porter. & came w[h] her parents & was after married to Philip Sharman of this church.

· Thomas Hills a man servant. he came in the yeare. 1633. he lived among us in good esteeme & Godly, & dyed about the 11[t] or 12[t] month. 1634 and left a good savor behind him, he was a very faithfull & prudent servant, & a good christian, he dyed in m[r] Eliots family.

Thomas Hale a single man, he lived but a short time w[h] buts u he removed to Hartford on Conecticott where God blessed him w[h]

a good measure of increase of grace, he afterwards returned & maryed Jane Lord one of oʳ members aboute the 12ᵗʰ month 1639 & the next spring returned to Conecticot

Edward Riggs

Walker the wife of John Walker.

Hues a maid servant

John Stow he arrived at N. E. the 17ᵗʰ of the 3ʳᵈ month año 1634. he brought his wife & 6 children: Thomas, Elizabeth, John, Nathaniel, Samuel, Thankfull.

Elizabeth Stow the wife of John Stow, she was a very godly matron, a blessing not only to her family but to all the church & when she had lead a christian conversation a few years among us, she dyed & left a good savor behind her.

John Cumpton

Abraham Newell he came to N. E. in the year 1634. He brought 6 children Ruth. Grace. Abraham. John. Isaak. Jaakob.

Freeborne

Sarah Burrell the wife of   Burrell.

Robert Potter

Isabell Potter the wife of Robert Potter.

Elizabeth Howard a maide servant.

Richard Pepper

Mary Pepper the wife of Richard Pepper

William Perkins

Robert Sever

Disborough the wife of Walter Disborough.

Christopher Peake a single man.

Edward Paison a man servant.

Nicholas Baker

Joseph Welde

Elizabeth Wise. a widdow.

Thomas Bell.

Mr. Tho. Bell and his wife had letters of Dismission granted & sent to England, año 1654. 7ᵐᵒ

Willia Webb

Adam Mott

Sarah Mott the wife of Aña Mott

Richard Carder

mʳⁱˢ Anna Vassaile the wife of mʳ Willia Vassaile. her husband brought 5 children to this Land, Judith, Francis, John, Margret Mary

Lawrenc Whittamore.

John Ruggles he came to N. E. in the yeare 1635, & soone after his coming joyned to the church, he was a lively christian. knowne to many of the church, in old England where many of the church injoyed society together : he brought his first borne John Ruggles w^h him to N. E & his second son was still-borne, in the 11th month 1636, of w^h his wife dyed

Barbara Ruggles the wife of John Ruggles. she was a Godly Christian woman, & joyned to the church w^h her husband, the pow^r of the grace of Christ did much shine in her life & death, she was much afflicted w^h the stone chollik in w^h sicknesse she manifested much patiens, and faith; she dyed in childbed, the 11th month, 1636, & left a godly savor behind her.

Isaak Heath

John Astwood.

Philip Eliot he dyed about the 22^d of the 8^t month : 57. he was a man of peace, & very faithful, he was many years in the office of a Deakon w^h he discharged faithfully. in his latter years he was very lively usefull & active for God, & his cause. The Lord gave him so much acceptanc in the hearts of the people y^t he dyed under many of the offices of trust y^t are usually put upon men of his rank. for besides his office of a Deakon, he was a Deputy to the Gen. Court, he was a Comissioner for the govñm^t of the towne, he was one of the 5 men to order the prudential affairs of the towne ; & he was chosen to be Feofee of the Publick Schoole in Roxbury.

Elizabeth Bowis

Martha Astwood the wife of John Astwood.

Jasper Gun

Thomas Bircharde.

John Cheny he came into the Land in the yeare 1635. he brought 4 children, Mary, Martha, John, Daniel. Sarah his 5^t child was borne in the last month of the same yeare 1635, cal^d February. he removed from o^r church to Newbery the end of the next sūer 1636.

Martha Cheny the wife of John Cheny

Mary Norrice a maide. She came into the Land

She was daughter to Mr Edward Norrice, who came into the land   & was called & ordained to be Teacher to the Church at Sāle^m where he served the Lord Christ

Henry Bull a man servant he came to the land   he lived honestly for a good season, but on the suddaine (being weake & affectionate) he was taken & transported w^h the opinion of familisme & runing in that siszme he fell into many & grosse sins of lying &c (as may be seene in the story) for w^h he was excomūnicate, after w^h he removed to the Ilaud.

Mr Thomas Jenner

——— Bell the wife of Thomas Bell

James How

——— How the Wife of Jam^s How

——— Birchard, the wife of Thomas Birchard.

John Graves he arrived in the 3^d month. 1633. he brought 5 children John, Samuel, Jonathan, Sarah, Mary. his wife quickly dyed, & he maryed Judith   a maid servant, by whom his first child Hañah was borne about the end of the 7ᵗ month. 1636

·Mʳ John Gore.

Mary Swaine a maide servant, her father lived in Watertown, & did remove wʰ them to Conecticott; whethʳ we recoⁿᵉᵈ her & she after did marrie to one at Newhaven, & she was dismissed to yᵗ church:

Jane Lorde a maide servant. she came over in the yeare she lived a Godly life among us; & in the yeare 1640 she was married to Thomas Hale, one of this church, who removed to Hartford on Conecticott, where they lived well approved of the saints.

Giles Paison, a single man. he maried oʳ sister Elizabeth Dowell.

Edward Porter he came in the yeare 1636. he brought two children wᵗʰ him: John about 3 years ould & Williã aboute a year ould: his 3ᵈ child Elizabeth was borne in oʳ church in the 10ᵗʰ month of the yeare 1637 his 4ᵗʰ child Hañah was borne in the 9ᵗʰ month, of year 1639.

Elizabeth Eliot the wife of Philip Eliot.

———— Newell the wife of Abraham Newell

Elizabeth Dowell a maide servant, she was maried to oʳ bro. Giles Paison

Phillis Pepper a maide servant.

Robert Williams

Judith Weld the second wife of Mʳ Thomas Weld

Samuel Hagbourne

Elizabeth Williams the wife of Robert Williams.

Katteren Hagbourne, the wife of Samuel Hagbourne

Abraham How,

———— How, the wife of Abraham How.

Arthur Geary

———— Geary the wife of Arthur Geary

Thomas Ruggles he came to N. E. in the yeare 1637, he was Eldʳ brothʳ to John Ruggles; children of a Godly fathʳ he joyned to the Church soone after his coming being as well knowne as his brothʳ his first born soñe dyed in England his second son John was brought over a servant by Phillip Eliot; & he brought two othʳ children wʰ him: Sarah & Samuell: he had a great sicknesse the yeare after his coming, but the Lord recovered him in mercy

Mary the wife of Thomas Ruggles. she joyned to the Church wʰ her husband & approved her selfe a Godly Christian, by a holy, & blamelesse conᵛation being conᵛted, not long before theire coming from England.

Edward Bridges.

———— Johnson the wife of Isaak Johnson

Christian Spisor a maide servant.

Mⁿˢ Rhoda Gore the Wife of Mʳ John Gore

Rachel Write a maide servant. She was married to o^r broth^r John Leavins.

Johaña Boyse a maide.

Thomas Mihill

—— Mibill the wife of   Mihill

Mathew Boyse

—— Boyse the wife of   Boyse

Greene widdow.

——Porter the wife of Edward Porter

Mr John Miller

Mrs Lidea Miller the wife of Mr John Miller

George Holmes.

William Chandler he came to N. E. aboute the yeare 1637. he brought 4 small childr, Thomas, Hañ. John, Willia : his 5^t child Sarah was borne here, he lived a very religious & Godly life among us, & fell into a consumption, to w^h he had bene long inclined, he lay neare a yeare sick, in all w^h time, his faith, patiens & Godlynesse & contentation so shined, y^t Christ was much gloryfied in him, he was a man of weake p^{ts}, but excellent fath & holyness, he was a very thankfull man, & much magnified Gods goodnesse, he was pore, but God so opened the hearts of his naybe to him y^t he never wanted y^t w^h was (at least in his esteeme) very plentifull & comfortable to him ; he dyed about the   in in yeare 1641. & left a sweet memory & savor behind him.

Hannah Chandler the wife of Willia Chandler

—— Webb : the wife of William Webb. She followed baking & through her covetuous mind she made light waight after many admonitions, & after sundry rebuks of o Court, & officers in the market, & after her speciall p̄ise to the contrary yet was ag   scandalously discovered in open market ; as also for an habit of lying & shifting, after much admonition, & also for a grosse ly in publik, flatly denying y^t after she had weighed her dough, she never   nimed off bitts fro^m each loaf, w^h yet was 4 wittnesses testified & after apped to be a cōmon if not a constant practis. for all w^h grosse sins she was excomunicated. the 23 day of the 8^t month ano. 1642. her ways having bene long a greif of heart to her Godly neighbors. But afterward she was reconciled to ye church & lived christianly & dyed comfortably.

Silenc Robbinson the wife of Thomas Robbinson.

M^{ris}   Sheafe a widdow.

M^r   Blackburne

M^{ris}   Blackburne the wife of Mr Blackburne.

Samuel Chapin

      Griggs

Richard Peacocke

Richard Peacock was dismissed to ye church at Boston, 9th 5to 1665

Jane Peacocke the wife of Richard Peacock.

John Roberts he came to New England in the yeare (1636) he brought wth him his aiged mother. wife & 7. children: Thomas & Edward soñs Elisabeth. Margery, Jones, Alce, Lidea, Ruth, Deborah, daughters. he was one of the first fruits of Wales, y^t came to N. E. calle to Christ by the ministry of y^t Reūend & worthy instrum^t Mr Wroth.

James Astwood he arrived at N. E. in the yeare 1638. the 3^d month he brought a young child wch was buryed here. James his first borne here, was borne about the 6^t day of the 10th month. 1638.

John was borne about the 15 of the 7^t month 1640. & dyed in the end of the 12 month the same yeare. John his 3^d son was borne about the begining of the 12^t month. 1641.

He was dismissed to ye new Ch at Boston.

Sarah Astwood the wife of James Astwood.

George Kilborne a man servant

Dorothy Harbeetle, a maide servant.

Ann Wallis a maide servant.

Mrs Martha Parks the wife of

M Thomas Dudly.

M^{ris} Dorothy Dudly

Mary Bridges. the wife of Edward Bridges.

John Trumell

———— Anderson

Robert Pepper a man servant

Mr John Hall

John Bowles.

Dorothy Bowles the wife of John Bowles.

Thomas Bumsted, he came to this Land in the 5^t month of the yeare 1640: he brought 2 small children Thomas & Jeremiah. Hañah his daughter borne the 25 day of the 11^t month año 1641.

He & his wife were dismissed to Boston.

Susane Bumsted the wife of Thomas Bumsted

———— Cheny the wife of William Cheny

Barbara Welde the second wife of Joseph Weld

Allis ———— a maide servant

———— Anderson the wife of Gowen Anderson

John Mays'

———— Mays' the wife of John Mays'

Lewis Jones

Ann Jones the wife of Lewis Jones

John Mathews He was convicted of notorious drunkeñnes & cast
    out of ye church 1. of 3^m 1659. But afterw^d restored
    aḡn upon his repentance.

—— Mathews the wife of —— Mathews

Richard Woddy

——Woddy the wife of Richard Woddy.

—— Stebbins the wife of Martin Stebbins. She was so vyolent in her passion. y^t she offered vyolence to her husband, w^h being divulged, was of such infamy, y^t she was cast out of o Church but soone after she humbled her selfe & was received in againe.

—— Holmes the wife of George Holmes

Judith Graves the wife of John Graves

—— Totman the wife of John Totman.

Thomas Baker

William Lewis

—— Lewis. the wife of William Lewis

Sisly Chapin the wife of Samuel Chapin

Elizabeth Roberts the wife of John Roberts

Mr Hugh Prichard recōmended frō the Church at Cape Ann.

M^{ris} Elnor Prichard the wife of Mr Hugh Prichard

—— Scarbro the wife of John Scarbro.

Bridget Dennison the wife of George Denison

Elizabeth Baker the wife of Thomas Baker

Mary Jordan a maide servant.

Edward White

James Morgan

Thomas Roberts

Edmund Sheffield who was dismissed to ye Ch. at Brantry.

John Woody

Thomas Reives a man servant

Mary Turner. a maid servant

Mary Gorton the wife of John Groton

Richard Goard

Jonet Starkweather the wife of Robert Starkweather.

Grace Newell the daughter of Abrahā Newell

Phillip Torie

Richard Wooddy Junio^r.

Sarah —— the maide servant of bro Park.

Joane Atkins. the maide servant of Mr Prichard she married one —— Smith & had letters of Dismission to Maldon. this 13th 2^m 1669.

Hañah Roe the maide servant of M^r. Gore.

William Frankling. in whom we had good satisfaction in his godlynesse yet it pleased God to leave him to some acts of rigor & cruelty to a boy his servant, who dyed under his hand, but sundry siñs he was guilty off, & the scandal was so greate, y^t he was ex·

communicated y^t day month y^t he was received the 21 of the 2^d 1644 & shortly after executed.

Elizabeth Williams. daughter of John Williams

Henry Farnham

Elizabeth Pepper the wife of Robert Pepper

Ann Direton. a maide servant

Thomas Gardiner

Widdow Gardiner

Elizabeth How, daughter of Abrahā How

Ann Brewer daughter of Dan: Brewer.

Mary Paison wife of Edward Paison

Hannah Wilson wife of ——— Wilson, she is bro: Crofts daughter.

Elizabeth Clark, wife of James Clarke. she is bro wrights daughter

——— Stonehard, the wife of John Stonehard.

Mary Wise the wife of Joseph Wise.

John Stebbin

Ann Stebbin the wife of John Stebbin

Goodwife Farrow joined in 1647

Goodwife Reade

Mary Heath.

John Stonhard

Robert Harris

John Turner.

Edward Dennison.

Martha Medcalfe.

Georg Brand

Samuel Williams, betwene 15 & 16 y of age.

John Weld

Elizabeth Davis wife of William Davis

Thankfull Pearepoynt, wife of John Peirpoint.

Hannah Heath. daughter of Williā Heath.

March, 1649 M^ns Barker a Gentlewoman that came from Barbados hither for the Gospells sake we found her not so well acquainted wth her own heart & the wayes & workings of Gods spirit in converting a sinner unto God, yet full of sweet affection, & we feared a little too confident, we received her notw^th out feares & jealousyes.

Goodwife Gardiner, ye wife of Thomas Gardiner

Goodwife Gardiner the wife of Peter Gardiner

Goodwife Lyon the wife of William Lyon (she had been sometime distracted.)

Goodwife Patchin a poor old woman

May 12. 1650. Samuel Danforth recomended & dismissed frō Cambridge Church & admitted here.

M͚ Sarah Alcock wife of M͚ John Alcocke.

Elisabeth Denison wife of Edward Denison (shee was y͏ daughter of M͚ Joseph Weld) confirmed

↙ Susanna Polly the wife of John Polly.

June 30. 1650. M͚ John Alcock confirmed.

Hugh Thomas

John Polly

October 20. 1650 Hugh Roberts

Novembʳ 17. 1650 John Perepoint

June 15. 1651 Nicholas Williams

Nov. 23. 1651 William Garee sonne to brothʳ Arthur Garee confirmed

Isaac Heath son to William Heath confirmed

March 23. 1651 Daniel Welde recom̄ended unto us frō the Church at Bantrey

3ᵐ 23ᵈ 1652. Peleg Heath son of Will. Heath confirmed

4ᵐ 6ᵈ '52 Sister Peake

Sister Devotion

4ᵐ 20 Joseph Grigs

Lydia Eliot daughter to Deacon Eliot confirmed. Since dismissed to yᵉ Church at Taunton. Anno 1666.

1653 3ᵈ 2ᵐ 1653 Abraham Newel junior confirmed

4ᵐ 26ᵈ — Susanna Heath y͏ wife of Peleg Heath

Hannah Garee y͏ wife of Will Garee confirmed

Magdalen Bullard A maid servant of Brother Williams Dismissed to Medfield this 22ᵈ of 3ᵐ. 1670. being married to John Parrich of Medfield.

John Ruggles junior confirmed.

29ᵈ 11ᵐ 1653 Tho. Weld confirmed. sonn to M͚ Tho. Weld some time Pastor of this Church.

Margaret Weld y͏ wife of John Welde.

Theodea Williams wife of Samuel Williams daughter to Deacon Park, confirmed.

14ᵈ 3ᵐ 1654 Abraham How confirmed.

3ᵈ 3ᵐ 1657 Goodman Griffin

19ᵈ 5ᵐ 1657 M͚ Rebecca Burrows who came frō Virginia y͏ she might enjoy God in his Ordin. in N. E.

Elizabeth Clerk y͏ wife of Hugh Clark. being dismissed frō Water town Church.

20. 10ᵐ 1657. ——— Huntley y͏ wife of John Huntley.

11. 2ᵐ 1658. John Hanchet

12. 7ᵐ 1658. Edward Morris admitted.

17. 8ᵐ 1658. John Maloh was confirmed.

14. 9ᵐ 1658. John Watson was confirmed.

21. 9^m 1658.   Isaac Williams was confirmed.

23. 11^m 1658   Mary Childe ye wife of Benjamin Childe, Mary Ruggles ye wife of John Ruggles junior, Mary Heath ye wife of Isaac Heath junior, Mary Griggs ye wife of John Griggs, Admitted. Martha Parkes, daughter to Deacon Parkes confirmed.

13. 12^m (58)   Samuel Ruggles was confirmed.

15 3^m (59)   Samuel Mayes was confirmed.

Sarah May wife to John May was confirmed

22. 3^m (59)   Bridget Davis wife to Tobijah Davis, Susanna Newell wife to Abraham Newell junior.   Grace Morris, wife to Edw. Morris.   Exercise Felton a maid of Salem.   Admitted.

11. 7^m (59)   Hugh Clarke was admitted.

12. 12^m (59)   Elisabeth Bowen personally & solemnly owned ye Couenant & thereupon had her child Baptised.

29^d 2^m 1660   Mrs Mary Danforth, being dismissed frō Boson church, joyned in covenant here.   Mrs Dorothie Welde being dismissed frō Lyn, was admitted here.   Sarah May, being dismissen frō Dorchester, joyned here, an aged woman.   Hanna Hopkins, dismissed frō Dorchester, joyned to this Church.

27. 3^m 1660   John Mayes junior was admitted to full Comūnion.

3^d 12^m 1660.   Isaac Newell was admitted to full Comūnion.

7^d 2^m 1661   Mary Griffin wife of bro. Griffin joyned to this church.   Elizabeth Brewer wife to Nath. Brewer joyned to this Church.

22. 7^m 1661.   Hanna Ruggles wife to Samuel Ruggles.   Anne Garee wife to Nath. Garee.   Elisabeth Newel wife to Isaac Newell. Mary Watson wife to John Watson jun.   Sarah Peak wife to Jonathan Peake.   Hanna,Mayo wife to John Mayo

24^d 9^m 1661 Remember Palfrey a maid servant since wife to Peter Aspinwall.   Dorcas Watson daughter to John Watson sen. Dismissed to Medfield 10^d 3^m 1670.

6th 5^m 1662 M^{rs}Sarah Eliot wife to Mr John Eliot jun.   Elisabeth Speare

22^d 1^m 166⅔   John Bridge, JohnMore

5th 2^m 1663.   Elisabeth Harris wife to Robt Harris, Rebecca Craft wife to John Craft.   Martha Newell wife to Jacob Newel, Prudence Bridge wife to John Bridge. Elizabeth Brewer wife to Nath. Brewer.

7th 4^m 1663.   Richard Meede, Alice Davis wife to William Davis.

1^r 9^m 1663.   Hanna Brewer wife to Daniel Brewer, daughter to Isaac Morral, was admitted to full Comūnion.

24 2^m 1664.   Thomas Woodward

4th 12^m 1664.   Sarah Frissell wife to James Frissell.

5th 1^m 166⅘.   William Cheany, Robert Hawes.

16. 2^m 1665.   John Chander, Jacob Newell, solemnly downe ye covenant.

28. 3ᵐ 1665. Mary wife to Job Tyler, she was dismissed to Mendhā. 4ᵐ 1672. Sarah wife to Richᵈ Chamberline, Elizabeth wife to John Chandler, Saɪah wife to Thomas Foster, admitted to full Comunion

18. 4ᵐ 1665. Thomas Foster.

20. 6ᵐ 1665. Edward Bugbee an old man, Maria Pierrepoint wife to Robᵗ Pierrepont.

24ᵗʰ 7ᵐ 65. John Prentice son to ōr sister Watson.

5ᵗʰ 9ᵐ 65. William Lyons admitted to full Comunion, Samuel Craft solemnly owned yᵉ Covenant.

12ᵗʰ 9ᵇᵉʳ 65. Benjamin Eliot, batchelor of arts, was admitted to full Comunion.

1ˢᵗ 5ᵐ 1666. John Gorton an old man admitted to full Comunion.

8ᵗʰ 5ᵐ 1666. Mary Polly yᵉ wife of John Polly, Desire-truth ⟩ Acrees yᵉ wife of John Acrees.

22. 5. 1666. Jacob Newell Admitted to full Comunion.

23. 7. 1666. ‒‒‒‒ More yᵉ wife of John More, ‒‒‒‒ Sharp yᵉ wife of John Sharp, Elizabeth wife of Joseph Buckmaster solemnly owned yᵉ Covenant.

12ᵐ 1666. Timothy Stevens solemnly owned yᵉ Covenant.

24. 1ᵐ 1666. Sarah Stevens, Mary Marshcraft, solemnly owned yᵉ Covenant.

20. 8ᵐ 1667. ‒‒‒‒ the wife of John Parker.

1. 10ᵐ 1667. Elizabeth Parker, recᵈ to full Comunion. 26. 11ᵐ 1667. Mary Bolstone solemnly owned yᵉ Covenant.

22. 1ᵐ 166⅞. Elizabeth yᵉ wife of John White jun. solemnly owned yᵉ Covenant.

5. 2ᵐ 1668. Steven Williams & Sarah his wife solemnly owned yᵉ Covenant.

28. 4ᵐ 1668. James Clark joyned himself to this church.

22. 9ᵐ 1668. Moses Craft & Rebecca his wife solemnly owned yᵉ Covenant.

21. 1ᵐ 166⅞. Mary wife to Nathaniel Johnson admitted but not to full Comunion.

30. 3ᵐ 1669. Joanna Davies grandchild to Mʳ Nicholas Parker, owned yᵉ Covenant.

1. 8ᵐ 1669. Mary wife of John Hemingway, Joanna wife of Joshua Hemingway, were admitted members of this church tho' not to full Comunion.

10. 6ᵐ 1669. ‒‒‒‒ wife to Tho Andrews solemnly owned yᵉ Covenant.

13. 12ᵐ 1669. Mʳ Joseph Dudley & Mʳˢ Rebecca his wife solemnly owned yᵉ Covenant. as also Mary Parker daughter to Edmund Parker.

20. 12. 1669. Maɪtha, daughter to James Clark was admitted to full Comunion.

3. 2ᵐ 1670. Mary, wife to Caleb Lamb solemnly owned the Covenant.

3. 5ᵐ (70.) Samuel Craft admitted to full Comunion.

17. 5ᵐ 70. Hanna wife to Joseph White solemnly owned yᵉ Covenant.

4. 7ᵐ 70. Patience wife to Thomas Swan solemnly owned yᵉ Covenant.

23. 8ᵐ 70. Patience wife to Nathaniel Homes admitted but not to full Comunion.

18. 10ᵐ 70. Decline Lamb alias Smith solemnly owned yᵉ covenant.

8. 11ᵐ 70. Deborah wife to Jabesh Tatman owned yᵉ covenant.

19. 12ᵐ 70. Andrew Gardiner & Sarah his wife, Sarah Cleaves wife of William Cleaves, solemnly owned yᵉ covenant.

2ᵈ 2ᵐ 71 Susanna wife to John Bennet solemnly owned yᵉ covenant.

23 2ᵐ 71. John Holdbroke being dismissed frō Dorchester, was admitted here, tho' not to full Comunion.

30. 2ᵐ 71. Elizabeth Whitney daughter to Robᵗ Harris. Mary wife to John Davis, daughter to bro. Devotion, Hanna wife to Isaac Curtis, daughter to John Polly, solemnly owned the covenant.

Sarah wife to ——— Sabin, daughter to bro. Polly dismissed to Rehoboth.

11. 3ᵐ 71. Tho. Lyons absolved frō censure & solemnly owned yᵉ covenant.

23. 5ᵐ 71. Mary Evans was admitted but not to full comunion.

23. 5ᵐ 71. Edward Porter, Ann his wife, his son William Porter, his daughter Elizabeth Nash, Hanna Dinely, Mary Bennit & Deborah Porter were all dismissed to the third Church in Boston.

15. 8ᵐ 71. Isaac Johnson jun. dismissed to the Church at Middleton on yᵉ River.

22. 8ᵐ 71. Mʳ Joseph Dudley was admitted to full comunion.

29. 8ᵐ 71. Mʳˢ Rebecca Dudley wife to Mʳ Joseph Dudley, Mary Goard wife to Richᵈ Goard, Mary Evans wife to John Evans, Mary Davis wife to John Davis, admitted to full Comunion.

4. 12. 71. Mary Hewes dismissed to the 3ʳᵈ Church in Boston.

24. 1ᵐ 7½ John Lyons & Abigail his wife, John Pason & Bathshebah his wife, Rebecca yᵉ wife of John Curtis. Mary wife to Tho. Bacon. Hanna, wife to Shubal Seaver. Abigail wife to John Clark. Solemnly owned yᵉ Covenant.

4ᵐ 72. Mary yᵉ wife of Job Tyler dismissed to yᵉ church at Mendham.

20ᵗʰ 2ᵐ 73. William Davies admitted to full Comunion.

John Harris & Mary his wife, Mary, Hanna, Sarah Denison, Experience Pierpoint, Mary Bowles, Abigail and Hanna Heath, Solemnly owned yᵉ Covenant.

8ᵗʰ 4ᵐ 1673. Jane wife to William Davies, Esther wife to Thomas

Woodward, Mary wife to Thomas Bacon, Mary Parkes a maide, Admitted to full Comunion.

23. 9^m Samuel Davis dismissed to North-Hampton.

21. 10. Samuel Lyons dismissed to Rowley.

4. 11^m Nathaniel Brewer admitted to full Comunion.

25. 11^m Thomas Bacon admitted to full Comunion.

8: 12^m Margaret Mason daughter to sister Denison, Sarah the wife of Joseph Davis, Sarah daughter to Deacon Pason Solemnly owned ye Covenant.

8th 1^m 7¾ Richard Woody with his sons Samuel & Richard & daughters Mary, Martha & Elisabeth were dismissed to the 3^d Church in Boston.

1674

29. 1^m 1674. Joseph White admitted to full Comunion.

5. 2^m —. Shubal & Caleb Seaver, solemnly owned ye Covenant.

12. 2^m 1674. Mr George Burrows admitted to full Comunion.

19. 2^m —. Susanna Bennet dismissed to the hithermost Church in Boston.

3. 3^m —. John Ruggles sen. admitted to full Comunion.

3. 3^m —. Joanna wife to Robt Harwood dismissed to the third Church in Boston.

24th 3^m —. Nathaniel Seaver, Sarah, wife to Nath. Seaver, Sarah wife to Caleb Seaver, Solemnly owned y^e Covenant.

30. 6^m John Winchester Sen. & Hanna his wife joyned to o^r Church.

John Winchester jun. & Joanna his wife, John Druse and Mary his wife, solemnly owned y^e Covenant.

25. 8^m —. Hanna wife to Isaac Curtis admitted to full Comunion.

9th month 15 $_{day}$. Samuel Perry & Elizabeth Holdridg, these Solemnly owned & tooke hold on the Covenant.

11 month 3 day. Samuel Scarbro & Rebecca his wife, Benjamin Tucker & An his wife, these solemnly tooke hold on the Covenant.

24 day. Mary Lambe wife to Joshua Lambe, Sarah Onion a maide servant daughter of Robert Onyon, Elizabeth Hawley, Dorothy Hawley, daughters of o^r Sister Hawley, all these y^l day did solemnly take hold on the Covenant.

1674. 11mo

31 day. John Ruggles junior, Martha his wife, Elizabeth wife of Samuel Crafts, Joshua Seaver, Hannah Devotion, these did this day solemnly owne, & take hold on the Covenant.

1 month $\frac{4}{5}$ 7th day. Admitted to take hold on the Covenant, John Davis junio^r, Mary his wife, Susanna the wife of Tho. Mory.

day 28 Received to take hold on the Covena^t, John Newel, Elizabeth wife of Joseph Weld, Mary the wife of Robert Baker, Abigail Gardner, Johanna Gardner, Bethiah Wise, Katherin Wise, Sarah Pepper.

day 18. Sarah Cleaves admitted to full Comunion

Month 2ᵈ, day 25ᵗ Received to take hold on the Covenant, Mʳ Tho Weld, Mʳ John Bowles

Month 4ᵗʰ On the 6ᵗ day the Church voted, & called bro Bowles to the office of a Ruling Elder. Also bro. John Peirpoynt was orderly nominated for yᵗ office.

day 27. Received to take hold on the Covenant, Elizabeth Onion, Hannah Onion, Abigail Clark, Mercy Clark, Abigail Griffin.

1675

Month 5. day 15. Experience Bugby the wife of Joseph Bugby was received to take hold on the Covenant.

Month 7, day 12ᵗ John Bugby was received to take hold on the Covenant.

Month 8ᵗ, day 17 Sister Griffen was dismissed to the first church of Boston.

M 9ᵗ, dy 28. Phillip Curtis his widdow made confession of her sins & hopeful conv'sion & was received to the full comunion of the church. her husband was slaine at Hassunnemesut.

M 12, dy 13. John Ruggles junioʳ son to John Ruggles, Samuel Ruggles son to Samuel Ruggles, these both took hold on the Covenant.

M 12ᵗ, dy 20. 75. Elizabeth the wife of John White, Sarah Onion a maide servant, were admitted to full Comunion.

1676

Month 5. day 2. Rebecca wife to Moses Crafts admitted to full Comunion.

Sarah Mayes, Abigail Mays, Hannah Porter, yᵉˢ 3 maids wʳ admited to take hold on the Covenant.

day 23. Mary Morie of Milton daughter of James Clark took hold on the Covenant among us & had her children baptized.

Month 7, day 10. Lidea Elder daughter of bro. Homes took hold on the Covenant & had 4 child'n baptized.

Mary Pepper widdow of Joseph Pepp. tooke hold on the Covenant.

Month 10, day 3. Elizabeth wife of Abiel Lambe was receiued to full Comunion.

day 31. Elizabeth Lawrenc, a godly maide admited to full Comunion & baptized.

Month 12, day 11. Abigail the wife of Williaᵐ Lyon, Johannah the daughter of Thom. Gardner, these two were admited to full Comunion.

Month 12, day 25. John Weld junioʳ took hold on the Covenant.

Month 8ᵗ, day 1. Mary Davis wife of John Davis admited to full Comunion.

1677

Month 2. 15 An Paison dismissed to the church of Dorchester.

day 29. John White Senioʳ of Muddy River was received wᵗʰ good acceptance.

Month 3, day 6. John Weld Junio^r was received to full Comunion wth good acceptance.

Jonathan Winchester, Mary his wife, both received to lay hold on the Covenant.

day 13. John Ruggles junio^r received to full Comunion wth good acceptance.

Month 5, day 29 Elizabeth the wife of Willia Gary, Abigal the wife of John Clark, both received to full Comunion.

Samuel Weld, John Weld, Edmond Weld, these 3 sons of M^s Tho: Weld took hold on the Covenant this day.

Month 6 day 19 William Lyon junio^r, Hannah Winchester, took hold on the covenant.

Month 7 day 30 Johh Clark was admited to full Comunion.

Month 9 day 25 Uriah Clarke took hold on the Covenant.

This day Samuel Williams was nominated to be called to be a ruling eld^r.

Month 11. 27. Expience Peirpoynt, Johanna wife of Joshua Hinningway, Ruth wife of John Grovnor, these 3 w^r admited to full Comunion.

1678

Month 1 day 17. Deborah the wife of Samuel Scarbrow, Mary the wife of John Hinningway. both admitted to full Comunion——

day 24 Abra How jun^r. received to take hold on the Covenant

Month 2 day 14. Sarah Gardner, Elizabeth Chandler tooke hold on the covenant y^i day.

Month 3 day 5. John Scot took hold on the covenant.

Mont 5 day 7. Mr Tho Boylstone admited full Comunion.

Month 4 day 16. Haña Hopkins was censured in the Church wth admonition for fornication wth her husband before y^{ei} w^r maryed & for flying away frō justice, unto Road Ilaud

Mon 5 day 11. Andrew Gardner confessed Christ & was received to full comunion wth good acceptan.

Mont 8 day 13. Sarah wife to Andrew Gardner, Mary wife to Joshua Seaver, Priscilla daughter of Robert Harris all y^{es} w^r received to full comunion wth good acceptan. blessed be the Lord.

Month 9 day 10. Robert Pepper was called afore the Church for the appearance of being drunk but his apologie is such as y^t we demur upon it & a 2^d demur month 10 day 8 a 3^d demur. Lord humblᵉ him. lastly he was accepted.

Month 10 day 8. Hannah Hopkins alias Goffe was called to confesse her sins & manifest her repentance for fornication & running away to Road Ilaud. she confessed & was absolved & received to take hold on the covenant.

1679

Mon 1 day 1. Joseph Lyon received to full comunion: he made a good confession.

Widdow Stevens was accepted in her confession.

day 30.   Timothy Stevens confessed Christ & joyned to full comunion

also, Jakob Newell, Isaak Newell. John Mayo, take hold on covenant.

Mont 2 day 13.   John Chandler confessed Christ & joyned to full comunion.

day 20.   Jabesh Totman confessed X & joyned to full Comunion.

Samuel & Elizabeth, Children of Samuel Willias took hold on the Covenant.

27.   Mr Tho Weld Junio^r confessed X & joyned to full comunion.

Mo: 3^d day 11.   y^{es} 3 maides, Elizabeth Gary, Mehitable Heath, Hannah Mayo y^{es} wth acceptance tooke hold on the Covenant.

Mon 4 day 1.   Epraim, Samuel, Mary Paison : children of Edward Paison all tooke hold on the Covenant.

John Devotion the son of ———— Devotion, tooke hold on the covenant.

Mon 6 day 17.   Marget Parker daughter to Widdow Cleaves tooke hold on the covenant.

Joseph Hawly dismissed to the church at Norhampton.

M. 9 d 2.   Admitted to full comunion, Sarah Saben, Mary Gardner.

1679

M 11. dismissed. Elizabeth Williams to the church at Rehoboth.

.   .   .   Mary Drew to the church at Cambridg. Village.

1680

M 1 day 7.   Admitted to full comunion John White junio^r.

M 1 day 14.   John Paison & Bathshebah his wife w^r dismissed to the church of Dorchester.

Josiah Winchester received to tak hold on the covenant

day 28.   Deliveranc Dunkan, Deborah Devotion, both y^{es} w^r admitted to lay hold on the covenant.

M 2 day 4.   Mr John Bowles received to full comunion.

M 3 day 2.   Edward Paison was received to full comunion

M 5 day 18.   Elizabeth Colton, Sarah Eliot, Mary Danforth, Dorothy Weld, these tooke hold on the covenant.

M 7 day 21. 1680 beloved Elder Bowles deceased having bene Elder of the church 5 years & 3 months he was killed by a cart wheele runing over his body.

M 11 day 23.   Thomas Woodward junio^r, Ester Woodward, Hannah Woodward, Sarah Devotion, all these take hold on the covenant.

1681

M 1 day 20.   Joseph Weld, Sarah Clark, Elizabeth White, Elizabeth Heath, Hannah Cleaves, all these were received to take hold on the Covenant this day.

M 1 day 27.   Elizabeth Pike, Mary Widdow Winchester, Elizabeth Gary, All these were this day received to the full Comunion of
the Church.

M 2 day 24.   Sarah the wife of Joseph Weld. Hannah Weld,
Johannah Brewer, Mehitabel Mayse, Hannah Brewer, Elizabeth
Morice, these 6 psons did all of y^m take hold on the Covenant this
day.

M 6 day 21.   Mary Weld, Grace Morrice, Elizabeth Bowen,
Prudence Bridg. these 4 maides took hold on the Covenant.

M 7 day 4.   Sister Cleaves (alias Stevens) was publickly admonished for unseasonable entertaining & corrupting other folks
servants & children. and hath corrupted Mr Lambs neger. who in
a discontent set her M^{rs} house on fire in the dead of the night &
also Mr Swans.   one girle was burned, & all the rest had much
adoe to escape wth their lives.

M 8 day 2.   Abigail Heath admited to full comunion.   She
made a good confession of Christ.

Naomi Mays received to lay hold on the covenant.

day 23.   Isaak Heath junio^r & his wife & Nathaniel Wilson took
hold on the Covenant. y^{es} did take hold on the Covenant.

M 11 day 15.   Jakob Pigg received to full Comunion.

1682

M 4 d 25.   Elizabeth Phillips tooke hold on the Covenant.

M 2 d 9   O^r sist Cheny was dismissed to the New Church in
Boston.

d 16   Isack Heath Seno^r confessed his sin in attempting to kill
hims: and was restored.

M 7 d 17.   Sister Danforth now Rock is dismissed to the first
Church at Boston.

Mary the wife of Joseph Lyon tooke hold on the Covenant.

Hannah the wife of Philip Searle received to full Comunion.

M 8 d 8.   Edward Paison was dismissed to Rowley.

M 10 d 11.   Joseph Gardner was admonished by the Church for
his wicked convsation.

d 31.   Mary Lyon wife of Joseph Lyon tooke hold on the Covenant.

M 12 d 25.   Benjamin Dowse & Jonathan Tory, these tooke
hold on the Covenant.

1683

M 1 d 11.   Joseph Wilson tooke hold on the Covenant.

d 15   Martha Sharp, Francis Prentice, tooke hold on the Covenant

M 2 d 22.   Narah Newel, Elizabeth Newel, both hold on the
Covenant.

M 8 d 7.   Martha Ramsie admonished for pride. disōbed to par-
ent & for fornication, unto w^h God left her, to shame & humble
her.

M 10 d 2. Sr Peirpont : son of John Peirpoynt, Sr Dennison. son of Edward Dennison, both tooke hold on the covenant wth good acceptanc.

M 11 d 6. John Williams & William Williams two hopfull young scholars. both of y^m tooke hold on the covenant wth good acceptance.

Mary wife of Joseph Gardner tooke hold on the covenant.

d 13. Sarah Parker (quoñda Cleaves) confessed her sin, was accepted & reconciled to the church & released of her censure.

M 12 d 17. Moses Draper confessed Jesus Christ, was received to full Coṁunion & Baptized.

Rebeccah Hubbard confessed her sin & repentanc & faith in Christ, was recēd to full Coṁunion & Baptized.

d 24 Benjamin Tukker confessed Christ, & was received to full coṁunion.

Thomas Lyon confessed Christ & was received to full coṁunion.

1684

M 1 d 2. John Davis Senior confessed Christ, & was received to full coṁunion.

d 9 Benjamin Saben, Steven Williams, Samuel Scarbrow, all these confessed Christ & were received to full coṁunion.

d 16. Sr Pierpoynt confessed Christ & is received to full coṁunion.

d 23 John Grigs Senio^r, Thomas Bishop these confessed Christ & are received to full coṁunion.

allso these male youth John Peirpoynt, Josep hGriffin, Jonathan Davis, Nathaniel Brewer, Joseph Weld Junio^r, Joseph Pairpont, Benjamin Pairpont. Joseph Bukmaster, all y^{es} tooke hold on the Covenant y^l 23 day of the first month.

Mary Searl wife of John Searl allso these female youth, Rebecca Ruggls daughter of John Ruggles jun'^{r}, Margret Searl, Rebecca Newel, Mary Gardner wife of, Joseph Gardner, Leah Fisher, Mary Newel, Elizabeth Newel, Rebecca Mayo.

d 30 Abraham Gorton, John Chandler, Eliezer Mays, Daniel Druer junio^r, Phillip Searl junio^r, Jakob Parker, these male youths took hold on the Covenant.

Also the same 30 day of the first month Sarah Gāry, Mary Davis, Sarah Brewer, Rebecca Polly, Mary Baker, Hannah Chandler, All these female youths took hold on the Covenant.

Also the same day Samuel Williams junio^r, Joseph Weld Senio^r, John Whitney, these 3 confessed Christ & were received to full Coṁunion.

M 2 d 6. Richard Hall, Francis Youngman, y^{es} confessed Christ, & were received to full coṁunion.

Allso this day Elizabeth Crafts, Hanna Crafts, Ann Tukker, Hannah Grigs, these w^r received to full coṁunion, having confessed Christ at the day appoynted.

Mary Swan, Mary Lambe, Sarah Bowles, Hannah Weld, Sarah

Williams, these confessed Christ this weeke & were received to full Comunion these all besides their oral confessions, gave in theire confessions in writing reade in the Church with good acceptanc.

d 13. Y^{es} young p'sons, males, John Mays, Thomas Chany, Williã Chany, John Chany, Daniel Harris, Benjamin Child, these all did publickly by y^r owne consent & desire take hold on the Covenant, wait^g for more grace.

d 13 Margrt Weld, Sarah Stevens, Abigail Wise, Annali Goare, Abagail Davis, Faith Newel, Deborah Williãs, Sarah Williã, Mary Williãs, Sarah Homes, Anna Goare, these young p̄sons females were received to take hold on the Covenent.

d 20. Daniel Brewer Senio^r, Samuel Ruggs junio^r, John Harris, these confessed Christ & w^r received to full comunion.

d 27. Nathaniel Homes, John Davis, Samuel Lyon, these confessed X & w^r received to full comunion.

m 3 d 4. Hannah Ruggles, Sarah Willia^s, Patienc Homes Hannah White, all these confessed Christ & were received to full Communion.

Abial Lamb, Joseph Bugby senio^r, John Crafts, Nathaniel Sanger & his wife, these confessed y^r sĩs y^t w^r publik, & so w^r admited to take hold on the covenant.

d 11. Joseph Bugby junio^r, Ebenezer Merice, Timothy Stevens Ebenezer Williãs, Thomas Boylston junio^r, Thomas Gardner, junio^r, these males w^r receiued to tak hold on the covenant.

Abigal Davis, Mary Williãs, Mary Davis, Rebecca Bugby, Elizabeth Child, Mary Sangor, Mary Boylston junio^r, Mary Duncan, Melatiah Hawkins, all y^{es} femals w^r received to take hold on the covenant.

m 4 d 15. Mary Boylston senio^r, Elizabeth Gore, Mary Lyon, Sarah Weld, Mary Baker, Hannah Chamberlain, Mary Lambe, these 7 did orally confesse &c. & also gave in the substance of their confessions in writ^g all which were pblikly read y^t day, & y^{ei} w^r received into the full comunion of the church by y^t gospel act o renewing theere explicit covenant.

m 4 d 22. Anna Goare, Elizabeth Hall, Mary Mashcraft, John Leavens, Abiel Davis, John Simonson, John Seaver, John Stevens, all y^{es} were received to take hold on the covenant.

John Williams confessed Christ & was received to full comunion,

d 29. Caleb Lamb, Joshua Lamb, Richard Davis, these w^r receiued to take hold on the covenant.

Williã Williams confessed Christ & was received by covenant to full comunion.

m 5 d 6. Uriah Clark confessed Christ, & was received to full comunion by covenant.

d 20. John Clark, Lidea Clark his wife, Mary Bukmaster, these took hold on o covenant.

m 6 d 42. Iaaak Curtis confessed & was received to full comunion.

m 7 d 7., Joseph Griffiñ confessed & was received to full com̄union.

m 9 d 22.   Hannah Goffe was excom̄unicate, though absent, for 3 great scandalous sins. 1. wicked fornication. 2. baudery. 3. contumasy, refusing to come to the church.

m 10 d 14.   Sister Hayward was dismissed to the South Church in Boston.

d 28.   Hannah Wilson wife of Nathaniel Wilson tooke hold on the covenant.

m 12 d 15.   Martha Ramsy confessed her sin, & was absolved of her censure.

año 1685

m 1 d 8.   Abigail Newail & Sarah Burdon received to take hold on the covenant.

Jakob Chamberlin did y^t day take hold on o covenant.

m 1 d 15.   Thom. Baker, Joseph Baker, Thomas Ruggles, Edward Bugby, ye^s 4 did y^i day owne & take hold on the covenant.

d 22.   Thomas Mory, Elizabeth Cotton, Johannah Winchester, y^{es} confessed Christ & were received to full com̄union.

Mr James Pairpont dismissed to Newhaven church.

m 2 d 5.   Hannah wife of John Devotion, Mehitabel Aspinal, Elizabeth Aspinal, these females took hold on the covenant y^t day.

Peter Aspinal, Nathaniel Aspinal, Samuel Aspinal, these males took hold on the covenant y^t day.

Nathaniel Bruer y^t day confessed Christ & was received to full com̄union.

d 12.   Benjamin Douse confessed and admitted to full com̄union.

m 3 d 10.   Willia^m Heath, Margret Bowin, Sarah Bullard, Marget Morrice, Sarah Brakket, Elizabeth Whitny, Rachel Davis, all y^{es} w^r y^s day received to take hold on õ covenant.

d 17.   Matthew Brand received to full Com̄union.

m 4 d 7   John Marcy, Hannah Newel, Mary Crafts, Elizabeth Crafts, Susanna Pike, all y^{es} took hold on the Covenant.

d. 14   Susanna Mory was accepted to full Com̄union.

d 14.   Sarah Erizal, Mary Woodward, Mary Burden, Mehitabel Mayo, all these, some formerly, some y^i day, were accepted to take hold on the Covenant.

m 5 d 12.   Mary Murreene, Rebecca Murreen, Elizabeth Grigs, Sarah Grigs, these w^r received to take hold on the Covenant.

m 7 d 20.   Phillip Mareen, William Mareen, Elizabeth Mareen, Mary Mareen, y^{is} day all y^{es} children of   Mareen were received to take hold on the Covenant.

m 9 dy 22.   Josiah Winchester confessed X & was received to full Com̄union.

d 29.   Thom. Hanshet confessed, was absolved & took hold on the Covenant.

Towards the end of this yeare some naughty $\bar{p}$son made and divulged a filthy lible for wch 3 w^r censured by civil^e authority.

The Church take notice of Six, who humbled y^{m}selves by publik confession in the church & we have cause to hope y^t the full $\bar{p}$ceeding of discipline, will doe more good y^n theire sin hath done hurt.

1686

m 1 d 7. Elizabeth wife of Andrew Watkins was received to take hold on the Covenant.

m 2 d 4. the wife of Joseph Lyon was called to fulfill her penitent confession of her sin in pilfering money frō her grandfath^r, & hiding it wth lying; wch confession shee made & was accepted & forgiven.

Sister Accor dismissed to the Church at Dunstable.

m 3 d 30. 3 women received to full Comūnion. Sarah the wife of Mr John Gore, Sarah the wife of Joseph Griffen, Hannah the wife of John Devotion

m 4 day 27. Sarah Peakok was received to take hold on ō Covenant.

m 5 d 4. Abigal Bowin was received to take hold on the Covenant.

d 25 Mary Bowin, Jane Davis, y^{es} two w^r admitted y^i day to take hold on the Covenant.

m 8 d 10. Sarah Hadlock received to take hold on ō covenant being adult.

d 24 y^s Sarah was Baptized.

d 31. Isaak Howe received to take hold on the Covenant.

m 9 d 14 Nathaniel Gary received to take hold on the Covenant.

m 10 d 5. wife of Samuel Paison received to full Comūnion.

d 26 Mary Feilder received to take hold on ō Covenant.

1687

In y^s yeare my ancient dearly beloved wife dyed, I was sick to death but the Lord was pleased to delay me, & keep in my service w^h was but pure and weak.

m 8 d 16. Mr Denison confessed & was received to full Comūnion.

d 26. My son Benjamin was buryd

m 9 d 26 Mr John Gore confessed Christ & was received to full Comūnion.

m 11 d 1. Eliezer Mayes & John Merey Sarah & the wife of John Merey. y^{es} confessed ye sin of fornication & were accepted.

y^i day Hannah Smith, Prudence Wade, Katherein Chikkerin, Hannah Ellis, all these took hold on the Covenant.

m 12 d 12. the wife of Thomas Cheany jun^r. Received to full Comūnion.

m 12 d 13.   Elizabeth the wife of Caleb Phillips Received to
ᶜull Comunion.

m 12 d 19.   Mʳ Jonathan Peirepoint confessed Christ & was
received to full Comunion.

1688.

m 3 d 13.   Received to take hold on the Covenant.

Hannah Williams. Elizabeth Williams daughter of Stephen
Williams.

Sarah Crafts daughter of John Crafts

Marget Pairpoynt tooke hold of ō Covenant.

Sarah Bullard alias Mays confessed her fornication & reconciled.

June 10   John Baker made confession of Christ & was received
to full Comunion.

July 8.   Hannah Brewer made confession of her sin of fornic-a
tion & the church forgave her.

July 8.   The Church voted that out of two persons viz. Mʳ John
Rogers & Mʳ. Nehemiah Walter they would make their choice as
God should direct for a standing help in the Dispensation of the
word of God & in order to office.

July 15.   The Church Elected by Papers & the voice of God by
the Church was for Mʳ Walter.

We also calleᵈ Mʳ Bowles to officiate among us. ō office of a
Ruling Elder, until such time as God please to restore his health
& capitate him to the ministry.

Septeber 9ᵗʰ The Church & congregation gave Mʳ Nehemiah
Walter a call to accept of office.

October 17ᵗʰ Nehemiah Walter ordained by the imposition of
hands & prayer.

— 21 Martha Williams, Patience Draper, Martha Ramsey,
Joseph Kingsbury. John Davis, Mary Holebrook, Nathaniel Holmes,
Ebenezer Holmes, Samuel Knight, Sarah Knight, Thomas Aspinal,
Joseph Crafts, — these took hold of the Covenant.

October 28ᵗʰ Elizabeth Morrice, Sarah Mayo, Mehittabel Mayo,
— were received to full Comunion.

1689

March 2   Caleb Sever & the wife of Moses Draper received to
full Comunion.

April   John Mayo & the wife of Jacob Pepper received to full
Comunion.

May 13.   Mehittabel Heath & Abigail Bowen received to full
Comunion.

June 30.   Benjamin Griffin & Sarah Davis received to full
Comunion.

PERSONS ADMITTED TO FULL COMUNION.

A.D. 1689.

Aug. 4. —
John Lyon
Hannah Morrice
Grace Child
Elizabeth Child
Nov. 24. — Elizabeth Child Jun.ʳ

1690

Feb 25 —
Sarah Newel
Elizabeth Newel
Hannah Newel
Ap. 13. —
John Newel
John Davis
Pennel Bowen.
Joanna Harris
Mary Chamberlain
Sarah Brewer
May —
John May
Prudence May
Elizabeth Nuel
Elizabeth Weld
July —
Mehittabel May
Naomi May
August —
Hannah Heath
Jonathan Curtis
Septʳ —
Elizabeth Bracket
Sarah Davis
Mary Mascraft
Decembʳ. —
Joshua Gardiner.

1691

Febʳʸ —
Mary Gardiner.

March —
John Winchester.
Sarah Haws
Mary Bridges
May — Edward Morrice
June — Robert Baker
Octobʳ — John White M.A.
Febʳʸ —
Joshua Hemmingway
Margarett Hemmingway.
Anna Goard

1692

March — Elizabeth Hall
April—Timothy Stevens M.A.
May —
Josiah Dwight M.A.
Thomas Ruggles, A.B.
Grace Onion.
August—Daniel Brewer M.A.

1693

April —
Samuel Weld
Susanna Weld
Elizabeth Mascraft
May —
Ebenezer Morrice
John Johnson
Hannah Newel [Excommuni-
cated for adultery most hei-
nously circumstanced 1695.
She was restored June 1708.]
Hannah Mascraft
August — Ruth Greerson
Novʳ 20 — Hannah Ruggles
Decembʳ — Mary Winchesteɪ

1694

July — Katharine Mather
Decemʳ 9. —
Christopher Peake
William Davis

John Simeson [Excommunicated
for open drunkennes 1696;
upon his publick confession of
his sin & profession of repentance he was some while after
restored to the church]

1695

June 9 — Mary Holland
July 7 — Matthew Davis
Sept[r]
Susanna Pike
Sarah Crafts [Was guilty of
fornication & lying some
months under the afflicting
hand of God which prevented
her being called before y[e]
church and during y[es] time
giving hopefull evidences of
her repentance was laid under
a suspension for y[e] probation
of y[e] truth of her repentance
some months after (carrying
it persistently) she was called
forth to confess her sin and
profess her repentance & was
absolved & restored 1698]
Experience Newel.
Decemb[r].
Tryphena Woodward
Hannah Gary
January —
Joseph Green A.B.
Abigail Williams
Hannah Merryfield

1696

✗   March — Patience Polly
June — Susanna Sabin
July — Prudence Swan
Decemb[r] — Paul Dudley, M.
A., and Mary Baker

1697

Febry 7th — John Druce
15th — Elizabeth Sanders
March — Faith Nuell

May —
Mehittabel Crafts
Sarah Aspinall
Mary Allen
June — Lyddia Bishop
Septemb[r] Hannah Parker
Octob[r] —
James Baily Sen[r] Dismissed from
the Church of Salem & rec-
ommended to this Church.
James Baily jun[r].

1698

Novemb[r] 13. — Deborah Warren, Elizabeth Tucker, Priscilla Williams

1699

April —
Joseph Buckminster
Bathiah Scarborough
Sarah Phipps
May — Dorothy Denison
Sept[br] — Ebenezer Newell

1700

Octob[r] — Mercy Kingsbery
Nov[r] 10th — Joseph Davis
[Was admonished and sus-
pended from y[e] L[ds] table
for scandalous drunkness
Feb[ry] 28th 170⅔. Afterwards
restored.]
November 17. —
Joseph Goddard & his wife
Deborah Goddard
Decemb[r] — Rebecca Johnston

1701

Jan[ry] — Bethiah Davis
May — Charity Davis
June —
Sarah Butcher
Mary Bacon
Sept[r] — John Ingram
Decem[r] Isaac Morice

1702

May 19th — Ichabod Davis

Feb^{ry} 21—Elizabeth Holbrook

1703

March —

Benjamin White, son of Joseph

Nathaniel Crafts

Patience Crafts

July — Susanna Willis

Octo^r — Huldah Ruggles

March — Lucy Ruggles

May —

Theodah Williams

Thomas Weld A. B. [pius juvenis prematurè objït in Christo urcitur viginti anuos natus]

Nov^r — Isaac Bowen Dismissed from ye church at Frammingham.

1705

Jan^{ry} —

Joanna Stevens

Lucy Gardiner

Rebecca Boylston

Francis White

April —

Dorothy Weld

Abigail Story

June — Mary Bacon

1706

Feb^{ry} —

Mrs Rebecca Sewall

Mrs Anne Dudley

March —

Jacob Bacon

Benjamin Crafts

Jarvis Pike

May —

Caleb Stedman

Hannah Bowen wife of Isaac Bowen

Abiel Bacon

Sarah Bugbee

Sept^r — Mary Williams wife of Stephen Will^{ms} jun^r

Decem^r — John Payson and his wife Elizabeth

1707

Feb^{ry} — Samuel White

May — Margaret Griggs

Dec^r — Mary Davis

1708

April —

Park Williams

Joseph Williams

May — Abigail Williams

July — Susanna Whitney

August — Abigail Harris

Octo^r — Mary Gardner jun^r

1709

Feb^{ry} 20 —

Samuel Stevens

Hannah Gore

March 20 — Benjamin Eaton

April 17 — Deborah Weld

May 29 —

Sarah Weld

Mehittabel Curtis

Patience Holmes

June 12 — Mr Samuel Sewall

July 10 —

Timothy Ruggles, A. B.

Hannah Ruggles

Patience Ruggles

August 7 —

John Bowles, A. M.

Lyddia Bowles

1710

Octob 1 —

Shubael Sever

Abigail Sever

Martha Ruggles

8 — Dorothy Davis

Dec^r —

Samuel Williams jun^r

Anne Charter

1711
Feb^{ry} 19 —
Samuel Davis
John Bailey
Sarah Williams
    May —
Eleazer Aspinwall
Mary Tucker
Mehittabel Howard
    June — Sarah Hartness
    July — Sarah Ruggles
    Octo^r — Caleb Gardiner &
      Abiel Gardiner.
    Nov^r — Esther Alcock
    Dec^r — Elizabeth Weld wife
      to Joseph Weld jun^r
1712
August 3^d —
Ebenezer Williams A.M.
    Nov^r —
Mary Holbrook
Lyddia Harris

1713
March 15 —
Anne White wife of Samuel
    White
    April 27—Ichabod Woodward
    June — Roger Adams

1714
May 9 —
Robert Stanton, A.B.
    Aug 1 —
James Grant
Alice Loverain

1715
April 9 —
Edward Sumner
Elizabeth Sumner
Elizabeth Weld Junr
    June —
Thomas Cobbett
Benjamin Payson

Mary Payson
    July —
Thomas Gardner
Joshua Seaver
    Octo^r — Joseph Ruggles
    Nov^r — Martha Williams,
      daughter of Isaac Williams
    Dec^r — Hannah Turner

1716
Febry —
Joseph Stevens
Abiel Chamberlain
Margarett Chandler
    May —
John Winchester
Samuel Healy
Mary Williams
    August — Ichabod Griggs
    Sept^r —
Jacob Howe
Elizabeth Bernard

1717
Feb^{ry} —
Sarah Gardner
Huldah Lamb
    Septr 21 —
Thomas Walter A.M.
    Nov^r —
Ebenezer Pierpont, A.M.

1718
June 22 —
Hannah Bowen
    Aug. 17 —
Josiah Holland
Sarah Walter
Hannah Walter
Joseph Warren
    Sept^r —
Stephen Williams
Abraham Howe
Jacob Payson
    Dec^r — Joseph Holland

1719

April 5 —
Ebenezer May
Benjamin West.
Elizabeth Holland
October —
Hannah Seaver
Hannah Meers
Elizabeth Holbrook

1720

March —
Hannah Norcross
April —
Joseph Mayo
Elizabeth Mayo
July — Abigail Greenwood.
30 — Samuel Davenport
Sept^r — Mary Stevens

1721

July —
Anna Pepper

1722

March —
Abigail Cheney
Aug. 19. —
Thomas Weld, Senior Sophister

Decr. 9
Elizabeth Shed
Elizabeth Craft

1723

March 3 —
Abijah Weld, Senr Sophister
17 — Susanna Gore
April 7 —
Joshua Lamb
Susanna Lamb
21 — Rebecca Davenport
August — Eunice Ruggles
Nov^r — Sarah Payson
Jan^ry — Katharine Meers

1724

29 March —
Joseph Warren jun^r
April —
Noah Perrin
Patience Perrin
May — Eleazar Williams
Novr 8 — Elizabeth Bowen

1725

July 25 —
Abigail Bugbee
Decr 5 — John Sumner, A.B

PERSONS ADMITTED TO CHURCH FELLOWSHIP.

1726

Jan^ry 30th Edmund Weld
Clemence Weld
March 27 Dorothy Dorre
April 24 Elizabeth Pierpont
May 8 Hannah Mather
Aug. 14 William Bosson, A.B.

1727

June 3 Timothy Parker
John Hely
Hannah Hely

Septr 3 Ebenezer Dorre
Mary Dorre
10 Mehittabell Meers
Octob^r 9 Mary Tompson
15 Isaac Curtis
Mehittabell Curtis
November 12 Elizabeth Crafts
December 10 Ebenezar Tucker
24 Ebenezar Gore
Samuel Gore
Mary Gore
Mary Mayo

December 31 Daniel Williams
Hannah Williams

1727-8

Jan^{ry} 7 Ebenezer Warren
James Meers
Hannah Curtis
Abigail May
Waitstill Payson
14 Andrew Bordman
Deborah Williams
Sarah Bordman
21 Joanna West
Mary Sever
Susanna Warren
28 Mary Bowles
Elizabeth Payne
Feb^{ry} 4 Samuel Craft
Mehittabel Craft
Sarah Lathbridge
Bethiah Rice
11 Mercy Eaton
18 Phillip Bacon
Patience Bacon
Jonathan Craft
Thankfull Craft
Rachel Davis
29 Joanna Rugles
Anna Bayley
March 3 Anne Pierpont
Joanna Stevens
Susanna Stevens
Elizabeth Payson
Mary Harkness
Martha Newel
17 Paul Davis
24 Mary Parker
Sarah Williams
31 John Prentice
Elizabeth George
Anne Wainwright
April 14 Peleg Heathe, A.M.
Elizabeth Hinks
21 Sarah Craft

May 19 Mary Gore
Sarah Pierpont
26 Jemimah Woods
June 23 Mary Bosson
Sarah Seaver
30 John Lovel
July 28 Francis Richey
Mary Richey
Septr 15 Ebenezer Seaver
Octob^r 13 Mary Hall
Mehittabel May
20 Elizabeth Tucker
Novr 10 Dorothy Williams
Margaret Seaver

1728-9

Jan^{ry} 5 Experience Cobbet
Feb^{ry} 16 Nathaniel Newel,
A.B.

1729-30

8th March Samuel Curtis. Dis-
missed from y^e
first church in Bos-
ton and recommen-
ded to ye church.
April 12 Abigail Hewes
June 21 John Searle
Mary Searle
Aug 2. Abigail Green
Septr 13 Sarah Mayo
Hannah Curtis

1731

July 26 Sarah Scott
August 15 Samuel Bayley
Anna Bayley
July 22 Ebenezar Davis
Sarah Davis
Octob^r 3 Thomas Seaver
Elizabeth Seaver

1732

Jan^{ry} 9 Rebecca Abbot
May 14 Mary Stevens

August 20 Anna Heathe

Dec.̃ 3. Joseph Heathe, dismissed from ˙yᵉ
church at North
Yarmuoth

_ 31 Nathaniel Walter,
A.M.

1733

August 13 Joseph Williams

Martha Williams

20 Aaron Davis

Mary Davis

1734

March 3 Abigail Table

Dec.̃ 16 John Bowles jun.̃

1735

March 23 Thomas Baker

Hannah Baker

April 12 Timothy Stevens

Oct. 16 Abigail Bugbee

Nov.̃ 16 Robert Loveren

1736

May 9 Ebenezer Crafts

Susanna Crafts

June 6 Samuel Griggs

July 4 Debora Warren

Hannah Warren

Nov.̃ 17 Eleazar May

Dorothy May

1737

May 1 Mary Williams

Sept.̃ 19 Noah Perrin

Mary Perrin

Mary Sumner

1738

Jan.ʳʸ 8ᵗʰ Abigail Stevens

19ᵗʰ Abigail George

April 16 Elizabeth Williams

Aug. 13. Bethiah Parker

Sept.ʳ 17 Rebecca Davis

Mary Woods

1739

Jan. 6 Phillip Curtis, A.M.

Mary Curtis

Feb.ʳʸ 25 Sarah Stevens

April 15 Susanna Crafts

May 20 Joanna West

June 24 Bethiah Scarborough

1739–40

March 16 Hopestill Monk

May 11 Robert Pierpoint

Hannah Pierpoint

Deborah Searle

Octob.ʳ Rebecca Choate

1741

May 3 Maria Walter

17 Mary George

Aug. 14 Samuel Heath

Octob.ʳ 7 Abigail Dorr

Sarah Dorr

1741–2

Jan.ʸ 24 Lucy Winthrop

31 Samuel Williams

March 21 Ebenezar Eaton

Susanna Woods

April 18 Mary Draper

Abigail Parker

May 2 Joseph Curtis

30 James Pierpoint

Samuel May

Abigail Robinson

June 13 Nathaniel Sumner,
A.M.

Aug. 15 Sarah Sumner

Octob.ʳ 2 Sarah Cole

Nov. 1 Joanna Ruggles

Elizabeth Ruggles

Sarah Payson.

1743.

Janʸ 16. John Giles dismissed from yᵉ Old South Church in Boston.

March 6 Sarah Williams
     Mary Williams

May 15 Priscilla Gore

June 26 Elizabeth Crafts

July 10 Ebenezer Newel
     24 Benjamin Curtis.

Sepᵗ 18 Susan Perriana

1744–5

Janʸ 27 Elizabeth Weld

March 3 Edward Ruggles

April 7 **Martha Perrin**

May   Guinea Negro servᵗ maid to Judge Dudley

Sepᵗ 15 Elizabeth Heathe

Octobᵉ 27 Abigail Sumner

1746–7.

Febʸ 1 **John Williams.**

May 24 Katharine Williams

June 28ᵗʰ John Salmon

1747–8

Janʸ 3 Samuel Williams

Sepᵗ 25 Lydia Gannet

1748 —

1750

    John Williams Jʳ
    Oliver Peabody Jʳ, Pastor Novʳ 17.

1751

April 28 Katharine Ruggles
     Mary Smith

Aug 11 Dorothy Halbrook
     Ann Williams

May 29ᵗʰ 1752 Died the Revᵈ Mʳ Oliver Peabody Pastor of yᵉ 1ˢᵗ Chᵗ in Roxbury

1752

Janʸ 19ᵗʰ Jonathan Sever

1733

Sepᵗ 12ᵗʰ Amos Adams admitted to full Communion, & ordained Pastor

Oct 14. Edmund Weld

Novʳ 11. Abigail Reves
     Abigail Besson

Novʳ 18. Joseph Howard

Dec. 28. Deacon Stephʳ Williams Reconfᵗ

Dec 30. Sarah Weld

1754

March 31 Daniel Sever
     Abial Sever

Sepᵗ 29 John Hewet
     Margrett Hewet

Oct 6. Jonas Merian A.B.

1755

Febᵗ 16. Elizabeth Williams
     Anna Williams

April 20. Anne Pierpoint
     Mary Pierpoint

June 8ᵗʰ Hannah Williams

June 15 Jane Williams

June 22. William Heath
     Prudence Heath

June 29. Jeremiah Williams

Sept. 7. Jeremiah Parker
     Martha Parker

Octʳ 5. Isabal Mosher

Decʳ 28 **Ann McClure**

1756

Jan 25. Abigail Williams

Feb 22. Ebenezer Cheney
     Mary Sever
     Susannah Seaver

March 21 Ebenezer Mary
     Sarah Duff
     Elizabeth Walker

May 6	Mary Parker
	Ann Mears
	John Bowen
	Mahetable Bowen
Augt 26	Daniel Bugbee
	Joseph Williams
	Susannah Williams
Octr 28	Sarah Fellows

1765

April 7th	William Bugbee
May 5	John Brewer

1766

July 20th	Noah Davis
27	Benjamin May
	Mary May
Augt 24	Elizabeth Davis
Novr 23	Mary Thompson

1767

April 5	Elizabeth Davis
	Abigail Davis
	Abigail Parker
Decr 13	Sarah Gridley
	Martha Gridley
	Susannah Gridley

1768

Feb 7	Hannah Pierpont
April 3	Phillis, a Negro woman.
Augt 2	Nath! Ruggles
	Martha Ruggles
	Rebecca Ruggles
Septr 18	Sarah Coolege

1769

March 5	Peleg Heath
	Patience Heath
April 2	John Bowen
30	John Pierpont
	Nath! Eaton
July 23	Joseph Heath

1769

July 22	Martha Dana
Augt 20	Increase Sumner A.B.
	Samuel Cheney A.B.
	Lydia Coolidge
Septr 17.	Joshua Felton
	Mary Felton
Octr 8	Abigail Dow
	Deborah Cheney
	Abigail Mears
	Catherine Parker
	John Davis Williams
	Hannah Williams
	John Williams
	Mary Williams
	Priscilla Craft
	Sarah Craft
	John Graeton
	Sarah Graeton
Novr 12	Anne Williams
	Joseph Smith
	Mary Smith
	Robert Champney
	Rebecca Champney
	Clarissa Kent
Decr. 10	Mary Hayward

1770

Feb. 4	Lemuel May
March 4	Joshua Bowen
	Joshua Bradley
	Sarah Bradley
	Mary Gore
April 1	Nath! Felton
	Mary Felton
	Nath! Felton jun^r
	Mary Felton
29	Mary Shed
Decr. 2	Moses Davis
	Hannah Williams
	Mary Newell

1771

Feb 3	Abigail Newell

Oct.r 13 Jemima Winslow
         Sarah Williams
         Abigail Williams
Nov.r 10 Abigail Whitney

1772

Jan.y 5 Samuel Langley
         Esther Langley
March 28 Lucy Sumner
April 12 Samuel   Whittemore
         jun.r
May 24 Margarate Seaver
         Samuel Bowen
         Mary Bowen
         Elizabeth Adams
Aug.t 16 Stephen Williams
         Mary Williams
Sep.t 27 John Ward
Nov.r 8 Mary Cheney

1773

Feb 28 Caleb Hayward
         Catherine Williams
April 25 Job Bearce
         Abigail Parker
         Sarah Parker
May 23 Thomas Clark
         Ebenezer Bugbee

Nov.r 7th Charles Belknap
         Mary Belknap

1774

Jan.y 4 Rev.d Jonathan Bow-
         man Dismissed from
         Dorchester
   30 Sarah Kelton
         Anna Pike
March 27 Joanna. Williams
         Hannah Hunt
May 22 Levy Whitman
         Patty   Howard [Dis-
         missed   from   Pom-
         fret]
Oct.r 9 William Felton
         Eunice Felton
         Anna Pierpont
         Mary Pierpont
         James Ireland
Nov.r 6 Joseph Ruggles
         Sarah Ruggles
         Samuel Weld
Dec.r 4 Samuel Heath
         Mary Heath

1772

Jan 1th ·Elizabeth Williams
April 9 Adam Patty
         Louis Patty

PERSONS THAT HAVe OWN'D THE COVENANT — 1750.   FROM NOV.B

      John Richards   Feb. 24.
      John Dean & Edward King   March 10.
      Edward Kelton   May 5.
      Obadiah Coolidge   July 21
      Thomas Dana   Oct.r 6.

PERSONS WHO OWNED THE COVENANT.

Sept.r 23. 1753   Jeremiah Mosher
                   Isabel the wife of Jeremiah Mosher

Jan.ʸ 27. 1754	Isaac Gardiner A.M. of Brookline
June 16. 1754.	Mary Shortlief the wife of Henry Shortlief
July 14. 1754.	Joseph Williams jun.ʳ
Dec.ʳ 22. 1754.	John Slack
Dec.ʳ 21. 1755	Sarah Prince
Jan 18. 1726.	Eleanor Bosson the wife of John Bosson.
April 18. 1756.	Fortune, a negro man belonging to Cap. Newell.
May 16. 1756.	Dinah, a negro woman belonging to Deacon Craft.
Aug.ᵗ 1. 1756.	John Searl.
	Margaret Searl.
Sept.ʳ 12. 1756	Keturah, a negro woman belonging to Tho. Seaver.
Nov.ʳ 7. 1756.	Samuel Woods & Mercy Woods the wife of Sam.ˡˡ Woods
March 20. 1757.	James Orr.
April 10. 1757.	Solomon Ayers & Elizabeth the wife of Sol.ⁿ Ayers.
April 17. 1757.	John Dinsdill & Abigail the wife of John Dinsdal
July 31. 1757.	William Blaney
Jan. 15. 1758.	Moses Winchester
	Mary the wife of Moses Winchester.
Dec.ʳ 3. 1758.	John Mears
April 2. 1758	James Mears
Feb 10. 1760	Joseph Worsley
17. 1760	Tho.ˢ Raymour.
	Mary the wife of Tho.ˢ **Raymour.**
June 21. 1761.	Richard Fox
Oct.ʳ 4	William Thompson
Dec.ʳ 27.	Enoch Hancock
May 29. 1762.	Henry Payson
June 6.	William Patrick
Oct.ʳ 17	Nicholas Seaver
	Mary Seaver
	Deborah Searle
	Ruth Searle
Oct.ʳ 3.	Tobias, a negro **man** belonging to William Williams
1764. Oct.ʳ 7.	Ishmael & Venus, Negro Servants of Joseph Ruggles
Nov.ʳ 18	Moses Dorr
	Eleanor Dorr
1765 May 26	Abijah Seaver
March 10.	Deborah Bosson
June 9.	Paul Gore

1766 Feb 2	Daniel Tombes
March 23	James Cornish
April 13	James Bird
Augt 31	Andrew Floyd
Octr 19	Elizabeth Johnson
Novr 23	Joshua Felton
Decr 21	Phillis, the Negro woman of Capt. John Williams
1767 Feb 15.	Eliphalet Downer
May 3	Brill Johnson
10	Mary Doyle
Augt 30	Joseph Smith
Sept 13	Benjamin Baker
Octr 25	Joseph Muncrieff
1768 Feb 28	James Gould
March 27.	Hannah How
August 7.	Mary Bosson
28.	Francis Dana
	Robert Champney
Septr 25.	Samuel Heath
Decr 18.	Richard Rowen
1769 March 23.	Martha Mills
July 15.	Hannah Tucker
Octr 8.	Thomas Weld
1770 June 3.	John Williams
Decr 16	Samuel Gore
1771 Feb 10.	Eben^r Wales.
24.	Benjamin Cotterel & Mary his **wife**
March 10	Anne Johnson
1762 April 26	James White
July 5	Aaron Blaney
Septr 27.	Samuel Croxfort
Octr 4th	Nathl Scott
	Stephen Jennings
	Mary Jennings
1773 Feb 7.	Noah Parker
	Eleanor Parker
March 21.	Enoch Hyde
Augt 22.	Nathan Shed
1774 Feb 20.	John Whitney
April 17.	Joseph Payson
Octr 9.	Benjamin Stevens
Novr 6	Nathl Healy
Decr 25.	Joseph Richardson

1775 Jany 22. James Howe
 Feb 12. Daniel Brown
 March 5th. Ephrahim Hyde and Abigail Hyde

1641.

BAPTIZED.

Month 10^t day 26. Abiel Prichard the son of Mr. Hugh Prichard.
Month 1 day 6. Samuel Perry the son of John Perry.
     John Astwood the son of James Astwood.
  day 13. Martha Park the daughter of Willia Park.
     Caleb Peakok the son of Rich. Peakok.
     Mary Gamlin the daughter of Rob. Gamlin.
  day 20. Sarah Denison the daughter of George Denison.

1642.

  day 27. John Parker the sone of Judith Parker some-
     time the wife of Richard Bugby who God
     tooke.
Month 2 day 10. Mary Johnson the daughter of Isack Johnson.
  day 24. Jams the son of John Leavins.
     Mary Bumsted the daughter of Thom. Bumsted.
Month 3^d day 29. Mary Porter the daughter of Edward Porter.
Month 4^t day 5. Hañah Hagborne the daughter of Sam. Hag-
     borne.
Month 5^t day 24. John Scarbro the sone of John Scarbro.
Month 6th day 5. Zachariah White the sone of Edward White.
Month 7^t day 25. Daniel Weld the son of Joseph Weld.
Month 8^t day 15. Japhet Chapin the son of Samuel Chapin.
Month 9^t day 28. Joshua Lambe the sone of Thomas Lambe.
Month 10^t day 18. Hañah Morgan the daughter of James Morgan.
  day 25. Mary Wood ⎫ twins : daughters of
     Sarah Wood ⎬ Wood of the church of
     Brantree who maryed o^r bro. Pigs daughter
     and she lying in childbed in this towne,
     they were baptized here by comunion of
     churches.
Month 12 day 5. Mary Stebbin the daughter of Martin Stebbin.
  day 12. Hannah Peake the daughter of Christopher
     Peake.

[1643.]

Month 1 day 12. Martha Pig the daughter of Thomas Pig.
Month 2^d day 9. Joshua Hinningway the son of Rãph Hiñing-
     way.
     John Bell the son of Thomas Bell.
Month 3^d day 7. Abigal Gore the daughter of Mr John Gore.
  day 21. Hañah Dennison the daughter of George Den-
     nison.   *K*

Month 4 day 4. Mehittabell Cheyny the daughter of Williã Cheyny.

day 11. Mary Gorton the daughter of John Gorton.

day 18. John Paison the son of Edward Paison.

Month 5 day 1. Aña Goarde the daughter of Richard Goard.
John Goarde the son of Richard Goard.

day 23. Elizabeth Starkweather the daughter of Rob. Starkweath.

Month 6 day 6. Gerrard Bourne the sone of Gerrard Bourne a member of Boston, & living at Muddy River was here received by comunion of churches.

Month 8 day 22. Zebediah Prichard the son of Mr. Hugh Prichard.
Elizabeth Mathews the daughter of Mathews.

Month 9 day 19. Sarah Park the daughter of Williã Park.
Joseph Astwood the son of James Astwood.
Elizabeth Seaver the daughter of Rob. Seaver.

Month 10 day 3. Hañah Scarbrough the daughter of John Scarbrough.

Month 11 day 7. Sarah Holmes the daughter of George Holmes
Isaak Johnson the son of Isaak Johnson.

day 21. Sarah Gorton the daughter of John Gorton.

Month 1 day 3. Aaron Eliot the son of Mr John Eliot.
James Morgan the son of James Morgan
Elizabeth Pepper the daughter of Robert Pepper.

1644

Month 2 day 14. Isaak Lewis the sone of   Lewis

day 21. Mary Speere the daughter of Georg. Speere. of the Church of Brantree, by Communion of Churches.

Month 3 day 5. Mary Watson the daughter of John Watson.
Peniel Bowen, the sone of Mr Bowen of Boston Church, by Comunion of Churches, he living at a farme neerer to us then to Boston. his wife was deliv̇d of this child by Gods mercy wthout the help of any othr woman. God himself helping his pore servants in a straight.
John Huise the son of Joshua Huise.
Joseph Porter the sone of Edward Porter.

Month 4 day 23. Mary Goard the daughter of Rich. Goard.
Lidea Starkweather the daughter of Rob. Starkweath.

Month 5 day 7. Hanna Hely the daughter of Williã Hely.

day 14. Israel How the sonne of Abrahã How.

Month 7 day 15. PeterLeavins & ⎫ Twins. the children of John
Andrew Leavins ⎬ Leavins in the 63 yeare of
⎭ his aige, a doble blessing.

		day 29.	Mary Lambe the daughter of Tom. Lambe.
Month	8	day 20.	Phebe Prichard the daughter of Mͬ Hugh Prichard.
Month	10	day 22.	Jonathan Paison the sonne of Edward Paison.
Month	11	day 26.	Samuel White the sone of Edward White
Month	12	day 9.	Joseph Weld the sone of Joseph Weld
			Elizabeth Paison the daughter of Giles Pason.
Month	1	day 2.	Deborah the daughter of Mͬ Thom. Dudly.
		day 23.	Joseph the sone of Christopher Peake.

John the sone of Edmund Sheffeild

Nathaniel the sone of Martin Stebbin

Desire truth the daughter of Will. Thorne living at Muddy River, whose wife is of Boston Church.

1645

Month 1 day 30. Elizabeth the daughter of Mͬ Daniel Gookins recom̄ended to us frō Boston.

John the sone of James Morgan.

Month 3 day 18. Hannah the daughter of John Gore.

Month 4 day 1. Elizabeth Pepper the daughter of Robert pepper.

Month 4 day 8. Elizabeth Hinningway the daughter of Ralph Hinningway.

Month 5ᵗ day 6. John Parke, the sonne of Williā Park.

Month 7ᵗʰ day 28. Mary Bell the daughter of Thom. Bell.

Month 8 day 19. Thomas Hanshet sonne of John Hanshet.

Month 9 day 9. Deborah Holmes daughter of Georg. Holmes.

Joseph Johnson sone of Isaak Johnson.

Month 11 day 1. Samuel Scarbrough sonne of John Scarbrough.

Phebe Jones daughter of   Jones.

day 8. Nathaniel Seaver the sonne of Robert Seaver.

day 14. Samuel Heli sonne of William Heli.

Abigal Gardner daughter of Thom. Gardner

Month 1 day 14. Phebe Goard daughter of Rich. Goarde.

1646

Month 1 day 29. Mehitable Johnson daughter of Humphrey Johnson.

Month 1 day 5. Hañah Gorton the daughter of John Gorton.

Month 3 day 3. Deborah Porter the daughter of Edward Porter.

Joseph Wise ⎫
Jeremiah Wise ⎬ the sonns of Joseph Wise

Elizabeth Clarke ⎫ the daughters of
Mary Clarke ⎬ Clarke.

Month 4 day 14. John Denison the sonne of George Denison.

day 14. Sarah Astwood the daughter of James Astwood.

day 28. Hañah Buckmaster daughter of   Buckmaster.

Month 5 day 5. Thomas Reives the sone of Thomas Reives

Month 6 day 2.   Marah Weld the daughter of Mr Joseph Weld now in great affliction by a soare on his tongue.

Rachel Leavins the daughter of John Leavins.

Marie Lewis daughter of   Lewis

John Starkweather the sonne of Robert Starkweather.

Abiel Lambe the sonne of Thom. Lambe who was not long fore deceased, & left his children to the Lord, y^t he might be theire fath^r.

Month 9 day 29.   Joseph Morgan the sonne of James Morgan.

Month 10 day 12.   Eliezer White the sonne of Edward White

Month 11 day 16.   Deborah Park daught^r of William Park.

Month 1 day 13.   Hannah Mekins daughter of Thom. Mekins.

1647.

day 28.   Bethiah Farrow ⎫ children of   Farrow

Hannah Farrow ⎬ whose wife joyned to o^r church at this time.

Hannah Hanshet daught of John Hanshet.

Month 2 day 11.   John Pepper the sonne of Rob. Pepper.

day 18.   Mary Hinningway daughter of Ralph Hinningway.

Month 3 day 2.   Ann Paison daughter of Edward Paison.

Nathaniel Johnson sonne of Isaak Johnson.

Hannah Wilson daughter of   Wilson.

day 9.   Hannah Thorne daughter of William Thorne.

day 23.   Hannah Gookins daughter of Mr Dan: Gookins

Month 5 day 25.   [blank]

Month 6 day 8.   Elizabeth Harris ⎱ child^m of Rob: Harris, who

Harrs John   ⎰ now joyned to o^r church.

day 29.   Susan Miller daughter to Mr John Miller. one an Eld^r of o^r church, afterwards at Rowley he p'ched & thenc. was called to Yarmouth.

Month 7 day 12.   Martha Johnson daughter Humfery Johnson.

day 19.   Joseph Goard sone of Richard Goard.

day 26.   Joseph Dudley sonne to Mr Thomas Dudley

Month 9 day 14.   Elizabeth Heli, daughter of Willia Heli.

Month 10 day 26.   Mary Astwood daughter of James Astwood.

Rebeka Read daughter of   Read

Sarah Wise daughter of Joseph Wise

Month 11 day 9.   Jeremijah the sonne of Edwad Dennison.

Month 12 day 6.   Hannah Seaver daughter of Rob: Seaver.

day 27.   Joseph Baker sonne of Thomas Baker.

1648

Month 2 day 2.   Elizabeth Parker daughter of Edmond Parker.

day 9.   Mary Gardner daughter of Thomas Gardner

	day 16.	Mary Chamberlin daughter of Edmund Chamberlin.
Month	5 day 16.	Sarah Paison daughter of Giles Paison.
Month	6 day 27.	Debora Starkweath^r daughter of Rob. Starkweath^r
Month 7	day 3.	Abraham Morgan sonne of James Morgan.
		Mary Gorton daughter of John Gorton.
Month	9 day 12.	Thomas Wooddy sonne of Richard Woody Junio^r
Month	10 day 3.	Gershon Culver sonne of Ed Culver.
	day 10.	Sarah Farrow daughter of Farrow.
Month	11 day 14.	Debora Turner daughter of John Turner.
	day 28.	John Mekins sonne of Thom. Mekins
Month	12 day 25.	Mary Devotion, of ye church of Boston at Muddy River.
Month	1 day 11.	John Woody sonne of John Woody.
	day 18.	Joseph Pepper sonne of Rob: Pepper
		Hannah Lewis daughter of William Lewis
	day 25.	Obadiah Gore sonne of Mr John Gore.
		Johanna Paison daughter of Edward Paison
		Sarah Goard daughter of Richard Goard

1649

Month	2 day 8.	Joseph Dennison sonne of Edward Dennison.
	day 29.	Elizabeth Parker daughter of Edmund Parker.
Month	3 day 20.	Ann Dennison daughter of Georg. Dennison.
	day 13.	John Park, sonne of Williā Parke.
Month	5 day 15.	Joseph Tory sonne of Phillip Tory.
Month	6 day 12.	Joseph Weld sonne of John Weld.
Month	8^t day 11.	John Davis ⎫ Children of William Davis Samuel Davis ⎬ whose wife was admitted & so Joseph Davis ⎭ brought her children to p'take of this blessed ordinance.
	day 14.	Hannah Hanshet, daughter of John Hanshet.
Month	10 day 2.	Thankfull Pairpoynt daughter of Thom: Pairpoynt.
	day 23.	Hannah Clark daughter of Clark.
Month	11 day 20.	Deborah Johnson daughter of Humfrey Johnson.
Month	12 day 3.	Isack Woody sonne John Woody.
		Mary Wise daughter of Joseph Wise [This and *all* the following entries in handwriting of Revd Mr Danforth, colleague Revd Mr Elliot.]

1650

Month	1 day 24.	Peter Gardiner the sonn of Peter Gardiner
		Rebecca Gardiner daughter of Peter Gardiner.
		Lyons
		Joseph Patchin ⎫ sons of Joseph Patchin John Patchin ⎭
Month	2^d day 28.	Sarah Baker ye daughter of Thomas Baker.

Month 3ᵈ day 26.   Anna } Alcock, daughters of Mʳ John Al-
                    Sarah }   cocke.
Moneth 4ᵗʰ day 2ᵈ   Mary } Polly, daughters of John Polly.
                    Sarah }
        day 16.   Samuel Lyons the son of William Lyons.
Moneth 5 day 14.   Timothy Harris son of Robert Harris.
        day 21   Mary Wooddie, daughter of Rich. Woodie.
Moneth 7 day 8.   Paul Dudley son of Tho. Dudley Esqʳ p'sent
                    Governour.
        day 15.   Joseph Weld, son of John Weld. There was
                    no help present wⁿ the mother was deliⱴ
                    of this child.
Moneth 8 day 23.   Hanna Seaver daughter to Brothʳ Seaver.
                    Roberts   of Hugh Roberts.
Moneth 9 day 17.   Morgan daughter of James Morgan.
Moneth 10 day 8.   Peter Gardiner the son of Thomas Gardiner.
        day 15.   Margaret Dennison daughter of Edw. Den-
                    nison.
        day 29.   Mary Parker.
Month 12 day 2.   Sarah Heley daughter to brothʳ Hely.
        day 23.   Elizabeth Bowles daughter of John Bowles.

1651

Moneth 2 day 6.   Deborah Park daughter to Will. Parke.
        day 13.   Joseph Goard the sonn of Richard Goard
        day 27.   Mary Pepper daughter of Robert Pepper.
Moneth 4ᵗʰ day 8.   John Turner son of John Turner.
        day 22.   Jonathan Torry son of Philip Torry.
Moneth 5 day 6.   Peter Hanshet son of John Hanshet.
        day 20.   Samuel Welde yᵉ son of Mʳ Thomas Welde.
Moneth 9 day 30.   Anne Pason daughter of Edw. Pason.
Moneth 11 day 25.   Martha Woodie daughter to Rich. Woodie,
                    junior.
Moneth 12 day 15.   Hanna Polly daughter of John Polly.
Month 1 day 8.   Alice Gorton daughter to John Gorton.

1652

Moneth 2 day 11.   Ephraim Peak son to brother Peake.
                    James Clark son of Brother Clark.
                    Hanna Culver daughter of Neighbor Culver.
        day 18.   Benjamin Chase son of William Chase.
        day 16.   Isaac Bowles sonne of John Bowells.
Moneth 3ᵈ day 23.   Daniel Harris son of Robert Harris.
                    Thomas Gardiner son of Peter Gardiner.
Moneth 4ᵗʰ day 6.   Mary Baker daughter to Brother Baker.
                    Mary White daughter to Sister · White· of
                    Watertowne.
Moneth 5 day 11.   William Hely sonne to William Heli.
        day 18.   William Lyon sonne of Neighbor Lyon.
Moneth 6 day 15.   Mary Alcock daughter of Mʳ John Alcock.
                    John Wise sonne to Joseph Wise.
Moneth 7 day 5.   Abraham Parker sonne of Edmund Parker.

Moneth 8 day 31.	John Perepoint sonn to John Perepoint.
Moneth 10 day 5.	Mary Sharp daughter to Goodman Sharp of Moody River.
	Susanna Heath daughter to Peleg Heath.
day 26.	Abigail Gardiner daughter of Tho. Gardiner.
Moneth 11 day 14.	Samuel Danforth yᵉ son of Samuel borne about 9 o'Clock at night and baptised at Boston upon yᵉ Sabbath following which was yᵉ 16 day of January.
day 30.	Reuben Keeble son to Goodman Keebie whose wife is sister of yᵉ church at Boston.
	Joseph Hawly son of Thomas Hawly.
Moneth 12 day 27.	Lydia Goard daughter to brother Goard.

1653

Moneth 1 day 13.	Mary Heath daughter to Isaac Heath.
	Martha Devotion.
day 27.	Mary Denison daughter to Edward Denison.
Moneth 3ᵈ day 8.	Nathaniel Wilson sonne to Nath. Wilson.
15.	Benjamin Pepper sonn of Robert Pepper.
Moneth 4 day 12.	Thomas Weld yᵉ sonn of Thomas Weld.
day 26.	John Weld sonn to John Weld.
Moneth 5 day 17.	John Bowles son to John Bowles.
Moneth 6 day 28.	Susanna Pason daughter to Edw. Pason.
Moneth 7 day 11.	Mary Baker daughter to brothʳ Baker.
25.	Abraham How son to Abrah. How.
Moneth 8 day 19.	Priscilla Harris daughter of Robert Harris.
Moneth 11 day 22.	John Ruggles son to John Ruggles.
day 29.	Sarah Gardiner daughter to Peter Gardiner.

1654

Moneth 2ᵈ day 9.	Samuel Clark sonn to James Clarke.
	Mary Torry daughter to Philip Torry.
Moneth 3ᵈ day 28.	Mary Danforth daughter to Samuel Danforth.
	She was born ye 24 day of May.
✗ Moneth 4ᵗʰ day 4.	Abigal Polly daughter to John Polly.
day 11.	Joseph Hawly sonn to Tho. Hawly.
Moneth 2 day 30.	Gorton daughter to John Gorton.
Moneth 7 day 3.	Hanna Glover daughter to Mʳ Hab. Glover.
Moneth 8 day 1.	Hanna Heath daughter to Peleg Heath.
day 8.	William Parke sonne to William Parke.
Moneth 10 day 3.	Joseph Lyons sonne to Will. Lyons.
	Benjamin Goard sonne to brothʳ Goard.
	Hanna Devotion.
Moneth 11 day 28.	Thomas Ruggles sonn of John Ruggles junior.
Moneth 12 day 11.	Lucia Gardiner daughter to Tho. Gardiner.
	Elizabeth Williams daughter to Sam. Williams.

Moneth 1 day 4.   Henry Wise sonn of Joseph Wise.
                   Elisabeth Keeble daughter to Goodm̄a Kee-
                   bie.
        day 18.   Experience Peirpoint daughter of John Peir-
                   point.

1655.

Moneth 1 day 25.   George Alcock sonn to Mʳ John Alcock.
Moneth 2 day 29.   Mary Bowles daughter to John Bowles.
                   Robert Pepper son of Rob. Pepper.
Moneth 3 day 20.   Josias Winchester sonne to Goodman Win-
                   chester of Scituate.
Moneth 5 day 1.   Susanna Pason daughter of Edw. Pason.
                   Isaac Heath son of Isaac Heath junior.
        day 29.   Rebecca Glover daughter to Hab. Glover.
Moneth 6 day 19.   Samuel Weld sonn to Tho Welde.
Moneth 7 day 16.   Hanna Denison daughter to Edw. Denison.
Moneth 9 day 18.   Elisabeth Welde daughter to John Welde.
Moneth 10 day 30. John Gardiner son to Peter Gardiner.
Moneth 12 day 17. Joseph } Wilson, sons of Nath. Wilson.
                   Benjamin }
        day 24.   John Gorton son of John Gorton.

1656

Moneth 1 day 9.   Sarah Peak daughter to Xtopher Peake
        day 16.   Benjamin } Welde Twins of Daniel Welde.
                   Mehetabel }
        day 23.   John Clarke son to James Clarke
        day 30.   Isaac How sonn to Abraham How
Moneth 2ᵈ day 6.   Susanna Newell daughtʳ to Abrӓha N. junior.
        day 27.   Samuel Williams sonn to Samuel Williams.
Moneth 4ᵗʰ day 22. Mary   ) Parker, daughters of Edmund
                   Esther }   Parker.
                   Deborah)
        day 29.   Elisabeth Hawly daughter to Tho. Hawly
Moneth 5 day 13.   Elisabeth Danforth daughter to Samuel Dan-
                   forth was borne, beinge yᵉ Sabbath
                   day, about 6 at night & was baptised yᵉ
                   Lords day following, viz, the 20ᵗʰ of July.
Moneth 7 day 7.   Benjamin Goard, sonne of Richard Goard.
Moneth 8 day 5.   Samuel Griggs sonne of Joseph Griggs
Moneth 11 day 25. Joanna Gardiner daughter to Tho. Gardiner.

1657

Moneth 1 day 8.   Samuel Gardiner son of Peter Gardiner.
                   Sarah Lyons daughter of W. Lyons.
        day 15.   John Alcock son of Mʳ John Alcocke.
Moneth 2ᵈ day 19. Bethiah Wise daughter to Joseph Wise.
Moneth 3ᵈ day 17. Mary   )
                   Elisabeth } Griffin
                   Joseph   )

Moneth 4 day 28. Edward Pason sonn to Edwd Pason.
Moneth 5 day 26. Elisabeth Heath daughter to Isaac Heath.
Moneth 6 day 23. Samuel Ruggles sonn to John Ruggles.
Moneth 8 day 11. John Welde ye sonn of Tho. Welde.
                  Margaret Welde daughter of John Welde.
Moneth 9 day 22. Mary Griggs daughter to Joseph Griggs.
Moneth 10 day 6. Sarah Denison daughter to Edw. Denison.
         day 27. Moses   ⎫
                  Aaron   ⎬ Huntley.
                  Elisabeth   ⎭
Moneth 1 day 21. Abigail Clark daughter to James Clark.

1658

Moneth 1 day 28. Martha Williams ye daughter of Saml Williams
Moneth 4.th day 20. William Pool son to Mr Williã Pool of Taunton.
                  Dorothy Hawly daughter to Tho. Hawly
Moneth 5 day 25. Joseph Newell sonn to Abrahã Newell junior.
Moneth 6 day 29. Isaac Wilson son to Joseph Wilson.
Moneth 7 day 19. Isaac Morrice ye sonn of Edw. Morrice
         day 26. Hanna Parks daughter to Deacon Parks.
Moneth 8 day 10. Katharen Wise daughter to Joseph Wise
                  Abigail Heath daughter to Peleg Heath.
         day 17. Daniel Welde ye sonne of Daniel Welde.
                  Barnabas Beeres ye son of Anthony Beers.
Moneth 9 day 7.   Sarah Danforth ye daughter of Samuel Danforth was baptised. But she was borne ye 30.th of 8.^m about 4 in ye morning.
Moneth 11 day 16. Joseph Gardiner son to Peter Gardiner.
         30.   John   ⎱ Ruggles ye children of John Ruggles
                  Mary   ⎰ junior.
Moneth 12 day 20. Ephraim sonne to Edward Pason.
                  John sonne to John Mayob.
                  Samuel sonne to Samuel Ruggles.
                  Bethjah daughter to John Polly.
         day 27. Ephraim   ⎫
                  Benjamin   ⎬ children of Benjamin Childe
                  Joshua   ⎭
Moneth 1 day 13. Edward sonn to Edward Morrice.

1659

Moneth 1 day 27. Elisabeth daughter to Mr John Alcocke.
                  Hanna daughter to Joseph Griggs
                  John, sonne   ⎱ to John Griggs
                  Mary, daughter ⎰
Moneth 3.^d day 1. Isaac Pepper sonn to Robt Pepper.
         day 8.   Joshua Gardiner sonne to Tho. Gardiner.
                  Abraham Gorton sonne to John Gorton.
         day 29. Sarah Mayes daughter to John Mayes junior
                  Abigail daughter to Samuel Mayes

Moneth 4 day 12.   John ⎫
                 Tobias ⎬ sons to Tobias Davis
                 Isaac ⎪
                 Samuel ⎭

Moneth 7 day 11.   Sarah daughter of John Mayes jun.
            18.   Abigail Griffin daughter to bro. Griffin.
Moneth 8 day 2.   Edmund sonn unto Mᵣ Tho. Welde.
       day 23.   Hanna daughter to John Griggs.
Moneth 9 day 20.   Mary daughter of Aarō Knap of Taunton.
Moneth 11 day 8.   James sonn unto John Pierpont.
       day 12.·   Henry, sonn of Henry Bowin.
       day 19.   Joseph son to Samuel Ruggles.
       day 26.   Elisabeth daughter to Samuel Williams.

1660

Moneth 2 day 8.   Mary daughter to John Welde.
Moneth 3 day 6.   Johannah daughter to Mᵣ John Alcock.
                 William ⎫
                 Thomas ⎬ sonnes ⎫
                 Hanna daughter ⎬ to William Hopkins.
Moneth 6 day 26.   Abigail daughter to Isaac Heath junior.
Moneth 7 day 2.   Mercie yᵉ daughter of James Clarke.
       day 23.   Deborah daughter to Edwᵈ Denison.
Month 8 day 7.   Benjamin son to Joseph Wise
         28.   Mary daughter to Benjamin Childe.
Moneth 9 day 11.   John yᵉ son of Samuel Danforth was bap-
                 tised, being borne yᵉ 8ᵗʰ day about 5 at
                 night.
Moneth 10 day 30.   Joseph son of Peleg Heath.
Moneth 11 day 6.   Isaac son to Isaac Williams.
       day 27.   Elisabeth daughter to Henry Bowen.
Moneth 12 day 3.   Mary daughter to John Huntley.
       day 17.   Grace daughter to Edw. Morrice.
       day 24.   Hanna daughter to John Mayo.
Moneth 1   day 24.   Samuel son to Tobias Davis.

1661

Moneth 2 day 14.   Mary daughter to Abraham Newel jun.
Moneth 3 day 5.   Esther daughter to brother Griffin.
Moneth 4 day 23.   Mary daughter to Goodman Wilson.
Moneth 6 day 4.   Jacob son to Robᵗ Pepper.
Moneth 7 day 22.   Abigail daughter to John Griggs.
Moneth 8 day 13.   Joseph Griggs son to Joseph Griggs.
                 Mary   ⎫
                 Elisabeth ⎬ daughters to Nath. Garee.
Moneth 10 day 22.   Ebenezer son to John Pierpoint
                 Hanna daughter to Samuel Ruggles.
                 Susanna daughter to John Polly.
Moneth 11 day 19.   Sarah daughter to Edward Devotion.

Moneth 12 day 16.   Eleazer son to John Mayes junior.
Moneth 1 day 9.   William son to Joseph Wise.
                     Mehetebel daughter to Peleg Heath.
         day 16.   Daniel son to M.ʳ Tho. Welde.
                     Isaac son to Isaac Williams.

1662

Moneth 1 day 30.   Mary daughter to William Hopkins.
Moneth 2 day 13.   Caleb son to Thomas Gardiner.
Moneth 4 day 15.   Hanna daughter to Jonathā Peake.
         day 8.   Sarah daughter to Pèter Gardiner.
Moneth 5 day 20.   Palsgrave son to M.ʳ John Alcocke.
Moneth 6 day 3.   Theodoe daughter to Samuel Williams.
Moneth 7 day 7.   John son to Henry Bowin.
         day 21.   Sarah daughter to M.ʳ John Eliot jun.
                     Samuel son to Edward Pason.
         day 28.   Rebecca daughter to John Ruggles jun.
Moneth 10ᵗʰ day 7.   Josiah son to Isaac Newell.
Moneth 11 day 25.   Samuel son to brother Griffin.

1663

Moneth 1 day 1.   Aaron son to James Clarke.
         day 15.   Mary the daughter of Samuel Danforth.
                       She was borne yᵉ 13 day about 5 at night.
                     Ebenezer son to Isaac Heath.
         day 29.   Mary, daughter to John Bridge.
Moneth 2 day 12.   Jacob son to Jacob Newell.
                     Martha daughter to Jacob Newell.
                     Joanna daughter to Nath. Brewer.
Moneth 3 day 17.   John, son ⎫
                     Rebecca ⎬ daughters ⎫ to John Crafte
                     Mary ⎭   ⎬
         day 24.   John son to John Mayes.
         day 31.   Rebecca daughter to Jacob Newel.
Moneth 4 day 14.   William, sonne ⎫ to William Daviss.
                     Elisabeth, daughter ⎭
Moneth 5 5ᵗʰ day   Nathanael yᵉ son of Nathanael Garec.
          12ᵗʰ day. Edward son to Edward Devotion.
          19ᵗʰ day. Thomas son to Abraham Newell jun.
Moneth 7 day 6.   Abigail daughter to John Welde.
         13.   Margaret yᵉ daughter of M.ʳ Gutts a member
                       of Salem Church, but resident in Kene-
                       bek.
Moneth 8 day 18.   Jonathan son to Jonathan Peake.
Moneth 9 day 15.   Samuel sonn to William Hopkins.
         day 22.   Sarah daughter to Samuel Ruggles.
Moneth 10 day 27.   Thankfull daughter to John Pierrepoint.
Moneth 11 day 24.   Matthew, son to William Daviss.
Moneth 12 day 7.   Jonathan son to Samuel May.
         day 21.   Elisabeth daughter to Benjamin Childe.

1664

Moneth 1 day 6.   William, son to Peleg Heath.
      day 20·   Benjamin son to Joseph Wise.
Moneth 2 day 3.   Benjamin, son to bro. Griffin.
      day 10.   Abigail daughter to Nath. Wilson.
                Martha daughter to Isaac Williams.
      day 17.   Ebenezer sonne to Edward Morrice.
      day 24.   Dorothy daughter to Mr Tho. Welde.
Moneth 3 day 1.   Thomas, son / Esther, daughter } to Thomas Woodward
      day 22.   Benjamin sonne to Peter Gardiner.
Moneth 4 day 12.   Prudence daughter to John Bridge.
      day 19.   Peter son to Peter Aspinwall.
Moneth 5 day 3.   Rebecca daughter to John Mayoh.
Moneth 7 day 18.   William sonn to Edward Denison.
                George sonn to John Griggs.
Moneth 10 day 18.   John son to Samuel Williams.
Moneth 11 day 1.   Esther daughter to John Welde.
Moneth 12 day 9.   Elisabeth daughter to Samuel Danforth, born about 9 in ye morning & baptized on ye Lords day following yt same day were baptized.
      day 12.   James, John, Joseph & Mary children of James Frissell.
1m 1664⅗ day 12.   John, sonne, / Mary, daughter } to Robt Hawes.
      day 19.   Mary, daughter to Edward Pason.

1665

Moneth 1 day 26.   Sarah daughter to Isaac Newell.
Moneth 2 day 3.   Sarah daughter to James Frissell.
      day 23.   Elizabeth / John } Chandler, childr. of John Chandler.
Moneth 3 day 7.   Mehetabel daughter to John Mayes.
      day 14.   Hanna, daughter to Thomas Woodward.
      day 28.   Margaret daughter to Henry Bowen.
Moneth 4 day 4.   John, / Samuel } sons to Job Tyler.
                Benjamin, Joseph, Mary, Rebecca, Anna, } the children of Richd Chamberlain.
                Thomas sonne to Thomas Foster.
      day 25.   Peleg, son to Isaac Heath.
                Sarah daughter to Nath. Garee.
Moneth 5 day 2.   Mercy daughter to Jacob Newell.
      day 9.   Hanna daughter to Daniel Brewer.
Moneth 6 day 20.   Jonathan son to Robt Pierrepoint.
Moneth 7 day 10.   Ebeneser sonne to Peter Gardiner.

Moneth 9 day 19. Hanna
               Elizabeth } daughters to Samuel Crafts.
Moneth 11 day 14. Sarah
               Richard } Davies children of Rich.ᵈ Davies.
               Abiel
      day 28. Margaret daughter to Benjamin Childe
               Mehetabel daughter to Rich.ᵈ Chamberlaine
Moneth 12 day 4. Jonathan sonne to William Davies.
Moneth 12 day 4. Hanna daughter to brother Griffin.
      day 11. Joanna daughter to Samuel May.
      day 18. Sarah daughter to Edw.ᵈ Devotion.
               Margaret daughter to William Hopkins.

1666

      day 25. Elizabeth daughter to Edward Morrice
Moneth 3.ᵈ day 6. Joseph son to M.ʳ Thomas Welde.
         13. Joseph son to John Craft.
Moneth 4.ᵗʰ day 10. Nathaniel son to Peter Aspinwall.
               Sarah daughter to Thomas Foster.
      day 17. Samuel son to Joseph Wilson.
      day 24. Abigail daughter to Joseph Wise.
Moneth 5 day 15. Elizabeth
               Desire-truth } daughters to John **Acrees**.
      day 22. Margaret daughter to John Bridge.
Moneth 6 day 12. Joseph son to John Pierpoint.
               Elisabeth daughter to Abraham Newel jun.
      day 19. Sarah daughter to John Griggs.
Moneth 7 day 2. Christopher son to Jonathan Peake.
      day 9 Jonathan son to William Lyons.
      day 16. Joseph son to Peleg Heath.
               Hanna daughter to John Welde.
      day 23. Mary daughter to Henry Bowin
               Robᵗ son to John Sharp.
               Joseph son to Joseph Buckmaster.
Moneth 8 day 14. Sarah daughter to James Clarke.
         21. William son to William Bartholomew.
Moneth 9 day 4. Deborah daughter to Edward Denison.
Moneth 10 day 9. Ebenezer son to Samuel Williams
               Mary daughter to Samuel Ruggles.
      day 13. Samuel Danforth born yᵉ 18ᵗʰ of yᵉ 10 month
                 about 1 in yᵉ morning, and baptized the
                 30ᵗʰ of 10ᵐ.
Moneth 11 day 13. Joseph son to John Mayo.
Moneth 1 day 3.ᵈ Timothy yᵉ son of Timothy Stévens.
               Abraham, son of Isaac Newell.
      day 10. William, son of Nathaniel Garee.
      day 24. Mary daughter to Daniel **Marshcraft**.

1667

Moneth 2.ᵈ day 14. Samuel son to Henry Stevens.
               Joseph son to John Chandler.

Moneth 3ᵈ day 5.   Benjamin son to James Frissell.
day 26.   Naomi, daughter to John May.
Elisabeth, daughter to Mʳ Jachin Reyner.
Moneth 4ᵗʰ day 2ᵈ   Martha daughter to John Sharp.
day 23.   Samuel, son to Samuel Craft.
Moneth 5 day 21.   Nathanael, son to Nathanael Brewer.
day 30.   Elisabeth, daughter to Thomas Woodward.
Moneth 6 day 4.   Samuel son to Jacob Newel
day 11.   Thomas, son to Robert Pierrepont.
Moneth 7 day 1.   Jonathan son to Peter Gardiner.
day 29.   John, son to John Prentice.
Moneth 8 27ᵗʰ day.   John
              William
              James
              Jacob } children of John Parker.
              Sarah
              Mary
Moneth 9ᵗʰ day 10.   Daniel son to Daniel Marshcraft.
Moneth 11 day 26.   Thomas son to Peter Aspinwall.
Thomas son to Tho. Boltstone.
Moneth 12 day 23.   Jabesh son to   Corban
Moneth 1 day 1.   Margaret daughter to Henry Bowin.
Christopher son to Jonathan Peake.
day 8.   Benjamin son to Joseph Griggs.
John, son to Benjamin Childe.
Joseph son to William Hopkins
Eleazar son to Samuel Mayes.
Sarah daughter to Timothy Stevens.
day 15.   Edward son to Edward Devotion.
day 22.   Elizabeth daughter to John White jun.

1668

Moneth 2 day 5.   Sarah daughter to Steven Williams
day 19.   Joseph
            Jonathan
            Peter } children of John Prentice
            Steven
            Esther
Moneth 6 day 2.   Benjamin son to John Pierpoint.

1668

Silence daughter to Henry Stevens.
day 16.   Rebecca daughter to John Polly.   ×
day 30.   Jonathan son to James Pemberton.
Moneth 7 day 13.   Edward son to John Bridge.
day 27.   Margaret daughter to Edward Morrice.
Moneth 8 day 18.   Experience daughter to John Parker.
Moneth 9 day 1.   Mary daughter to William Bartbelomew.
day 22.   Peleg son to Peleg Heath.
Deborah daughter to Samuel Williams.
Elizabeth daughter to John Acrees.

Rebecca daughter to Moses Craft.

Moneth 11 day 10. Elizabeth yᵉ posthumous daughter of Joseph Buckmaster.

day 17. Mary daughter to Thomas Woodward.

day 24. Elizabeth daughter to Isaac Newel.

day 31. Rebecca daughter to Nath. Garee.

Moneth 12 day 7. Daniel son to Daniel Brewer.

day 28. Mehetabel daughter to John Mayo.

Ruth daughter to Abraham Newel junior.

1669

Moneth 1 day 21. Elisha son to John May.

John son to Nathaniel Johnson.

Mary daughter to Thomas Boltstone.

Moneth 2 day 25. Thankfull daughter to John Capin junior of Dorchester.

Moneth 3 day 16. Icabod son to Jonathan Hide.

Grace, daughter to Thomas Oliver.

John, son to John Sharp.

day 30. Joanna Davies a little maid grandchild to Mʳ Nicolas Parker.

Moneth 4 day 13. Jane daughter to Thomas Cheany.

day 27. Thankful daughter to Sergeant Badcock of Dorchester.

Moneth 5 day 18. John son to John White junior.

Joseph son to Samuel Craft.

Thomas son to Thomas Stedman of Cambridge Village.

day 25. Joseph son to Isaac Heath.

Hanna daughter to Thomas Foster.

Moneth 6 day 1. Abigail daughter to Henry Bowin.

Joshua son to Joshua Hemingway.

day 8. Thankful daughter to John Hemingway.

day 29. Mehetabel daughter to Benjamin Childe.

Moses son to Moses Craft.

Moneth 7 day 5. Sarah daughter to Samuel Ruggles.

day 19. Hanna daughter to John Chandler.

Moneth 3 day 17. Thomas son to Thomas Andrews.

day 31. Ruth daughter to Henry Leadbetter of Dorchester.

Moneth 10 day 5. Margaret daughter to Mʳ Tho. Welde.

Faith daughter to Jacob Newel.

day 19. Mehetabel daughter to Peter Aspinwall.

day 26. Joseph son to John Ruggles.

Mary daughter to Steven Williams.

Hanna daughter to James Frissell.

Moneth 11 day 2. Esther daughter to Enoch Wiswall of Dorchester.

Moneth 12 day 27. Sarah daughter Samuel Danforth.

She was born upō yᵉ 21 of 12ᵐ.

Moneth 1 day 13. Joanna daughter to John Polly.

1670

	day 27.	Thomas son to Mr Joseph Dudley.

Moneth 2 day 3.   Joseph son to Joseph Weekes of Dorchest^r.
                   Josiah sonne to John Parker.
                   Elizabeth daughter to Will. Hopkins.
         day 24.   John son to Jonathan Peake.
Moneth 3^d day 1.   Thomas son to Edwd Devotion.
         day 8.   Nathaniel son to Nath. Johnson.
                   Susanna Bradly of Dorchester.
         day 15.   Thomas son to Caleb Lamb.
                   Mary daughter to Henry Stevens.
                   William Swift } of Dorchester.
                   Mary Clap   }
Moneth 4th day 12. John White of Dorchester.
         day 19.   John son to Samuel May.
Moneth 5 day 10.   Mehetabel daughter of Isaac } both of Dor-
                      Jones   } chester.
                   George son to John Homes   }
         day 17.   Daniel Michee   } both of Cambridge Vil-
                   Francis Prentice } lage.
                   Mary daughter to Joseph White
         day 24.   John son to Timothy Stevens.
         day 31.   Experience daughter to Saml Clap of Dor-
                      chester.
Moneth 6 day 21.   Abigail daughter to Henry Bowen.
Moneth 7 day 4.   Thomas son to Thomas Swan.
Moneth 8 day 2.   Joanna daughter of Joshua Hemingway
         day 23.   Sarah daughter to Nath. Brewer.
         day 30.   Nathaniel } sons to Nath Homes.
                   Ebenezer }
Moneth 9 day 13.   Dorcas daughter to   Corban.
                   Mary daughter to John Hemingway.
         day 20.   Thomas son to John Mayoh.
                   Samuel son to Samuel Paul   } Dorchest^r.
                   Sarah daughter to Nicholas Clap }
         day 27.   Rachel daughter to Tho. Woodward.
Moneth 10 day 11. Andrew son to William Bartlomew.
                   Sarah daughter to John Gapin of Dorchester.
         day 18.   Steven son to Decline Smith alias Lamb
         day 26.   Dorothy daughter to Peleg Heath.
                   Ephraim son to John May.
Moneth 11 day 8.   Joanna daughter to Jabesh Tatman.
         day 15.   John son to John Bridge.
         day 29.   Richard son to Thomas Boltstone.
Moneth 12 day 19. Joseph son to Thomas Cheany.
                   Nathaniel Hammond of Cambr. Village.
                   Hanna daughter to Isaac Newel.
         day 26.   Deborah daughter to John Acrees.
Moneth 1 day 5.   Rebecca daughter to Moses Craft.
         day 12.   Thomas son to Samuel Ruggles.
                   Ebenezer son to James Frissell.

1671

Moneth 2 day 9.	Samuel son to Edward Morrice.
	John, son to Nath. Clap of Dorchestsr.
day 16.	John Stedman Samuel Stedman } of Cambridge Village
day 30.	Elisabeth daughter to Mr Tho. Mighil minister.
	John, son Elizabeth, daughter } to John Holbrook
	Susanna daughter to John Bennet.
Moneth 3 day 14.	John son to John Davies.
day 21.	Martha daughter to Samuel Williams
	Sarah daughter to Andrew Gardiner.
	Isaac, son to Isaac Curtis.
	Elisabeth daughter to John Whitney
Moneth 4 day 4.	Rebecca daughter to Will. Chaplin at Dorchester.
18.	Unite Mosely of Dorchester.
Moneth 5 day 9.	Hanna daughter to Nathaniel Garee.
day 30.	John, sonn to John Evans.
Moneth 6 day 20.	Elizabeth daughter to John Sharp.
Moneth 7 day 10.	Edward son to Mr Joseph Dudley.
	Abigail daughter to Tobiah Davies.
	James Trot of Dorchester.
day 24.	Jonathan son to Tho Foster.
Moneth 8 day 1.	John son to Benjamin Childe.
day 8.	Joseph son to Joseph White
day 22.	Mary daughter to Samuel Craft.
Moneth 9 day 26.	Elizabeth daughter to Peter Aspinwall.
Moneth 10 day 17.	James son to John Griggs.
day 29.	Joseph son to Jonathan Peak.
day 31.	Caleb son to Caleb Lamb.
Moneth 12 day 4.	Elisabeth daughter to William Cleaves.
	Gideon, son to Samuel May
day 18.	Mehetable daughter to John Polly.
Moneth 1 day 10.	Penuel, son to Henry Bowen.
	Smith, son to Nath^el Johnson.

1672

day 31.	Benjamin, son to John Mayo
	John, son to John Clark.
	Bathshebah, daughter to John Pason.
Moneth 2 day 7.	Thomas son to Samuel Danforth. He was born on the 3^d day of 2^m being Weddensday in ye evening.
	George son to Thomas Bacon
	John son to John Whitney
day 14.	John Thomas } sons to John Curtis Jonathan

Esther daughter to Andrew Gardiner.
Robert, son to Shubal Seaver.

Moneth 3 day 5. Margaret daughter to Robt Pierpoint.
Moneth 4 day 9. John, son to Abrahā Newel jun.
     30. Joseph, son to Shubal Seaver.
      Abigail daughter to Will Hopkins.
Moneth 6 day 18. Mary, daughter to Jacob Newel.
Moneth 8 day 6. Anna, daughter to Samuel Ruggles.
      Elizabeth, daughter to Steven Williams.
    day 27. Ruth, daughter to John Parker.
Moneth 10 day 8. Abigail, daughter to William Bartholomew.
Moneth 11 day 5. Dorothy, daughter to Tho. Swan.
      Joanna, daughter to John Pason.
    day 12. Joanna, daughter to Joseph Griggs.
    day 26. Edward, son to Thomas Boltstone.
Moneth 12 day 9. Joanna, daughter to   Corban.
Moneth 1 day 2. Charity, daughter to Nath^{li} Homes.
    day 23. Margaret, daughter to John Bridge.

1673

Moneth 2^d day 13. Moses, son to Moses Craft.
      Joseph, son to Timothy Stevens.
      Sarah, daughter to John Curtis.
    day 20. Thomas } Lyons, children of Thomas Lyons.
      Sarah, }
    day 27. Peter, son to John Evans.
Moneth 3 day 4. John Hammond of Camribdge Village.
    day 11. Caleb Stedman of Cambridge Village.
    day 18. Mary }
      Jane } daughters to William Davies.
      Rachel }
      Rolph sonn to Joshua Hemingway.
      Robt sonn to John Harris.
      John son to John Polly jun.   ✗
    day 25. Sarah, daughter to Jonathan Peak.
Moneth 4 day 8. Samuel, sonn to James Frissell.
Moneth 5 day 13. Hanna, daughter to Tho Cheany.
     27. Ruth, daughter to John Griggs.
Moneth 6 day 10. John. sonn to John Acrees.
      Deborah, daughter to Jabez Titman.
    day 17. William, sonn to John Davies.
    day 31. Joseph, son to Benjamin Childe.
      Experience, daughter to Saml May.
      Mehetabel, daughter to John Chandler.
Moneth 7 day 7. Samuel, son to Nathaniel Garee.
Moneth 8 day 12. Eleazar } Twins of Peter Aspinwall.
      Joseph }
    day 19. Elisabeth, daughter to Samuel Danforth.
      [She was born on ye 16th day, being ye 5th
       day of ye week, about 11 oClock in y^t
       morning.]
      Robert, son to Thomas Woodward.

Moneth 9 day 2.   Isaac, son to John White jun.

day 9.   Joseph, son to M: Joseph Dudley.

day 16.   Thomas, son to John Mayo.

Joseph, son to Caleb Lamb.

Moneth 10 day 7.   Abigail, daughter to Samuel Craft.

day 14.   Richard, son to John Clark.

William, son to   Gravener.

day 21.   Mary, daughter to John Harris.

Moneth 11 day 25.   Rhoda, daughter to John Polly.

Moneth 12 day 1.   Ebenezer, son to Isaac Newel.

day 15.   Rob! son to Isaac Williams.

Mary, daughter to Nath. Johnson.

day 22.   Joseph } Davies, of Joseph Davies.
Sarah }

Moneth 1 day 22.   Hanna, daughter to M: Tho. Mighill.

1674

Moneth 2ᵈ day 12.   Rebecca Burrows, daughter to Mr. G. Burrows.

Hanna, daughter to Joseph White.

day 19.   Caleb, son to Caleb Seaver.

Moneth 3ᵈ day 10.   William, son to John Sharp.

day 17.   Hanna Deering, baptized at (Hingham)

day 31.   Jeremy, son to John Parker.

Moneth 4 day 7.   Benjamin, son to William Davis.

Robert, son to Abraham Newel.

John, son to Nathaniel Seaver.

day 31.   Peter, son to John Evans.

Moneth 5! day 5.   Ebenzer, son to William Hopkins

day 19.   Abigail, daughter to Samuel Williams.

Moneth 6! day 9.   Hanna, daughter to Shubal Seaver.

day 23.   Jonathan, son to Thomas Lyon.

day 30.   Abigail, daughter to John Holdbrook.

\ Moneth 7 day 6.   Mary, daughter to John Hemingway.

Joanna, daughter to John Winchester jun.

Ruth, daughter to John Whitney.

day 13.   John, sonne } to John Drnse.
Mary, daughter }

day 20.   Grace, daughter to Jacob Newel.

George, son to Thomas Bacon.

day 27.   Priscilla, daughter to John Pason.

Hanna, daughter to John Druse.

Moneth 8 day 25.   James, son to Robert Pierpoint.

Moenth 9 day 1.   Joseph, son to Thomas Andrews. [Last entry of Baptism in Rev.ᵈ M: Danforths' writing.]

day 15.   Andrew, son to Andrew Gardner. [This and following entries in Rev.ᵈ M: Eliot's writing.]

Abigail, daughter of Thoˢ Boylston

Abigail, daughter of John Clark

day 22. John ⎫ All these are the little children
Sarah ⎪ of Elizabeth Holdridg, who
Thomas ⎬ was received last Sab. to
Elizabeth ⎪ owne & lay hold on the cove-
Mary ⎭ nant.

Ichabod, the son of Nathaniel Holmes.

day 29. Nathaniel, son of Samuel Ruggles.

Samuel ⎫ All these are the litle children of
Sarah ⎬ Samuel Perry, lately received
Elizabeth ⎭ to owne & lay hold on the cove-
nant

Month 11 day 3. Martha, daughter of Edward Morice.
day 17. Willia, son of Jonathan Peake.
day 24. Elizabeth, daughter of Caleb Seaver.
day 31. Abiel, daughter of Mr Sam. Danforth. borne
after her father's decease.
Mary, daughter of John Harris.

Month 12. 14^d Rebeccah, daughter to John Curtis.
28^d Harbottle the son of Abiel Lambe.

1675.

Month 1 day 7. Joshua, the son of Joshua Lambe.
day 14. Ester, daughter of Henry Bowen.
Benjamin ⎫ the son & daughter of Benjamin
Ann ⎭ Tukker.
Mary, daughter to John Davis junior.

day 21. Elizabeth daughter of Willia Bartholmew.
Margret, daughter of Clement Corbin.

day 25. Mehittabel, daughter of Thom. Woodward.

Month 3 day 16. Jonathan, son to Benjamin Tukker.

Month 4 day 6. John, the son of John Gravener.
day 27. Abigail, daught. of John Ruggles junio^r

Month 5 day 15. Peter, the son of Mr Tho. Swan, Cambridge.

Month 7 day 5. Paule, the son of Mr Joseph Dudley.

Joseph ⎫ the children of Joseph Bugby
Rebecca ⎪ whose wife was lately admitted
Edward ⎬ to take hold on the covenant.
Samuel ⎭

Month 8^t day 10. Ichabod, son of Joseph Griggs
William, son of Willia Lyon junio^r

day 17. Mary, daughter of Robert Baker.

Month 9 day 7. Margret, daughter to Joseph Weld.

M 9. day 25. George, the son of Mr George Burrows.

M 10 day 5. Bethia, daughter to Willia Hopkins.

Josiah, ⎫ Children of Philip Curtis, lately
Hollard, ⎬ Slaine in warre.
William ⎭

day 12. Hannah, daughter of Samuel Scarbrow.
Mary daughter of Joseph Davis.
Elizabeth, daughter of Jabesh Tatman.

Month 11 day 23. Samuel the son of Phillip Curtis, lately killed
in warre. .

Mercy, daughter to Robert Grundye.
day 30.   Benjamin, the son of Thomas Cheny.
Month 12 day 20.   Marah, daughter of Daniel Weld.
day 27.   Job, the son of Peter Aspinall.
Benjamin, the son of Joseph White.

1676

Month 1 day 5.   Abiel, daughter of Phillip Curtis.
day 12.   Samuel son of Elizabeth Holdridg.
day 19.   Joseph, son of Tho. Andrews of Dorchest!
Jakob, the son of Daniel Makoe.
Deborah, daughter of Nath Gary.
Month 2 day 2.   Ichabod, son of Willia Davis.
Isaak, son of Nathaniel Johnson.
day 9.   Daniel, son of Daniel Mason of Norwich.
Mathew, son of Hep. Tiler.
Mary, daughter of   Beamsly of Nashoway.
day 16.   Mary the daughter of John Davis Smith
Thomas son of Thomas Gardner.
Moneth 6 day 11th   Benjamin the son of John Ruggles.
Month 7 day 22.   Mary, daughter to   Chamberlin.
day 29.   Ebenezer son to Samuel Lyon.
Month 8. day 13.   Jonathan son of John Paison.
Mary daughter of John Winchest!
day 20.   Benjamin son of Benjamin Wilson.
day 27.   Sarah. daughter of Ephraim Savage of Boston Church.
Month 9 day 3.   Samuel son of Thaddeus Mackarty of Boston.
Ebenezer son of Thomas Cheny.
day 10.   John, the son of Samuel Gore.
day 17.   Joseph son of   Holloway of Boston.
Month 10 day 1.   Elizabeth, daughter of Abra How junior.
Mo 11 day 12.   Rosamund, son of Rosamund Drue.
Mo. 12. day 16.   Phillip the son of Phillip Gos.
day 23.   Joshua, son of Joshua Seaver.

[No entries of either Baptism or Burials for 2 years owing to the war.
See entry under " Burials."]

1679

Month 1 day 2.   John the son of Mr Joseph Dudly.
Nathaniel son of Sam. Ruggles.
day 9.   Zabdiel son of Tho. Boylcston.
day 16.   Hannah, daughtr of Phillip Goss.
day 30.   Henry, son of Thomas Swan.
Mon 2 day 20.   Sarah, daughter of   Stevens deceased.
27.   Elizabeth, daughter of Robert Grundy.
Mon 3 d 25.   Jeremiah the son of Caleb Lambe
Mon 3 day 8.   Dorothy daughter of Joshua Lambe.
Ester daughter of Tho. Lyon.

		Samuel, the son of Elizabeth Holdridg.
	day 29.	Williā, the son of Akkers.
Mon.	6. day 24.	Elizabeth the daughter of John Hinningway.
	day 31.	Mehitabell, daughter of Joseph Bugby.
M	7. d 28.	Samuel son of Tho. Lyon.
M	8. d 12.	Shubael the son of Shubael Seaver.
	d. 19.	Ebenezer the son of Benjamin Tukker.
M	9. d. 2.	Jeremiah son of John Wise.
	d. 16.	Marget the daughter of John Parker.
	d. 30.	Thomas, son of Brian Claɪk.
		Sarah, daughter of Benjamin Saben.
M	11. d. 4.	Williā son of William Davis.
		Abiel Lambe son of Abiel Lamb.
	d. 11.	John, the son of Tho. Gardner.
M	12. d. 1.	Benjamin son of John Lyon.
		Susanna, daughter of Isaak Curtis.
M 11 (12?) d. 8.		Ebenezer son of Samuel Crafts.

1680

M 1.	d. 7.	Dorothy, daught. of Ralfe Bradhurst.
	d. 14.	Josiah son of Isaak Newell.
		John, son of John Howard.
	d. 21.	John the son of Midle John Ruggles.
		Hannah, daughter of Joseph Davis.
	d. 28.	Francis, daughter of Joseph White.
		Hannah, daughter of Josiah Winchester.
M 2.	day 4.	Marget the child of John Clark.
		Abigal daughter of Tho. Mory.
	day 11.	Jabesh, son of Samuel Dunkan.
		Thomas son of Sister Booth of Stratford.
	day 18.	Nicolas the son of Caleb Seaver.
	day 25.	John son of John Weld juniʳ.
		Biel son of Joseph Lyon.
M 3.	day 16.	Margret daughter of Tho. Bakon.
	day 29.	Sarah, daught' of Robert Peirpoynt.
M 4.	day 27.	Rebecca, daught. of Nath. Johnson.
M 5.	day 4.	Edward the son of Dor.
	day 18.	Robert son of Steven Williams.
		Hannah, daughter of John Rugls minimus.
	day 25.	Sarah, daughter to John Polly. x
M 6.	day 8.	Abigal daughter of Mary Mory of Milton.
	day 15.	Elizabeth, daughter of Jonathan Peake.
	day 22.	Mary, daughter of Phillip Goffe.
	day 29.	Hannah, daughter of Timothy Stevens.
M 7.	day 5.	Thomas, son of Samuel Perry.
	day 12.	Martha, daughter of Richard Hall.
	day 26.	Johannah daughter of John Bugby.
M 8.	d. 3.	Thomas, son of Thomas Bishop.
	day 31.	Abigail, daughtʳ of Andrew Gardner.
M 9.	day 7.	Joseph, son of Robert Baker.
	day 28.	William the son of Clay of Dorchesteʳ
M 10.	day 5.	Sarah, daughter of John White junʳ

day 12.   Samuel, son of Samuel Scarbrouhg.
day 26.   Sarah, daughter of Tho Boyleston.
          Mary, daughter of Jabesh Totman.
M 11. day 2.   Abraham son of Abraha How jun.
day 23.   Nehemiah, son of Benjamin Saben.
day 30.   Obedience, daughter of Nathaniel Homes.
M 12. day 13.   Susanna, daught. of John Gravner.

1681

M 1. day 13.   John, son of Bobert Grande.
          Mary, daughter of Caleb Lambe.
day 20.   Timothy, sone to Richard Mather of Doichest.
day 27.   George, son of Joshua Lambe.
          Margret, daught. of Joseph Weld.
          Sarah, daughter of John Harris.
M 2. day 3.   Susanna ⎫ These child'n of Sister Pike who last
          Sarah   ⎬ Sab. joyned co X, w. baptised.
          John   ⎭
          also Marget, daughter of Daniel Preston of Dor-
          chest. by Comunion of Churches.
day 10.   Samuel, son of Samuel Willia⁸ junior.
          Elizabeth, daughter to Nathaniel Mather of Dor-
          chester.
day 24.   Joseph, son of Tho. Mozly of Dorchester.
          Mehitabel, daughter of Tho. Lyon.
M 3. day 15.   Richard, son of James White of Dorchester.
day 22.   Rebekah, daughter to M. Joseph Dudley.
M 4. day 5.   Daniel, son of James Lovet of Mendon.
day 12   Mary, daughter of M. Tho. Swan.
day 26.   Samuel, son of John Davis senior
M 5. day 17.   Jonathan son of Ebenezer Billing ⎫ both of Dor-
          Joseph, son of Roger Billing   ⎭ chester.
day 31.   Sarah, daughter of Thom⁸ Trot of Dorchester.
M 6. day 14.   Hannah, daughter of Willia Lyon junior.
M 8. day 2.   Deliveranc, daughter of Sam. Dunkan.
          Sarah, daughter of Charles Danforth of Dor-
          chest
day 23.   Samuel, the son of Samuel Gore.
M 9 day 6.   Mary, daughter of Isaac Curtis.
M 10. day 4.   Daniel, son of John Whitny.
          Samuel, son of Sam. Ruggls junior
day 11.   John, the son of John Leavens.
day 18.   Hannah, daughter of John Weld junior
day 25.   Mary, daught. of John Ruggles minim⁸
M 11. day 1.   Josiah, the son of Josiah Winchester.
15.   Nathaniel, son of Nathaniel Wilson.
day 29.   Mercy, daughter of Jacob Hewin of Dorchester.
M 12. day 5.   James, son of James Clark.
day 12.   John, son of Uriah Clark.
day 19.   Allice, daught. of Sam. Crafts.
day 26.   Timothy, son of Timothy Foster of Dorchest.
          Joseph, son of Steven Williams.

1682

M	1. day 12.	Thomas, son of Jonathan Danford, of Dorchest.	
	day 19.	Samuel, son of Joseph White.	
		Sarah, daughter of Hix of Dorchest.	
	day 26.	Thomas, son of Caleb Seaver.	
M	2. day 2.	Mahitabel daught^r of Jabesh Totman	
	day 16.	Timothy, son to Peter Aspinal.	
	day 23.	Caleb, son of Tho. Gardner junio^r	
		Lucy, daughter of Thomas Boylston.	
	day 30.	Hañah, daught$_r$ of Nathaniel Glover.	
		Nathaniel son of Joseph Leeds both y^{es} of	
		Dorchester.	
M	3. day 7.	Patience, daughter of Benjamin Saben.	
		Joseph, son of John Scot.	
M	4. day 11.	Jonathan, son of Joseph Bugby.	
M	5. day 9.	Caleb, son of Caleb Phillips.	
	day 16.	Abigail, daught. of John Lyon.	
M	6. d. 20.	Mary, daughter of Benjamin Tukker.	
		Benjamin, son of Robert Baker.	
		Mary, daughter of Thomas Mory.	
M	7. d. 24.	Samuel, son of Faris.	
M	8. d. 8.	Experience, daughter of John Howard.	
		Annis, daughter of John Parker.	
	d. 15.	John, son of John Devotion.	
M	9. d. 5.	John, son of John Bowles.	
	d. 19.	Henry, son of Samuel Lion.	
		Daniel, son of Daniel Harris.	
		Abigail, daughter of Abraham How.	
M	10. d. 10.	Theoda, daughter of Sam. Williā junio.	
	d. 17.	Hannah, daughter of Ralf Bradhurst.	
	d. 24.	Mary, daughter of Isaak Curtis.	
11^m.	day 14.	Margaret, daughter of Tho. Bakon.	
		Samuel, son of John Browne.	
M	12. d. 4.	Richard, son of Richard Hall.	
	d. 18.	Joseph, son of Sam: Scarbrow.	
		James, son of James Atkins.	
	d. 25.	Benjamin, son of Joseph Davis.	

1683.

M	1. d. 4.	Elizabeth, daughter of Joshua Lamb.	
	d. 18.	Annah, daughter of Nathaniel Johnson.	
M	2. d. 1.	Mary, daught. of Joseph Grigs.	
		Samuel, son of Timothy Steevens.	
		Susanna, daught^r of Benjamin White.	
		Mary, daughter of Joshua Sever.	
	d. 22.	Isaac, son of Williā Davis.	
		Sarah } daughters of Joseph Wilson.	
		Abigail }	
		John, the son of Caleb Lamb.	
M	3. d. 6.	Joseph, son of John White junio^r	
	d. 20.	Mary, daughter of John Accors.	

M 4. d. 10. Joseph, son of John Chandler.
M 5. d. 15. Joseph, son of Joseph Weld.
      Robert, son of Robert Grundy.
M 6. d. 26. Mary, daughter of Uriah Clark.
M 7. d. 9. Lucy, daughter of Samuel Ruggls junior.
    d. 16. Abigail, daughter of John Harris.
    d. 30. Samuel, son of Joshua Hinningway.
M 8. d. 7. John, son of John Weld junior.
      Margret, daughter of Joshua Gardner.
    d. 28. Benjamin, son of Samuel Crafts.
M 9. d. 4. Patience, daughter of Nathaniel Homes.
    d. 11. Sarah, daught. of Jabesh Totman.
      John, the son of John Scot.
      Elizabeth, daughter of Nathaniel Wilson.
    d. 18. Edward, son of Edward Dor.
      Edward, son of Jo. Ruggls medius.
M 10. d. 23. Ephraim, son of Benjamin Child.
    d. 30. Jonathan, son of John Winchester.
M 11. d. 20. John, son of Steven Williams.
      Robert, son of Robert Mason.
M 12. d. 3. John, son of Caleb Phillips.
      Samuel } children of Daniel Mashcraft.
      Mehitabel }
    d. 17. Elizabeth daughter of Edward Morice, jun.
    $\frac{i}{y}$. day. Moses Draper } confessed X and were bap-
      Rebecca Hubbard } tized.

        1684.

M 1. d. 2. John, the son of Mr John Gore.
      Jarvis, son of   Pike.
    d. 9. Ebenezer, son of Josiah Winchest.
    d. 16. Jeremiah, son of Benjamin Saben.
      Rebecca, daught. of John Ruggls junior.
      Mehitabell daught. of Isaak Curtis.
    d. 30. John, son of Caleb Lambe.
      Rebecca, daughter of Joseph Gardner.
M 2. d. 6. James, son of James Atkins.
    d. 13. Thankfull, daught. of Shuball Seaver.
      John, son of John Searl.
      Rebecca } the children of John Hubbard.
      Rachel }
M 4. d. 1. Deborah, daughter of Samuel Weld.
    d. 29. Mercy, daughter of Elizabeth Holdridg.
M 5. d. 6. Hulda, daughter of Samuel Ruggles senior.
      Mehitabel daughter of Williã Lyon junior.
      John, son of John Browne.
    d. 27. Ephraim   }
      Mehitabel } Children of John Crafts.
      Sarah   }
      Peter, son of Thomas Gardner.
M 6. d. 3. Lidea, wife of John Clark.

Elizabeth } both children of John & Lidea Clark.
John

Mary Bukmaster

d. 10. Edward, son of Benjamin Tuker.
Sarah, daught. of John Whitny.

d. 17. Mary, daughter of Joshua Sever.

Mehitabel }
Mary } daughters of Nathaniel Sangor.
Jane }

d. 24. Peter, son of Thomas Goodwī junio.ᵣ
d. 31. An, daughtᵣ of Mᵣ Joseph Dudley.
M 7. d. 7. Francis, daughter of John White junio.ᵣ
d. 21. Sarah, daughter of John Hubbart.
M 8. d. 19. Ebenezer, son of John Devotion.
M 9. d. 2. Susanna, daughter of   Bostow
d. 9. Josiah son of Joseph Bugby.
d. 23. Josiah, son of John Leavens.
M 10. d. 14. Thomas, son of Andrew Gardner.
Samuel, son of Joseph White.
d. 21. Benjamin, son of John Lyon.
M 11. d. 4. Prescilla daughtᵣ of David Harris.
M 12. d. 3. John, a son of Joshua Lamb.
Francis, daughter of Joshua Gardner.
d. 22. Mehitabel, daughtᵣ of Joseph Davis

1685

M 1. d. 15. Jakob, son of Jakob Chamberlain.
Elizabeth, daughter of Edward Morice.
Abigail, wife of Abrahã Newel junio.ᵣ
Sarah Burden, a maid servant.
yᵉˢ two wᵣ adult psōns
d. 22. John, the son of John Bowles.
M 2. d. 12. Samuel, son of Abiel Lambe.
Phillip, son of Phillip Searle.
d. 19. John, a son of John Mayse.
M 3. d. 17. Mary, daughtᵣ of Abrahã Gorton.
Susanna, daughtᵣ of Thom. Mory.
d. 24. Johannah, daughtᵣ of Uriah Clark.
M 4. d. 14. An, daughter of Robert Baker.
d. 21. Edmund, son to Robert Grundy.
M 5. d. 5. Abigal, daughter of Raph Badhurst.
An, daughtᵣ of Benjamin White.
d. 26. John a son of John Grigs junio.ᵣ
M 6. d. 9. Jeremiah son of Samuel Scarbro
d. 30. Sarah, daughter of John Gore.
Isack son of   of Dedham.
Mary Burden, adult.
M 7. d. 13. Marget, daughter of Samuel Lyon.
d. 20. Rebecca, daughter of Tho. Boylstone.
Johanna, daughter of John Weld junio.ᵣ
Mary, daughter of Josiah Winchester.
M 8. d. 18. John, son of Jabesh Totman.

<table>
<tr><td></td><td>d.</td><td>25.</td><td>Hannah, daughter of Nathanel Wilson ⎫</td></tr>
<tr><td></td><td></td><td>24.</td><td>Elizabeth, daughter of Caleb Phillips ⎬ infants.</td></tr>
</table>

                Phillip Mareen
                Willià Mareen
                Elizabeth Mareen
                Mary Mareen

M 9.	d.	1.	John, son of Joseph Weld.
	d.	8.	Timothy, son of Samuel Ruggles junio.ʳ
	d.	15.	Isaak, son of Isaak Curtis.
	d.	22.	Eunice, daughter of Caleb Lambe.
	d.	29.	Abigal, daughter of Timothy Stevens.
M 10.	d.	20.	Thankfull daughtʳ of Nath. Homes.
	d.	27.	Nathaniel, son of Nathaniel Sangor.
M 11.	d.	3.	Nathaniel, son of Samuel Perry.
	d.	10.	Hannah, daughter of Thomas Bakon.
	d.	31.	Edmond, son of John Browne, of Dorchest.ʳ
M 12.	d.	21.	Samuel, son of John Clark.
	d.	28.	Steven, son of John Winchester.
			Sarah, daughter of Jo. Ruggles minimus.

1686

M 1.	d.	14.	John, the son of Abraham Gorton.
	d.	21.	Mary, daughter of John Searle.
	d.	28.	Edmond, son of Edward Dor.

M 2.   d.   11.   Samuel, son of Joshua Lambe.   ⎫ all yᵉˢ six
                    Henry, son of Steven Williams.   borne   yⁱ
all yᵉˢ w.ʳ   John, son of John Harris.   week w. bap-
baptized   Mary, daughter of   Hubbard   ⎬ tiz. o. same
yᵗ day.   Marget, daughter of Thomas Cheny.   week yᵗ we
                 Hannah, daughter of   Draper   sent out
                                                     youth   t.
                                                        make a new
                                                        ⎭ plantation.

                 Also yⁱ day o. children of Andrew Watkins were
                   baptized, their mother having taken hold of
                   the covenant.
                 Andrew Watkins
                 Peter Watkins
                 Samuel Watkins
                 Elizabeth Watkins
                 Mary Watkins
                 Sarah Watkins

	d.	25.	Isaak, son of John White junior.
M 3.	d.	16.	Ebenezer, son of Swan.
			Lidea, daughter of Widdow Crafts.
	d.	23.	Rebecca, daughter of John Mayo junio.ʳ
M 4.	d.	13.	Elizabeth, daughter of John Pike.
			Margery, daughtʳ of Dowse of Charleston.
M 5.	.d	11.	John Scot, son of John Scot.
	d.	25.	Isack, son of Thomas Gardner junio.ʳ

M 6. d. 8. Sarah Peakok, adult, baptized. ⎱ al y^{es} baptized
             Mary her first child.   ⎰ y^s day.
             Sarah, her 2nd child

     d. 15. Sarah, daughter of Caleb Seaver.
     d. 22. Thomas, son of Samuel Gore.
            Elizabeth, daughter of Sarah Peakok.
M 7. d. 5. Sarah, daughter of Joseph Griffin.
     d. 26. William, son of Williã Heath.
M 8. d. 10. Jonathan, son of Francis Youngman.
     d. 17. Mary, daughter of Joseph Lyon.
            Sarah, daught^r of James Atkins.
     d. 24. William, son of Mr Joseph Dudly.
            Thomas, son of Daniel Harris.
            Sarah Hadlock, adult.
M 9. d. 7. Joseph, son of Benjamin Tukker.
            Isaak, son of Isaac How.
     d. 14. Hannah, daughter of Edward Morie.
     d. 21. Sarah, daughter of Mr John Bowles.
     d. 28. James, son of Nathan^{el} Page.
            John, son of John May.
M 10. d. 26. Martha, daught^r of Jo. Ruggls, medius.
M 11. d. 1. Nathaniel, son of Joseph Bugby.
            Nathaniel son of Nathaniel Gary.
            Sarah daughter of Mary Fielder.
     d. 16. Rachel daughter of John Leavens.
     d. 30. Williã son of Benjamin Davis of Boston.
            Rebecca, daughter of Robert Grundy.
M 12. d. 20. Robert, son of Uriah Clark.

1687

M 1. d. 13. Elizabeth daught^r of Joseph Bukmaster.
M 2. d. 3. Mary, daughter of Joseph Good.
    day 17. Williã, son of Mr Chikly
            Dudly son of Thom. Boyleston.
            Robert son o Jakob Pepper.
M 3. d. 15. Caleb, son of Joshua Gardner.
     d. 22. Joseph son of   Stone of Dedham.
M 4. d. 5. Susannah, daughter of John Lyon.
     d. 19. Sarah, daughter of Joseph Weld.
M 5. d. 3. John, son of Robert Mason.
     d. 10. Thomas son of John Gravnor.
     d. 17. Deborah daughter of Samuel Scarborow.
            John son of Thomas Mory.
     d. 24. Sarah, daught^t of John Hinningway.
M. 6 d. 7. Ebenezer son of   Chamberlain.
            John son of Joshua Seaver.
     d. 14. George son of   Bosto .
     d. 21. Abigail, daught^r of John Weld junio^r
M 7. d. 18. Thomas ⎱
            Henry ⎰ Twins of Thomas Cheny.
            Johannah, daughter of Samuel Lyon.

M 8. d.   2.   Mehitabel, daught.ʳ of John Howard.
     d .30.   Samuel son of Samuel Weld.
            Hannah, daughter of John Aldis.
M 9.   Edward, son of Benjamin Child.
     d.   13.   Susanna, daughter of Nathaniel Wilson.
     d.   20.   Robert the son of Robert Baker.
     d.   26.   Hannah the daughter of John Searle.
M 11. d.   8.   An, daught.ʳ of John Merey.
     d.   29.   Ebenezer the son of Edward Dor.
M 12. d.   5.   Thomas the son of Williå Cheany.
            Isaac the son of Isaac Nuel jun.ʳ
     d.   19.   Abigail the daughter of John Davis.
   Item.   Robert the son of Robert Sharp.
   Item.   Thankfull the daughter of Jacob Parker.

1688

March d. 18.   Hañah the daughter of William Heath (Bap-
            tized)
March d. 25.   John, the son of John Grigs.
April   d.   1.   John, the son of Goodman Park of Stonington.
April   8.   Grace, the daughter of Stephen Williams
Item   d.   8.   Benjamin, the son of Nathaniel Sangor
Item   d.   8.   Amariah, the son of Josiah Winchester
Item   d. 15.   Abigail the daughter of Joseph Daviss
Item   d. 22.   Hanna the daughter of Samuel Ruggles.
Ite. the   ⎫
   same day   ⎬   Sarah the daught. of Nathaneal Holmes.
April d. 29.   Ebenezer son of Joshua Hemingway.
The same day.   Mary the daughter of Caleb Phillips
May: 20:   Sarah, the daughter of Samuel Williås jun.ʳ
M   4. d.   3.   Mary, daught.ʳ of Joseph Griffin
June. 10 d.   Nathan Stevēs
     Item.   Sarah Mayo
June   24.   Mary, the infant of Joseph Lion
July   d.   8.   Peter, the son of Joseph Gardner
July. s. d.   Eliezar son of Eliezar May.
July   15.   Obadiah the son of Samuel Gore
Item.   Martha the daughter of Hañah Brewer
Aug.⁵   12.   Eliphalet son of Thomas Lion
   ⸠ d. 19.   Dudley the son of Thomas Boilston
     d. 26.   Benjamin son of Benjamin Gamblin.
Item   Hañah daughter to Benjamin Gamblin.
Sept 2ᵈ.   Mary, daughter of Benjamin White
Item.   Cornelius son of Francis Youngmå
Sept 9ᵗʰ.   Samuel son of Isaac Curtiss [baptized]
Ite.   Abigail daughter of Andrew Watkins   [Last
          entry of Baptisms by Rev.ᵈ J. Eliot.

ANNO 1700. PERSONS Y^T HAVE OWNED YE COVENANT [WRITTEN BY REV^D N. WALTER.]

May   Sarah Henneway

1702

March 1   Margaret White
           Allice Crafts
           Elizabeth Crafts
           Francis White

1703

Jan^{ry} 31 Sarah Baker
           Mary Johnson
March   Steven Johns
           Robert Loverain
June   Elizabeth Brown
           Martha Brown
           Mehittabel Brown
June   Samuel Sewal
           Joshua Lamb
           Rebecca Sewal

1704

Feb^{ry}   Dorothy Bacon
June   Susanna Curtis
           Mehittabel Curtis

1705

March   Peter Boylston and
           Anne his wife
           Thomas Gardner jun^r
           and Mary his wife
           Shubal Seaver jun^r
           and Abigail his
           wife
           Robert and Sarah
           Sharp
July   Mary Aspinall
           Mary Stevens
           Hannah Stevens
           Abigail Stevens
           Roger Stainer and
           his wife Susanna.
Octo^r 28 Thomas Pope bap-
           tised adult

1706

May   Caleb Seaver and
           Hannah his wife
           Noah Perrin and Pa-
           tience his wife
           Elizabeth White
           Cornelius Youngman
June   Amos Hill   } Ne-
           Simon Gossan   } groes
July   Richard Hall
           Anne Baker
August   William Lezon
           Thankfull Lezon
           Mary Bugbee
           Joanna Bugbee
Octob^r   Deborah Davis
Dec^r   Samuel Lion
           Joanna Lion

1707

June   Grace Williams
           Caleb Gardiner
July   Sarah Gardiner
           Elizabeth Wood
Sept^r   Abigail Cole

1708

April 18   Josiah Winchester &
           Sarah Winchester
           his wife
           Esther Alcock bap-
           tised adult
May   2   John Frost baptised
           adult
May   Lydia Buddoono
Octob^r   Hannah Scott, bap-
           tised adult

1709

June 26   Jeremiah Rogers,
           baptised adult
Octo^r   James Trusty negro
           man baptised

1710

March	Sarah Hartnuss
June	Elisha Johnson
July	Joseph ⎫
	Mary ⎪ Adams
	Sarah ⎬ baptised
	Daniel ⎭ adult
Novr 5th	Ebenezer Dorr
	Mary Dorr
	Thomas Graves

1711

Feb^{ry}	James Shed
Octo^r	John Totman
Nov.^r	Sarah Pierpoint

1712

March	Thankfull Holmes
	Sarah Holmes
April	Lyddia Harris
July	Jacob Chamberlain
Nov.^r	Enoch Farley
Dec.^r	James Grant
	Hannah Blake
	Dan, negro serv.^t to
	Cap^{tn} Ruggles

1713

May	Abraham Woodward
July	George Woodward
	Nathl Woodward
August	Samuel Gardner
	Martha Gardner
Sept^r	Peter Gardner
	Mary Gardner
	Simeon Buttler
	Hannah Buttler
	Rebecca Adams

1714

July	John Wilson
	Sarah Wilson
	John Woods
	Jemima Woods
	Richard Cooms
	Hepsibah Cooms
	James Goddard
	Mary Goddard
Octo^r	Thomas Jones

Dec.^r	Elizabeth Jones
	Jacob Chamberlain
	Abiel Chamberlain

1715

Feb^{ry}	John Goddard
	Elias Monk
	Dorothy Monk
Octob.^r	Hezekiah Turner

1716

Jan^{ry}	Edward Clark
	Sarah Clark
	Amariah Winchester
	Sarah Winchester
Feb^{ry}	Ebenezer Seaver
	Margarett Seaver
	Peter Gardner
	Elizabeth Gardner
August	Isaac Leason
	Anne Leason

1717

John Williams

1719

Octo^r	Timothy Parker
	Mary Parker
	Titus Jones

1720

August	Joseph Craft
	Susanna Craft
Nov.	Margarett Tucker

1721

July	Sarah Lathgood
	Elizabeth Scutts

1723

October	Abigail Table
Nov.^r	William Bosson
Dec.^r	Elizabeth Pierpoint

1724

Jan^{ry}	John Craft
	Elizabeth Craft

Feb^{ry}	John Cheney	
	Mary Cheney	
March	Sarah Davis	
April	John Huit	

1725

July   Daniel Williams
        Hannah Williams

1726

Jan^{ry}   Samuel Crafts
        Mehittabel Crafts

1727

Jan^{ry}   Sarah Tilestone
July   Phillip Bacon
        Patience Bacon
Octob^r   John Lovel
Nov^r   Rebecca Smith

1728

March   3 Mary Cheney
          Elizabeth Hooper
July   21 Zipporah Towers
Nov^r   10 Rebecca Macthaden

1730

Octo^r   4 Ebenezer Cheney
Dec^r   12 Margaret Searle

1731

May   2 Joseph Woods

1732

April   2 Steven Choate
      30 John Ruggles
         Elizabeth Ruggles
June   18 James Tucker

1733

May   27 Barnabas Wilson
July   1 Joseph Gardiner
         Mary Gardiner
August 26 Peter Seaver
         Hannah Seaver
October 11 Moses Davis
         Rebecca Davis
      19 Thomas Cole
         Sarah Cole

March   10 Daniel Bugbee
          Abigail Bugbee

1734

Nov^r   10 Edward Bilbo
         Elizabeth Bilbo
         Richard Robertson
         Abigail Robertson
Dec^r   Sarah Ames

1735

April   28 Shubael Seaver
         Mary Seaver

1736

Feb^y   7 Benjamin Eaton
        Sarah Eaton
May   2 Ebenezer Payson
        Sarah Payson

1737

Feb^{ry}   6 Caleb Richardson
May   29. Ebenezer Dorre
Sept^r   Hannah Goald
Dec^r   11 Increase Sumner
         Mary Sumner

1738

Oct^r   23 John Holbrook

1739

May   27. Benjamin Draper
         Mary Draper

1740

Jan^y   27 Rebecca Pendle baptised adult
March 16. Sarah Manser baptised adult
      30 Lydia Manser baptised adult
         Susanna Manser baptised adult
Sept^r   7. Ambrose Searle
         Elizabeth Searle

1741

July   19 Ralph Holbrook
         John Salmon

Dorothy Holbrook

27 Bethiah Ramsel baptised adult

August 30. James Shed
        Mary Shed

1742

Feb^ry 14 Jeffery ⎫
            Bristol ⎬ negroes
            Guinea ⎭ baptised
July   11th Robert Lee
Septr 26 Samuel Sumner
Novr 14 Nathaniel Felton
            Hannah Felton

1743

Jany 23 Phillis a negro baptised

1744

April   1 Abraham Woodward
            Sarah Woodward
June   3 Thomas Grigs
            Margaret Grigs
            Jeremiah Parker
            Mary Parker
August 26 Jeremy Williams
            Catharine Williams
Septr 2 Samuel Clark
            Mary Clark
Novr 25 Jacob Reeves
            Abigail Reeves

1745

Jan^ry 13 .Samuel Healy
May   31 Edward Dorr
July   28 Ebenezar Bodoono
Decr 15 Ebenezar Gore

1746

May   27 William Bosson jun^r

1747

August 29. Jeane Linsdey
Novr 21 Mary Manser
            Rebecca Bidford

1748

January 17. Anne Tucker
March 20. Phillis negro serv^t of
            Mr Stedman
October 22. Daniel Sever
            Abiel Sever
Novr 11th Joseph Bodoono

1749

Feb^ry 26 Thomas Cheney
            Deborah Cheney
Novr 5th Joseph Ruggles

1750

June   30th Sam. Weld
            Ebenezar Pierepont
            jun^r.

[The following entries are in the handwriting of Revd Oliver Peabody junior.]
Saml & Lois Gridley baptised children of Deac. Gridley
Hannah, daughter of Saml Weld
Hannah, daughter of Eb^r Pierpoint j^r.
John, son of John Williams j^r
Hannah, daughter of John Williams
Mary, daughter of Beduna
All baptised by ye Revd Mr Walter at his own house, during his confinement before his death.
Revd Mr N. Walter died Septr 17. 1750.

BAPTISMS.

1750

Francis the son of Saml Clark Novr 11 Baptized
Thomas the son of Daniel Sever Nov. 18.
Abigail the daughter of John Richardson j^r Decr 2.
Edward the son of Ed^d Dorr Decr 23.

1751

Abraham ye son of Shubael Sever ⎫
Oliver the son of James Shed ⎬ Jany 6th
Mary the daughter of Willm Boson ⎭
Ebenezer ye son of Daniel Bugbee Feby 3^d
Hezekiah y^o son of Edward King ⎫ March 19.
& Rebecca ye daughter of John Richards ⎭
Elizabeth ye daughter of Samuel Perham March 24.
William ye son of John Dean April 7th
John the son of Ebenezer Gore April 21.
Elizabeth y^o daughter of Ralph Holbroke ⎫ May 5th
Sarah the daughter of Edward Kelton ⎭
Leonard Fisher the son of Richard & Hopestill Lethbridge
May 26th
Elizabeth the daughter of Samuel and Mary Gore ⎫ June 2
Thomas ye son of John Cheney ⎭
Samuel the son of Nathaniel & Hannah Felton June 9th
Henry son of Jeremiah & Katharine Williams June 16th
Lucy the daughter of Increase & Sarah Sumner June 30th
Abigail the daughter of Sarah & Abigail Williams jun^r ⎫ Augt 4.
Sarah the daughter of Obadiah & Sarah Coolidge ⎭
Mercy the daughter of Ebenezer Bedunah Aug$_t$ 11
William the son of Abraham & Susanna Dorr Aug$_t$ 25.
Nathaniel the son of Ebenezer & Abigail Newell ⎫ Octr 20
Thomas the son of Samuel & Hannah Weld ⎭
Martha daughter of Thomas & Martha Dana Octr 27
Nathaniel son of Ebenezer & Sarah Pierpoint ⎫ Decr 15. 1751.
Anna daughter of Joseph & Rebecca Ruggles ⎭
Patience the daughter of Edward Manning Decr 29.

1752

Henry ye son of   & Sibil Badcock Jany 19. 1752.
Joseph ye son of Joshua & Sarah Davis Jany 26
Ann ye daughter of John & Ana Williams Feby 23. 1752.
Elizabeth the daughter of   & Katherine Hovey March
1. 1752.
Sarah the daughter of John &   Bugbee March 15th
Joseph the son of Isaac & Elizabeth Bird April 5th
John the son of Joseph Warren Augst 5. 1753 .
N.B.   By reason of the vacation after the death of the Rev^d M^r
Peabody several of the children then baptized are not recorded.

1753

Sept 16. Benjamin Payson the son of Benjamin Weld & Sarah his wife

Samuel the son of Daniel Bugbee &   his wife

Sept 30 Elizabeth the daughter of Abraham Dorr & Susannah his wife

Nov. 4. Edmund Grindall the son of Edmund Weld & Sarah his wife

Abigail the daughter of Nath! Felton & Hannah his wife

Nov. 11. Abigail the daughter of Jacob Reves & Abigail his wife.

Sibil the daughter of Sam¹ Badcock.

Hannah the daughter of Jeremiah Mosher & Isabel his wife.

Dec. 11. Margaret daughter of John Newell } of Brookline.
James son of Isaac Winchester

Dec. 23. Anne, daught' of Eben! Pierpoint jun'. and Hannah his wife.

Dec. 30. Elizabeth daughter of Jacob Reves & Abigail his wife.

1754

Jan. 13. Olieve daughter of Joseph Morse of Boston and Olive his wife.

Jan. 20. Thomas son of John Williams jun' and   his wife.

John son of Benjamin Curtiss and Abigail his wife.

Feb. 17. Robert, son of Samuel Craft of Brookline.

Mary, daughter of Edward Dorr and Abigail his wife.

Anne daughter of Eben' Dorr jun' and Naomi his wife.

Sarah, daughter of Joseph Ruggles &' Rebecca his wife.

March 17. Joseph, the son of Ebenezer Pierpont Esq.'

April 7. Abigail the daughter of Benj^a May and   his wife.

May 5. Elizabeth the daughter of Ebenezer Newel & Abigail his wife.

19. Timothy son of Jeremiah Parker and Martha his wife

26 Sarah the daughter of Jonathan Parker and Abiga¹¹ his wife.

June 2 Patience the daughter of Aaron Davis.

July 14. Edward the son of Edward Manning

John the son of John Dean

28 Joseph the son of William Heath and Prudence his wife.

Susannah the daughter of Thomas Dana & Susannah his wife.

Augt 4. Elizabeth the daughter of Amos Adams & Elizabeth his wife.

11. Abigial the daughter of Henry Shortlief and Mary his wife.

18 Abigail the daughter of Ebenezer May

Sep^t 1. Ebenezer, the son of Ralph Holdbrook

8. Sarah the daughter of Shubal Sever jun^r

Decr 1. Susannah the daughter of Saml Clark

22 John the son of John Slack & Elizabeth his wife.

1755

Jan 5. Abigail the daughter of Jeremiah Williams

19. Susannah the daughter of Joshua Davis, Brookline.

Catherine the daughter of Saml Williams

Jeremiah the son of Jeremiah Mosher & Isabel his wife.

Lucy the daughter of John Cheney & Martha his wife.

26. William the son of Thomas Cheney.

Feb 9. Joshua, the son of Ebenezer Gore jun^r

Elizabeth, the daughter of Edward King.

23. Mary, the daughter of William Bosson & Abigail his wife.

March 30. the of Woodward, Brookline.

April 13. Jane the daughter of Richard Lathbridge

June 29. Samuel the son of Samuel Weld

Edward the son of Abraham Dorr

Lydia the daughter of Ebenezer Bedunah

Augt 17. Nathaniel the son of Nathl Williams and Jane his wife.

31 John Chandler the son of Sam^{ll} Williams jun^r & Hannah his wife.

Sept 7 Abigail the daughter of Benjamin Curtiss

14. Priscilla the daughter of John Bugbee

Octr 5. Ezekiel the son of John Williams jun^r

19 Paul, the son of John Bugbee

Novr 9. Amos, the son of Amos Adams & Elizabeth his wife.

16. Abigail the son [daughter?] of Ebenezer Newell.

Hannah, the daughter of Jerahmeel Wheeler.

30. William, the son of James Duffs and Sarah his wife

Decr 14. Thomas the son of Joseph Ruggles

Mary, the daughter of William Curtiss

21. Jeremiah the son of Samuel Badcock & Isabel his wife.

Sarah Prince, a young woman, aged 18 years.

28 Mary, the daughter of Jonathan Parker & Abigail his wife.

1756

Jan 4. Anne, the daughter of Edmund Weld & Sarah his wife.

18 Anne the daughter of Saml Gridley.

Eleanor Bosson the wife of John Bosson

John, the son of John Bosson and Eleanor his wife

William, the son of John Bosson & Eleanor his wife

Elizabeth, the daughter of John Bosson and Eleanor his wife.

Feb 1st Sarah, the daughter of Ebenezer Dorr jun^r & Naomi his wife

March 7 Jerusha, the daughter of Edward Dorr.

Sarah, the daughter of Sam^{ll} Perrin.

21 Naomi, the daughter of Jacob Reves and Abigal his wife.

Lydia, the daughter of Daniel Sever & Abial his wife.

28. William the son of William Heath & Prudence his wife

April 18. Fortune, a negro man belonging to Capt Newel.

Guinea, daughter of the s^d Fortune.

28. Mary, daughter of Eben^r Pierpoint & Hannah his wife.

May 2^d William the son of Thomas Cheney

May 9. Mary, the daughter of Isaac Gardiner A.M. of Brook-line.

Mary, the daughter of Jeremiah Parker and Martha his wife.

Elizabeth, the daughter of John Slack and Elizabeth, his wife.

Sarah, the daughter of Thomas Dana & Susannah his wife.

16 Dinah, a negro woman belonging to Deacon Craft.

23 Susannah, the daughter of John Richardson.

June 13 Samuel the son of Ephraim Seagar and Abigail his wife.

20 Hannah, the daughter of Elijah Whitney and Hannah his wife.

27 Mary, the daughter of Nathanel Felton.

Ebenezer the son of Ebenezer May and Susannah his wife

Mary, the daughter of Joseph Williams jun^r & Mary his wife.

Eleanor, the daughter of Jeremiah Mosher & Isabel his wife.

July 4. Edward the son of Daniel Bugbee.

Augt 1. William, the son of William Williams.

8. John Searl, a young man aged 17 years.

Margaret Searl, a young woman, aged 16 years.

29. Louis [? Lois or Louisa], the daughter of Saml Williams and Abigail his wife.

Bethiah the daughter of Capt John Williams and Bethiah his wife

Septr 5. Mary, the daughter of Ebenezer Seaver jun^r and Mary his wife.

Jonathan the son of Capt Newels negro man Fortune.

12. Keturah a negro woman belonging to Mr Thos Seaver,

Phebe, the daughter of s^d Keturah.

Susannah, the daughter of s^d Keturah.

26 Susannah, the daughter of Aaron Davis.

Oct[r] 24 William the son of William Gridley and Lydia his wife

Nov[r] 7. Mercy, the daughter of Sam[ll] Woods and Mercy his wife

21 Henry, the son of Henry Shortlief and Mary his wife

Dec[r] 26 Lucy the daughter of Jeremiah Williams

1757

Jan[y] 16 Hannah the daughter of Benjamin Williams and Elizabeth his wife.

March 6 Jonathan, the son of Jonathan Hall and Mercy his wife

13 Edmund the son of Sam[iel]. Weld.

Mary, the daughter of John Dowse.

Sarah the daughter of Joseph Muncrief and Sarah his wife.

20 James the son of Orr & Elizabeth his wife

April 10 John } The sons of Solomon Ayers & Elizabeth
Solomon } his wife.

17 Abigail, the daughter of John Dinsdell and Abigal his wife.

May 1 Thomas the son of Sam[ll] Williams jun[r] & Hannah his wife.

15 Sarah, the daughter of Edmund Weld and Sarah his wife.

22 Mary Benjamin, the wife of Daniel Benjamin & Mary his wife.

Katherine the daughter of Jonathan Parker & Abigail his wife.

29 Nehemiah, the son of William Bosson & Abigail his wife.

June 5 Job } Twin children of Job Walker and Elizabeth
Elizabeth } his wife.

12 Samuel, the son of Isaac Winslow Esq[re]. & Lucy his wife.

26 Stephen the son of John Williams jun[r]

July 3 Prudence the daughter of Benjamin May.

Daniel, the son of Daniel Benjamin & Mary his wife.

17 William the son of Ebenezer Dorr jun[r] and Naomi his wife.

31 Edward the son of Edward King.

William, the son of William Blaney and Mary his wife.

Aug[st] 7 Paul the son of Thomas Dudley and Hannah his wife.

28 Henry the son of William Dinsdell & Lucy his wife.

Sept[r] 11 Joseph the son of Joseph Williams jun[r] & Mary his wife.

18 Sarah, the daughter of Ebenezer Davis and Sarah his wife.

Oct[r] 9 Edward, the son of Edward Dorr.

16 Elizabeth, the daughter of Ebenezer Bedunah.

Nov.ʳ 13 John, the son of Samˡˡ Badcock, & Isabel his wife.
Dec.ʳ 4 Sarah, the daughter of Joseph Weld & Mary his wife.
      25 Stedman the son of Capt John Williams & Bethiah
         his wife

1758

Jan   29. Lucy, the daughter of William Gridley & Lydia his
          wife
          Isaac, the son of Moses Winchester & Mary his wife
Feb   5. Mary, the daughter of Jeremiah Mosher and Isabel
          his wife.
      19. Anne, the daughter of William Williams and Sarah
          his wife.
      26 Hannah the daughter of Capt Ebenʳ Newell.
          Lemuel, the son of Benjᵃ Curtiss and Abigail his wife.
          Mary, the daughter of John Slack & Elizabeth his
          wife.
          Isabel, the daughter of William Curtiss.
March 12. Martha the daughter of Jeremiah Parker and Martha
          his wife.
      26 John the son of Capt Ralph Holdbrook.
          Solomon, the son of Ebenezer May and Susannah his
          wife.
          Deborah, the daughter of Jerahmeel Wheeler.
April 2 Catharine the daughter of James Mears junʳ & Nancy
          his wife.
      16 Edward, the son of William Heath & Prudence his
          wife.
      26 Timothy the son of Thomas Cheney and
          his wife (privatim)
May   21 Nathaniel the son of Joseph Brewer and
          his wife.
July   2 Henry, the son of Amos Adams & Elizabeth his wife.
      16 Mary, the daughter of Jacob Reves & Abigail his
          wife.
      30 Elizabeth Gleason the daughter of Daniel Benjamin &
          Mary his wife.
Augᵗ 20 Samuel, the son of Samuel Williams & Abigail his
          wife.
Sept   3. Edward the son of Abraham Dorr & Susannah his
          wife.
          John the son of Job Walker and Elizabeth his wife.
      10 Edward Jackson, the son of Nathᵉˡ Felton.
      17 Elisha Bowers the son of Ebenezer Dorr & Naomi his
          wife.
      24 Susannah, the daughter of Edmund Weld & Sarah his
          wife.
Nov.ʳ 5 Hannah, the daughter of Ebenʳ Seaver junʳ and Mary
          his wife.
      19 Abigail, the daughter of John Dinsdell and Abigail
          his wife.

Decr 3 Daniel the son of James Orr and Elizabeth his wife.
Abigail, the daughter of John Mears and Abigail his wife.

1759.

Jan 21 Benjamin, the son of Benjamin May.

28 Susannah the daughter of Samuel Sumner jun^r. & Susannah his wife.

Feb 4 Daniel, the son of Benjamin Williams & Elizabeth his wife.

11 Ebenezer, the son of Joseph Williams & Mary his wife.

Jonathan, the son of Jonathan Parker and Abigail his wife.

18 Jeremiah the son of Jeremiah Williams and Catherine his wife.

March 4 Gardiner, the son of Sam! Williams jun^r. & Hannah is wife. [SO IN ORIG!]

Joseph, the son of Sam! Weld.

Ichabod the son of Daniel Seaver & Abial his wife.

April 8 Rebecai, the daughter of John and Mary Cotton his wife.

15 James the son of James Mears jun^r. & Sarah his wife.

22 Simon, the son of Peter a Negro man & Elizabeth his wife.

May 20 Ebenezer the son of Ebenezer Davis & Sarah his wife.

June 17. Elizabeth, the daughter of Isaac Winslow & Lucy his wife.

24. Thomas, the son of Jonathan Hall and Mercy his wife.

July 15 Abigail, the daughter of Sam¹ Whittemore & his wife.

30 James, the son of William Lampson & Catharine his wife.

Augt 5 Weld, the son of Henry Shortlief, and Mary his wife.

12 Mary, the daughter of John Williams jun^r and · his wife.

Walter, the son of William Dinsdel and Lucy his wife.

22 Ebenezer, the son of Capⁿ Eben^r Newel and his wife (Privatim)

Sep^t 9 Thaddeus, the son of William Bosson and Abigail his wife.

30 Mercy, the daughter of Samuel Badcock and Isabel his wife

William the son of Edward King and his wife.

Octr 14 Mary, the daughter of David Weld and Sarah his wife.

21 Ephraim the son of Ephraim Seagar and Abigail his wife

	28	Lucy, the daughter of Obadiah Coolege and Sarah his wife.
Nov^r	18	Lucy, the daughter of William Gridley and Lydia his wife
Dec^r	9	Sarah, the daughter of Job Walker & Elizabeth his wife.

Sa_n^muel, the son of Willm Blaney & Mary his wife.

	23	Theoda, the daughter of Eben^r May and Susannah his wife
	30	William, the son of William Williams and Sarah his wife.

1760

Jan.	13	Phillip, the son of Jeremiah Mosher & Isabel his wife.
	20	Charles, the son of Amos Adams & Elizabeth his wife.
Feb	3	Bethiah, the daughter of Capt John Williams & Bethiah his wife.
	10	Benjamin, the son of Benjamin Pierpoint and Elizabeth his wife.
	17	Thomas, the son of Thomas Raymour and Mary his wife.
March	2	Lucy, the daughter of Jeremiah Williams and Catherine his wife.
	9	Samuel, the son of William Heath jun^r & Sarah his wife.
	16	Sarah, the daughter of John Slack and Elizabeth his wife.
	23	Sarah, the daughter of Joseph Woorsley & Sarah his wife.
April	20	John, the son of Jere. Parker & Martha his wife.
May	4	John, the son of Aaron Davis & Mary his wife.
June	7	Elizabeth, the daughter of Joseph Muncrief & Sarah his wife.
July	6	Elizabeth, the daughter of James Orr and Elizabeth his wife.
		Asa, the son of Abraham Woodward and his wife.
		Martha, the daughter of John Foster, deceased, and Jane his wife.
	20	Benjamin, the son of Edward Dorr and Abigail his wife.
	27	Dorothy, the daughter of Capt Ralph Holdbrook and Dorothy his wife.
		Zebiah, the daughter of Joseph Williams jun^r and Mary his wife.
		Joseph, the son of Joseph Weld and Mary his wife.
Aug^t	24	Ebenezer, the son of Ebenezer Pierpoint & Hannah his wife.
	31	Elizabeth, the daughter of Isaac Curtiss and Anna his wife.
Sep^t	8	Sarah, the daughter of Jonathan Payson and his wife (Privatim).

14 Grizzel, the daughter of Isaac Winslow Esqr and Lucy his wife.

28 Susanna Pierpoint, the daughter of Capt Eben^r Newel and _____ his wife.

Octr 12 Clements, the daughter of Edmund Weld and Sarah his wife.

Novr 16 Elizabeth, the daughter of Benj^a Williams & Elizabeth his wife.

30 Jane, the daughter of Thaddeus Partridge & Jane his wife.

Decr 7 Rhode, the daughter of Jon^a Parker & Abigail his wife.

1761

Jan. 11. Stephen Williams the son of Willm Heath & Prudence his wife.

Feb 15 Catherine, the daughter of Will. Pike & Hannah his wife.

March 8 Hannah, the daughter of Saml Williams & Hannah his wife.

22 Increase, the son of Ebenezer Davis & Sarah his wife.

William Milberry, the son of Job Walker & Eliz^h his wife.

29 Susannah, the daughter of John Dowse & _____ his wife.

Lucy, the daughter of William Bossom & Abigail his wife.

April 19 John Waters, the son of Ebenezer Bedunah & _____ his wife.

May 3^d Samuel, the son of Benj^a Curtiss and Abigail. his wife.

24 Jonathan, the son of Ebenezer Seaver and Mary his wife.

June 7 Solomon, the son of Ebenezer May and Susannah his wife.

Ebenezer Hinsdell the son of Thomas Williams & Abigal his wife.

21 James, the son of Richard Fox and Elizabeth his wife.

28 _____ the _____ of Jerahmeel Wheeler & _____ his wife.

July 19 Elizabeth, the daughter of Samuel Williams & Abigail his wife.

Augt 2 Elisha, the son of Daniel Seaver and Abial his wife.

23 Elizabeth, the daughter of Benjamin Pierpoint and Elizabeth his wife.

Sep^t 13 Lucy, the daughter of William Dinsdel and Lucy his wife.

Joseph, the son of Joseph Payson and Abigail his wife.

Susannah, the daughter of Aaron Davis jun^r & Susannah his wife.

20   Mary, the daughter of Moses Winchester and Mary his wife.

27   Mary } The twin daughters of Abraham Dorr & Su-
Sarah }   saunah his wife.

     Jane, the daughter of Thomas Reymour & Mary his wife.

Oct.   4   William, the son of William Thompson & Mary his wife.

Nov^r   8   Margaret, the daughter of James Orr & Elizabeth his wife.

     15   Nathaniel the son of Joseph Ruggles and Rebecca his wife.

     29   Caleb, the son of Obadiah Coolege and Sarah his wife.

Dec^r   6   Susannah, the daughter of Sam! Perrin and Elizabeth his wife.

     Mary, the daughter of Sam! Weld & Hannah his wife.

     Polly, the daughter of Willm Gridley and Lydia his wife.

     13   John, the son of John Mears & Abigail his wife.

     20   John, the son of Thomas Dana and Susannah his wife.

     27   Enoch Hancock (adult)

     Bethiah, the daughter of Thomas Cheney and his wife.

     Abigail, the daughter of Enoch Hancock and Abigail his wife.

1762

Feb   14   Hannah, the daughter of Jeremiah Parker & Martha his wife.

     Benjamin, the son of Edmund Weld & Sarah his wife.

Jan.   24.   the   of Thaddeus Partridge & Jane his wife.

Feb   20   Caleb, the son of Caleb Howard & Mary his wife.

March   7.   Elizabeth, the daughter of Saml Whittemore &   his wife.

April   4   Joseph, the son of Joseph Woorsley and Sarah his wife.

May   2   Mary, the daughter of William Blaney & Mary his wife.

     16   Elizabeth, the daughter of Jos. Muncrief & Sarah his wife.

May   30   Henry, the son of Henry Payson and   his wife.

June   6   William Patrick (adult)

     Sarah, the daughter of Willm Patrick & Sarah his wife.

     27   Elizabeth, the daughter of Capt John Williams and Bethiah his wife.

     Jonathan Davis, the son of William Bossom and Abigail his wife.

July   25.   Catherine, the daughter of James Mears jun^r & Nancy his wife.

Aug. 1 Samuel, the son of Abraham Woodward and   his wife.

Sarah, the daughter of Thomas Wyman and Sarah his wife.

15 Joseph, the son of Joseph Williams & Mary his wife.

Mary, the daughter of Joseph Weld and Mary his wife.

26 William, the son of William Heath and Sarah his wife

Octr 17 Sarah, the daughter of Thos Williams & Abigail his wife.

Mary, the daughter of Nicholas Seaver & Mary his wife.

Deborah Searl (adult)

Ruth Searl (adult)

3 Tobias a negro man belonging to William Williams

Novr 14 Jeremiah, the son of Jeremiah Williams, (deceased) & Catherine his wife.

Mahitabel, the daughter of Isaac Curtiss and Anna his wife.

Decr 5 Samuel, the son of Ephraim Seagar & Abigail his wife.

26 Henry, the son of Ebenezer May and Susannah his wife.

Amos, the son of Amos Adams and Elizabeth his wife.

1763

Feb. 5 Ebenezer, the son of Richard & Elizabeth Fox

March 13 Timothy } The twin sons of Jonathan Parker & Abigail John   }   his wife.

Thomas, the son of Benj.^a Curtiss & Abigail his wife.

Benjamin the son of John Slack and Elizabeth his wife.

Charles, the son of William Dinsdel and Lucy his wife.

27 John, the son of John Brewer and   his wife.

Jane, the daughter of James Orr and Elizabeth his wife.

April 3. Mary the daughter of Benj.^a Williams & Elizabeth his wife.

17 Aaron the son of Aaron Davis jun.^r & Susannah his wife.

James, the son of Thomas Reymour and Mary his wife.

May 1st Isaac, the son of Isaac Winslow Esqr & Lucy his wife.

15 Sarah, the daughter of Joseph Payson & Abigail his wife.

Daniel, the son of Daniel Bugbee jun.^r & Mary his wife.

Samuel, the son of William Thompson and Mary his wife.

29 Lucy, the daughter of Saml Williams jun.^r & Lucy his wife.

July 10 Ebenezer, the son of Ebenezer Seaver and Mary his wife.

Sep: 25   Sibil, the daughter of Samuel Badcock and Sibil his wife.

       John, the son of Edmund Weld & Sarah his wife

       Hannah, the daughter of Wᵐ Curtiss and   his wife

October 9   Lucy, the daughter of Willᵐ Williams and Anne his wife.

Nov: 27   John, the son of John Lewis and Abigail his wife

Dec: 11   Thaddeus, the son of Thaddeus Partridge & Jane his wife.

       Mary, the daughter of Caleb Hayward and Mary his wife.

Dec: 18   Lucretia, the daughter of Capt John Williams and Bethiah his wife.

       Lydia, the daughter of William Gridley and Lydia his wife.

1764

Jany 15   Theoda, the daughter of Stephen Williams and Theoda his wife.

     22   Abiah, the son of Samuel Holdbrook (of Boston) & Elizabeth his wife.

       Mary, the daughter of William Patrick and Sarah his wife.

Feb   12   Robert, the son of Robert Pierpont and Anne his wife.

       Susannah, the daughter of Joseph Ruggles and Rebecca his wife.

     19   Anne Husk, the daughter of Edmund Quincy and Anne his wife.

     26   Susannah, the daughter of Lemuel Hutson (Boston) and   his wife.

May   20   Ruth, the daughter of Samuel Whittemore &   his wife.

     27   Thomas, the son of William Thomson & Mary his wife.

       Sarah, the daughter of Moses Winchester and Mary his wife.

June   3   Sarah, the daughter of Edward Dorr and   his wife.

       Thomas, the son of Thomas Williams & Abigail his wife.

     24   Joseph, the son of William Blaney and Mary his wife.

       Anna, the daughter of Isaac Curtiss and Anna his wife.

July   8   Thomas, the son of Amos Adams & Elizabeth his wife.

     22   Edith, the daughter of Tho: Wyman & Sarah his wife.

     29   Sarah, the daughter of William Heath & Sarah his wife.

Augᵗ 12   David, the son of Joseph Woorsley and Sarah his wife.

     16   John the son of James Mears junʳ & Nancy his wife.

Sepᵗ   9   Abraham, the son of Abraham Dorr (deceased) and Susannah his wife.

       Samuel, the son of Samᴸ Daniels and   his wife.

23 Joseph the son of Joseph Williams and Susannah his wife.

Oct.ʳ 7 Venus, an adult woman negro serv.ᵗ belonging to Joseph Ruggles.

Richard, the son of Ishmael & Venus the negro servants of Jos. Ruggles.

28 Caroline the daughter of Capt John Williams & Bethiah his wife.

Nov.ʳ 18 Moses, the son of Moses Dorr & Eleanor Dorr his wife.

Priscilla, the daughter of Moses & Eleanor Dorr

Dec.ʳ 16 Anne, the daughter of William Bosson & Abigail his wife.

Anne, the daughter of Thomas Dana & Martha his wife.

Joshua, the son of William Dinsdel and Lucy his wife.

29. Ezra, the son of Samuel Weld and Hannah his wife.

1765

Jany 20 Joanna, the daughter of John Brewer and   his wife.

Feb 10 Margrett the daughter of John Dowse and   his wife.

Rebecca, the daughter of Henry Payson and Abigail his wife.

17 Samuel, the son of Joseph Payson and Abigail his wife.

March 10 Deborah Bosson (adult)

31 Sarah Tyng, the daughter of Isaac Winslow Esq.ʳ & Lucy his wife.

Charles, the son of Eben.ʳ Pierpont and Hannah his wife.

April 21 Susannah, the daughter of Edmund Weld & Sarah his wife.

28 Rebecca, the daughter of James Orr & Eliz. his wife (Privatim)

May 5 Richard, the son of Richard Fox and Elizabeth his wife.

19 Nathaniel, the son of Samuel Perrin (deceased) & Elizabeth his wife.

John Ruggles, the son of Joseph Weld and Mary his wife.

26 William, the son of Abijah Seaver &   his wife.

June 9 Mary, the daughter of Paul Gore and Mary his wife.

July 7 Sarah, the daughter of Aaron Davis & Susannah his wife.

21 Abigail, the daughter of   Welsh and   his wife.

Sept.ʳ 8 Enoch, the son of Enock Hancock (deceased) and Abigail his wife.

22 Charlotte, daughter of William Gridley & Lydia his wife.

	29	Esther, the daughter of John Lewis and Abigail his wife.
Oct^r	27	William the son of Dan! Seaver & Abial his wife.
Dec?	1	Susannah, the daughter of Willm Patrick & Sarah his wife.
	8	Sarah, the daughter of Thaddeus Partridge & Jane his wife.

1766

Jan	5	Davis, the son of Obadiah Cooledge & his wife.
		Charles, the son of Caleb Hayward & Mary his wife.
Feb	2	Mary, the daughter of Daniel Tombs and his wife.
	9	Samuel, the son of John Slack and Elizabeth his wife.
	16	Hannah, the daughter of Davis Whitman and his wife.
March	2	Susannah, the daughter of Joseph Williams and Susannah his wife.
	23	Elizabeth, the daughter of James Cornish and Sarah his wife.
April	6	Joseph, the son of Capt William Heath and Sarah his wife.
	13	James, the son of James Bird & Deborah his wife.
	20	Joseph the son of Job Walker and his wife.
	27	John, the son of Joseph Williams and Mary his wife.
		Nathaneel, the son of Jeremiah Parker & Martha his wife.
		Susannah, the daughter of Isaac Curtiss and Anna his wife.
May	18	Roxbury, the son of Ishmael & Venus (Negroes belonging to the Wido. Ruggles)
June	8	Charles, the son of Ephraim Seagar and Abigail his wife.
July	20	Noah, the son of Noah Davis & Elizabeth his wife.
	27	Catherine, the daughter of Thomas Learned and his wife.
Aug^t	10	Thomas, the son of Thomas Hovey and his wife.
	17	Adams, the son of Richard Lathbridge & Hopestil his wife.
	24	William, the son of Joseph Payson and Abigail his wife.
	31	Andrew, the son of Andrew Floyd and his wife (privatim)
Oct^r	12	Elijah the son of Thomas Williams & Abigail his wife.
		Benjamin the son of Abial Seaver and his wife.
		Leocada, the daughter of Jacob Davis and his wife.
	19	Charlotte, the daughter of William Williams & Anne his wife.

Mary, the daughter of Daniel Bugbee jun.ʳ & Sarah his wife.

Elizabeth Johnson, a young woman.

Nov.ʳ 2 Benjamin Sharp, the son of William Blaney & Mary his wife.

23 Mary, the daughter of Joshua Felton & Mary his wife.

30 Mary, the daughter of Joseph Woorsley and Sarah his wife.

Dec.ʳ 7 Dorothy, the daughter of Edmund Weld and Sarah his wife.

21 Phylis, the Negro woman of Capt John Williams

1767

Jany 11 Paul, the son of Paul Gore & Mary his wife.

Thomas the son of Thomas Thompson & Mary his wife.

Anne, the daughter of Willᵐ Bugbee and Hannah his wife.

Feb 1ˢᵗ Joseph, the son of Edward Dorr and Abigail his wife.

15 Joseph, the son of Eliphalet Downer and his wife.

Mindwell, the daughter of Daniel Benjamin & Mary his wife

April 5 Abigail, the wife of Jeremiah Parker jun.ʳ

19 Stephen, the son of Stephen Williams & Theoda his wife.

May 10 Mary, the daughter of Phillip Doyle & Mary his wife.

3 Brill Johnson, a young man.

July 12 Joseph, the son of Amos Adams & Elizabeth his wife.

Augᵗ 23 James Clap, the son of Aaron Rumnie and his wife.

Jeremy, the son of Jeremy Parker jun.ʳ & Abigail his wife.

30 Elizabeth, the daughter of Richard Fox and Elizabeth his wife

Joseph, the son of Joseph Smith and Mary his wife.

Sepᵗ 13 Scarborough, the son of Jonathan Parker and Abigail his wife.

Anna, the daughter of Benjamin Baker and his wife.

Oct.ʳ 5 Elizabeth, the daughter of Thaddeus Partri'ge & Jane his wife.

18 the daughter of James Bird and his wife.

25 Joseph, the son of Joseph Muncrieff & Mary his wife.

John, the son of William Thompson and Mary his wife

Nov.ʳ 8 Benjamin, the son of Joseph Williams & Susanna his wife.

Theoda the daughter of William Dinsdel & his wife.

Dec.ʳ 6 Isaac the son of Isaac Curtiss and Anna his wife.

13 Oliver, the son of Willᵐ Gridley & Lydia his wife.

20 Daniel, the son of Daniel Bugbee & Sarah his wife.

1768

| Jany | 31 | Mary, the daughter of Peter Walker &   his wife. |

Jany 31 Mary, the daughter of Peter Walker & his wife.

Feb 7 Hannah, the daughter of Jõhua Felton and Mary his wife.

14 James, the son of Thomas Hovey and his wife.

28 Ruggles, the son of John Slack & Eliz. his wife.

James, the son of James Gould & his wife.

March 14 Charles, the son of Ephraim Seagar & Abigail his wife.

27 Charles, the son of William Boston & Ruth his wife.

Hannah How, a young woman.

April 3 Abigail, the daughter of William Blaney & Mary his wife.

17 William, the son of William Bugbee & Hannah his wife.

May 1 Anne, the daughter of Henry Payson & Abigail his wife.

15 Catharine, the daughter of Sam! Sumner & Mary his wife.

June 5 James Hervey, the son of William Pierpont & his wife.

19 Abigail, the daughter of Jacob Davis and his wife.

July 17 Rebeccah, the daughter of John Brewer & his wife.

24 Charles, the son of Daniel Cooledge & his wife.

August 7 Mary, the daughter of Mary Bosson.

14 Lucretia, the daughter of Moses Winchester and Mary his wife.

28 Eunice, the daughter of Francis Dana & Eunice his wife.

Oliver Royal, the son of Robert Champney & Rebecca his wife.

Sep! 4 Caleb, the son of Daniel Seaver & Abial his wife.

Abigail, the daughter of Thomas Williams & Abigail his wife.

Rebecca, the daughter of Caleb Hayward & Mary his wife.

Anne, the daughter of Abijah Sever & his wife.

(?) 14 Martha, the daughter of Nath! Ruggles & Martha his wife.

John Knight, the son of Thomas Learned &_____ his wife.

25 Elizabeth, the daughter of Samuel Heath &_____ his wife.

Oct' 9 Rebeccah, the daughter of Paul Gore & Mary his wife.

16 Mary, the daughter of Aaron Davis & Susannah his wife.

23 Priscilla, the daughter of Edmund Weld & Sarah his wife.

30 Mary, the daughter of Jos. Smith & his wife.

Decr 18 Rebeccah, daughter of William Thompson & Mary his wife.

John, the son of Richard Rowen and   his wife.

25 Mary, the daughter of Eliphalet Downer & his wife.

1769

Jan. 15 Mary, the daughter of Thomas Dana & Susannah his wife.

22 Michael Presbury, the son of James Bird & his wife.

Feb 1 Sarah, the daughter of Joseph Payson & Abigail his wife.

March 26 Sarah, the daughter of Amos Adams & Elizabeth his wife.

April 23 Martha, the wife of Stephen Mills.

May 20 Charles, the son of Joseph Williams and Mary his wife.

June 4 Henry, the son of Capt William Heath and *[illegible]* his wife.

11 Oliver, the son of William Dinsdel & his wife.

July 1 George, the son of Moses Dorr and Eleanour his wife.

15 Joshua, the son of Joshua Felton and Mary his wife.

James, the son of Hannah Tucker.

22 Samuel, the son of Joseph Williams and Susannah his wife.

29 Robert, the son of William Williams & Anne his wife.

Mary, the daughter of Jeremiah Parker jun^r & Abigail his wife.

Augt 6 John, the son of Co^l Joseph Scott and   his wife.

Elizabeth, the daughter of Jonathan Parker & Abigal his wife.

Sep^t 3 Cato, the son of London & Phillis, servants to Maj^r Bayard.

17 Mary, the wife of Joshua Felton.

John, the son of Daniel Bugbee and Sarah his wife.

Octr 8 Elizabeth, the daughter of Thomas Weld & Thankful his wife.

15 Lucy, the daughter of Peleg Heath and Patience his wife.

22 Sarah, the daughter of Isaac Curtiss & Anna his wife.

Novr 5 Abigail, the daughter of Lemuel May & Abigail his wife.

Benjamin West, the son of James Cornish & his wife.

Anne, the daughter of James Gould & his wife.

20 Benjamin Woodbridge the son of Benjamin Baxter &   his wife.

William, the son of Thadeus Partridge & Jane his wife.

Dec. 10 Abigail, the daughter of Stephen Williams & Theoda
        his wife.

        Prince, a negro man of William Bowdoin Esq' &
        Phillis his daughter.

     24 Lucretia, the daughter of John Graeton & Sarah his
        wife.

1770

Jan   21 Priscilla, the daughter of Richard Fox and
        his wife.

     28 Susannah, the daughter of Daniel Seaver & Abial his
        wife.

        John, the son of John Davis Williams & Hannah
        his wife.

Feb   11 Aaron, the son of Aaron Ruminee & Eliza his wife.

     18 Hannah, the daughter of Samuel Sumner & Mary his
        wife.

March   4 Mary, the daughter of William Thompson & Mary
        his wife.

     11 Elizabeth. the daughter of Benjamin Baker &
        his wife.

        Sarah, the daughter of Jacob Cummins & Sarah his
        wife.

     25 William, the son of William Bugbee and   his
        wife.

        Elizabeth the daughter of Stephen Mills &
        his wife.

April   1 Thomas, the son of   Welch (deceased) &
        his wife.

        Sam' the son of John Williams & Mary his wife.

     15 Anne the daughter of Joseph Muncrief and Mary his
        wife.

     29 Benjamin, the son of Edmund Weld and Sarah his
        wife.

May   13 John Shirley, the son of James Mears & Nancy his
        wife.

June   3 Eunice, the daughter of Dan! Coolidge & Lydia his
        wife.

July   1 Elizabeth, the daughter of Sam! Sumner and Su-
        sannah his wife.

      8 John, the son of Samuel Whittemore &   his
        wife.

     22 William, the son of Susannah Dorr.

Aug!   5th Lucy, the dang' Joshua Fulton & Mary his wife.

     12 Henry the son of William Blaney & Mary his wife.

     19 Susannah, the daughter of Sam! Heath &   his
        wife.

Sept!   2 Lemuel, the son of Thomas Davenport &   his
        wife.

     30 Martha, the daughter of John Slack and Elizabeth
        his wife.

        Nathaniel, the son of Nath' Eaton & Martha his
        wife.

Oct.ᵣ 14 Samuel, the son of Thomas Learned &   his wife.

      28 Ralph the son of Joseph Smith &   his wife.

Nov.ᵣ 4 Abigail, the daughter of Jeremiah Parker jun.ᵣ & Abigail his wife

      11 Deborah, the daughᵣ of Joshua Bradley & Sarah his wife.

Dec.ᵣ 2 William, the son of Moses Davis & Hannah his wife.

      9 Nathˡ the son of Nathˡ Ruggles & Martha his wife.

      16 Abigail, the daughter of Danˡ Bugbee junᵣ & Sarah his wife.

      23 Susannah, the daughter of Paul Gore & Mary his wife.

         Samuel, the son of Samuel Gore & Hannah his wife.

1771

Jan. 13 Nathaneel, the son of Nathˡ Felton & Mary his wife.

      20 Joseph, the son of Abijah Seaver and   his wife.

         Elijah, the son of Danˡ Whitney &   his wife.

Feb 10 Eben.ᵣ the son of Ebenezer Wales &   his wife.

      24 Eleazer, the son of Thomas Williams &   his wife.

         Henry, the son of William Thompson &   his wife.

         Asa, the son Jacob Davis &   his wife.

         Thomas, the son of Benjamin Cotterel & Mary his wife.

         Benjamin, the son of Benjamin Cotterel & Mary his wife.

March 10 Hannah, the daughter of Joseph Williams Esq & Hannah his wife.

April 10 Kendal, the son of Kendal Johnson (dec.ᵈ) & Anne his wife.

May 26 Peleg, the son of Peleg Heath & Patience his wife.

         Abigail, the daughter of Henry Payson &   his wife.

         Rebeccah, the daughter of Robert Champney & his wife.

         Sarah, the daughter of Ebenezer Swan &   his wife.

June 16 Aaron, the son of Aaron White &   his wife.

         Abigail, the daugᵣ of Thomas Weld &   his wife.

July 28 Samuel, the son of William Gridley & Lydia his wife.

         Mary, the daughter of   Thorp & his wife.

      14   the   of Thomas Safford &   his wife.

Aug.ᵗ 4 Elisha, the son of Joseph Williams junᵣ & Mary his wife.

John, the son of Isaac Curtis & Anna his wife.

Samuel, the son of Eliphalet Downer &   his wife.

11 Mary, the daughter of Caleb Hayward & Mary his wife.

Sep^t 15 Sarah, the daughter of Richard Rowen &   his wife.

Octr 8 John, the son of John Graeton & Sarah his wife

Benjamin, the son of Joseph Payson & Abigail his wife.

Novr 10 Mary, the daughter Joseph Williams & Susannah his wife.

24 Elizabeth, the daughter of Jeremiah Parker & Abigail his wife.

Decr 15 James, the son of Thadeus Partridge & Jane his wife,

Mary, the daug^r of James Gould &   his wife.

1772

Jany 26 Esther, the daug^r of Saml Langley & Esther his wife.

Feb 9 Lucy, the daug^r of John Williams & Rebecca his wife.

Ezekiel } The children of Peter Walker &
Elizabeth } his wife.

16 Thomas, the son of Isaac Winslow Esq & Jemima his wife.

William, the son of Wm Dinsdel &   his wife.

March 1 Ashael Plimpton, the son of Moses Dorr & Eleanor his wife.

Moses, the son of Moses Winchester & Mary his wife.

28 Henry, the son of Richard Fox & Elizabeth his wife.

April 5 Charles, the son of Aaron Davis & Susannah his wife.

12 Bethiah, the daughter of Jonathan Parker & Abigil his wife.

Susannah, the daughter of Joseph Smith & Mary his wife.

Abigail Sumner, the daughter of John Williams & 'Mary his wife.

19 Thomas, the son of Edmund Weld & Sarah his wife.

26 Elizabeth, daughter of James White &   his wife.

May 3 Hannah, daughter of William Bugbee & Hannah his wife.

10 Martha, the daughter of Jacob Cummins and Sarah his wife.

24 Joseph, son of Capt Nat.^l Ruggles & Martha his wife.

June 10 John, son of William Blaney & Mary his wife (privately)

14 Margartae, the daughter of Eben: Seaver & Margaret his wife.

John, son of Samuel Bowen & Mary his wife.

July 5 Caroline, daughter of Aaron Blaney & Eunice his wife.

Augt 2 Jeremiah, son of Joseph Williams Esqr & Hannah his wife.

William, son of Nath! Eaton & Martha his wife.

Sep^t 13 Catharine, the daughter of John Slack & Elizabeth his wife.

27 Joseph, the son of Joseph Curtiss & Catherine his wife.

Samuel, the son of John Ward &   his wife.

Samuel Croxford (a young man)

Octr 4 Eunice, the daug^r of Eben: Wales & Eunice his wife.

Polly, daug^r of Stephen Williams jun: & Mary his wife.

Nathanael, son of Nathl Scott &   his wife.

11 Mary, the daug^r of Sam! Sumner jun: & Susanna his wife.

Richard, the son of Richard Rowen & Sarah his wife.

Novr 8 Betsey, the daug^r of Thomas Shed and   his wife.

29 Elizabeth, daug^r of Stephen Jennigs & Mary his wife.

Decr 6 Elizabeth, daug^r of   Ridley and Elizabeth Ridley.

13 Samuel, the son of Samuel Sumner & Mary his wife.

Thomas, the son of Thomas Davenport &   his wife.

Polly, daughter of Ralph Smith & Mary his wife.

1773

Jany 17 Martha, daughter of Thomas Dana & Martha his wife.

Sarah, daughter of Benja. Cotterell & Mary his wife.

31 Turell, the son of Thomas Learned &   his wife.

Katie, the daug^r of John Graeton & Sarah his wife.

Feb 7 Anna Darby, daug^r of Noah Parker & Eleanor his wife.

14 Mary, daughter of Joseph Muncrief and   his wife.

March 14 Elizabeth, daug^r of Aaron White and   his wife.

21 Enoch, son of Enoch Hyde and Mary his wife.

Stedman son of John Davis Williams & Hannah his wife.

April 4 Benjamin, the son of Thomas Safford &   his wife.

18 Mary Willard, daughter of Benjamin Tucker &   wife.

Sarah, daug.ʳ of Daniel Bugbee & Sarah his wife.

Polly, daugʳ of John Williams & Polly his wife.

May   2   Sarah, daug.ʳ of Isaac Curtiss & Anna his wife.

Robert, son of James Morton &   his wife.

16   Nathanael, son of Abijah Seaver &   his wife.

Aug.ᵗ   1ˢᵗ Thomas, son of Thomas Shed &   his wife.

22   Samuel, son of Peleg Heath & Patience his wife.

Nathan, son of Nathan Shed &   his wife.

29   Olle, daughter of William Dindsdel & his wife.

Nathanael, son of Joshua Felton & Mary his wife.

Oct.ʳ   3   William, son of Thomas Maccarty & Sarah his wife.

11   Sally, daughter of Edward Payson Williams & Sarah his wife.

Nov.ʳ   28   Francis, son of Deacon William Gridley & Lydia his wife.

Dec.ʳ   26   Catherine, the daug.ʳ of Thadeus Partridge & Jane his wife.

1774

Jan.ʸ   2   Ebenezer, son of Luke Baker &   his wife.

16   Anne, daug.ʳ of Joseph Payson & Abigail his wife.

Lemuel Baker, son of Jacob Davis &   his wife.

Feb   20   Nathanael Whiting, son of Joseph Williams Esq.ʳ & Hannah his wife.

Jonathan, son of Jonathan Champney &   his wife.

Elizabeth, ⎰ Twin daughters of Joseph Smith & Mary
Sally   ⎱ his wife.

John, son of John Whitney & Mary his wife.

27   William, son of Sam.ˡ Gore & Hannah his wife.

Cuffe, a negro man belonging to William Fulton (privately)

Mar   27   Lemuel son of Joseph Williams & Susannah his wife.

April   3   Arnold, son of Aaron Blaney & Eunice his wife.

17   Mary, daug.ʳ of Joseph Payson jun.ʳ & Mary his wife.

May   1   Samuel, son of Joseph Curtiss & Catherine his wife.

Betsey, daughter of Eben.ʳ Wales & Eunice his wife.

Samuel, son of Samu.ˡ Whittemore jun.ʳ &   his wife.

Nancy, daughter of Noah Parker & Eleanor his wife.

15   Lydia, daugʳ of Doctor Thomas Williams & his wife.

29   Pamela, the daug.ʳ of Sam.ˡ Heath &   his wife.

Martha, the daugʳ of Nathˡ Eaton & Martha his wife.

Olive, the daugʳ of John Ward & Martha his wife.

June   5   Sally, dangʳ of William Thompson & Mary his wife

26   Samuel, son of John Williams & Rebeca his wife.

Bethiah Allen, daug.ʳ of Jeremiah Parker jun.ʳ & Abigail his wife.

Samuel, son of Samuel Bowen & Maiy his wife.

July   31   Stephen son of Stephen Jennings & Mary his wife.

Aug^t   7   Charles, son of Moses Winchester & Mary his wife.

Sep^t   4   Daniel, son of William Bugbee & Mary his wife.

Warren, son of Daniel Coolege &   his wife.

Francis, son of Enoch Hyde & Mary his wife.

Oct^r   2   Joshua, son of Ebenezer Seaver & Margaret his wife.

Elizabeth, daug^r of Thomas Kelton &   his wife (Dorchester)

       2   Benjamin Stevens (adult)

    23   Thomas Cotton, son of Caleb Hayward & Martha his wife.

Eleanor, daughter of Thomas Shed and   his wife.

Charles, son of Jacob Cummins & Sarah his wife.

Nov^r   6   Nathanael Healy (adult)

    13   Samuel, son of Benjamin Cotterel & Mary his wife.

Ileriot, daug^r of William Felton &   his wife.

Decr 18   Mary, daug^r of Stephen Williams & Theoda his wife.

    25   Susannah, daug^r of John Slack & Elizabeth his wife.

Abigail, daug^r of Joseph Richardson & Abigail his wife.

1775

Jany   1   Lulley daug^r of John Graeton & Sarah his wife.

    15   Lucy, daug^r of   Floyd and   his wife.

    22   Susannah, daug^r of James How and Susannah his wife.

Feb   5   Lucretia, daug^r of Joshua Felton & Polly his wife.

    12   Phanne, daug^r of Henry Payson &   his wife.

Thomas, son of Richard Fox & Elizabeth his wife.

Abigail, daug^r of James Morton &   his wife.

Betsey, daug^r of Daniel Brown & Ruth his wife.

    26   Hannah, daug^r of Tho. Learned &   his wife.

Ebenezer son of Ebenezer Smith & Abigail his wife.

March 5   Betsey, daug^r of Robert Williams & Elizabeth his wife.

    12   Ruth, daug^r of Nathl Scott &   his wife.

April 9   Joseph, son of Robert Champney and Rebeccah his wife.

The following is taken from Page 269 of the Records (at the end of Revd J. Eliot's Register of events.)

"Inasmuch as some things worthy of notice are not as I find mentioned in this Book, and others y^t are, are mentioned in divers places scattered up & down I have thot proper here to insert ye following articles, following the Revd Mr Eliot & Danforth's annals of events.

"Amos Adams."

1632 July		The first Church in Roxbury was gathered.
1632 July		The Rev.ᵈ Mʳ Thoˢ Weld was chosen & invested wᵗʰ yᵉ pastoral care of the church in Roxbury he was a Minister in England, att Terling in Essex.
1631 Novʳ		Mʳ John Eliot arrived in N England aged 27. Joyned to yᵉ Chʰ att Boston.
1632 Octʳ		Mʳ John Eliot was married.
Novʳ	5 or 9ᵗʰ	The Rev.ᵈ Mʳ Eliot was ordained Teacher of the Church in Roxbury.
1639		*The Rev.ᵈ Mʳ Weld upon advice of his friends returned to England.
1650 Sept	24	The Rev.ᵈ Mʳ Sam.ˡ Danforth was ordained Pastor of the Church in Roxbury.
1674 Novʳ	19	The Rev.ᵈ Mʳ Danforth dyed, aged 48.
1688 Octʳ	17	The Rev.ᵈ Mʳ Nehemiah Walter ordained Pastor of the Chʰ in Roxbury.
1690 May	20	The Rev.ᵈ Mʳ Eliot died.
1718 Octʳ	19	The Rev.ᵈ Mʳ Thoˢ Walter ordained· Pastor of the Chʰ in Roxbury.
1725 Jan	10	The Rev.ᵈ Mʳ Tho.ˢ Walter died.
1750 Sept	17	The Rev.ᵈ Mʳ Nehemiah Walter died.
1750 Nov	7	The Rev.ᵈ Mʳ Oliver Peabody was ordained Pastor of this Church.
1752 May	29	The Rev.ᵈ Mʳ Peabody dyed.
1753 Sept	12	Amos Adams was ordained Pastor of the first Chʰ in Roxbury.
1775 Octobʳ	5	The Rev.ᵈ Mʳ Adams died.
1782 Octʳ	2	Eliphalet Porter was ordained Pastor of yᵉ 1st Chʰ in R.
1830 July	7	George Putnam ordained Colleague.
1833 Dec	7	Rev.ᵈ Eliphalet Porter D.D. died aged 75½ years.

1641

Month 11ᵗ day 26.	Williã Chandler, a Christian & godly brothʳ dyed of a Consumption.
Month 1 day 3.	A new borne infant of Georg. Holmes.

1642

Month 2 day 30.	Abigail Gore the daughter of Mʳ John Gore.
Month 6ᵗʰ day 10.	John Scarbro the soñe of John Scarbro. this infant dyed of convulsions.
Month 7ᵗʰ day 21.	John Perry, a christian brothʳ he dyed of a Consumption p.tly & an extreame paine in his head.
Month 9.	There were 2 infants dyed in the birth, it was conceived to be through the unskilfullnesse of the midwife, none of the p.ents were of oʳ church.

---

*Rev.ᵈ Tho.ˢ Weld died at London, March 23ᵈ 1660.

Month 11th day 24. Samuel Hagbourne a christian & godly broth^r dyed of a feaver, upon a deepe could & stopt up with flegme.

Month 12 day 13. Whittamore, the wife of Laurenc Whittamore, She dyed of an Apoplexie, wch she had more then two years before, but it resolved into a palsy in all her left side, being voyd of sence & motion, but was cured of it againe, though she were aboute 60 years of age.

1643

Month 2 day 4. Mary Onion the wife of Rob. Onion died of a cold and sw̄et taken in childbed her child also dyed, because she was stubborne, and would not submitt to the paines, but she was after filled wth dredful horror of conscience and dyed under them, but I hope und^r some tokens of mercy

Month 4^t About the 1^t of this month Mary the maid serva^t of Mr Prichard was buryed. She was a godly maide & was to have joyned to the Church, but the Lord pvented her & tooke her to Heaven.

The last of this month John Bell, the son of Thom: Bell y^t was baptized about 2 month before, dyed.

Month 6 day: Bridget Denison, the wife of George Denison & a godly young woman dyed of a feaver & consumption.

Month 8 day 26. Goodman Stone, an old Kentish man dyed, he was not of the Church, yet on his sick bed some had some hopes of him.

Month 10 day 27. M^{ris} Dorothy Dudly dyed of the wind collik, a godly Christian woman & left a religeous sav̄ behind her.

day 30. Thomas Pig dyed of a dropsy, a godly Christian man. He had a fall & a bruise on his back, w^h hurt his kidneys & not carefully cured they utterly wasted away & many oth^r of his intrals.

Month 1 day 8. Elizabeth Pepper, the child lately baptized, dyed.

(Opposite entry of Baptism under date of Month 1. day 3.)

1644

Mrs Cuddington, who was not of the church, an ancient woman, she dyed of an Apoplexie.

Month 7 day 7. John Dennison the child of Edward Denison.

Month 9 day 4.   John Grave, a godly broth^r of the church, he tooke a deepe cold, w^h sweld his head wth rhume & o͞vcame his heart.

day 15.   Thomas Ruggles a godly broth^s, he dyed of a Consumption.

These two brake the knot first of the Nazing Christians. I meane they first dyed of all those Christians y^t came fr͞o y^t towne in England.

day 18.   Laurence Whittamore, an ancient Christian of 80 years of aige.

Month 11   Peter Leavins, one of the two twins dyed. (Baptized Month 7 day 15, 1644)

aboute the 24 day.   Old Mother Grave; died, she was about 80 years of aige.   —

1645

A girle, the child of broth^r Griggs of abo^{te} 12 years old dyed of a kahexie

Month 10 day 2.   Dorothy Jocelin, a maide servant of Mr Dudly, she was exceeding lively spirited in bitter paines & left a good savor thereby, she was first taken wth an apoplectical sleeping & at the resolution of it it fell upon her lungs w^h w^r weake afore, wth a paine like a plurisy.

day 5.   John Grave a godly young man, the eldest so͞ne of him who dyed the yeare afore, he dyed of an ulcer in his lunges.

day the 7   How, the wife of Abraham How, a godly woman, he dyed of a stoping in her lungs.

Joseph Weld the infant of Joseph Weld bap tized the su͞mer afore.

day 8   w^h was the Sab. Mr Henry Dingham dyed in the same ma͞ner as Dorothy Jocelin did. This was the most sad mortal weeke, y^t evei Roxbury saw, to have 5 dy in one week, & many more ly sick in the towne.

day 24   Joseph Johnson, baptized two months afore, dyed.

Month 11 day 7.   Old Moth^r Roberts, a Welch woman, she had lived about 9 years in this country & dyed the hundred and third yeare of her aige, she was above 90 years ould w^n she left her native country.

Month 12 day 2.   George Holmes a godly broth^r dyed of a fea͞v.

day 3.   Old Mother Dennison dyed.

day 9.   Hannah Wilson deliv͞erd of a dead borne child.

1646

Month 1 day 28. Bro. Lambe dyed of a Calenture, by a great could.

Bro. Brewer dyed of an Ulcer in his longes w^h p̄ced through into his bowels & emptyed thith^r to his great swelling & torment.

A lit [sic] litle infant also a twinn of Job Tilers dyed.

Month 3 day 7. Obadiah Gore a child of 10 years old dyed of a Consumption wth as sweete & gracious exp^{r}essions of faith as ev̄ we have heard.

day 23. Bro. Griggs who lay in a long affliction of sicknesse & shined like gold in it, greatly glorifying God & magnifying his grace in Christ.

Month 4 day 9. John Scarbrough slaine by charging a great gunn.

day 16 John Parke, the soñe of Williā Park not a yeare old.

Month 6 day 6. Ezbon, an Indian, hopefully godly, haveing lived 10 yeare among the English, could read, desired to serve God &^{c} dyed

day 7. Nan, Mr Weld's captive Indian dyed, who also was hopeful.

Month 7 day 29. Deborah Holmes dyed, a child not a yeare old.

Month 8 day 6. Dennison soñn of Edward Denison dyed of convulsions : of 17 [weks]

day 7. Mr Joseph Weld dyed of a Cancer in his tongue & jawes.

day 20. Egleden, daughter in law to Joseph Patchen she was about 10 y. old, she dyed of a paine first in her head, then in her back.

Month 9 Gorton, the daughter of John Gorton, dyed.

1647

Month 2 day 13. A new borne child of Christopher Peake dyed.

Month 6 day 2. Hannah Gookins, this infant, lately baptized, was buryed.

Month 8 day 7. Goodwife Turner dyed in child bed, a godly young woman, though not yet admitted, yet should had not her travail p^{r}vented.

Month 9. About the 1st day. A still borne child of Rich Wooddy's.

day 15. John Levens an ancient gōdy christian, dyed of a dead palsie.

1648

Month 3^d day 25. Hannah Hanshet a child dyed of windy convulsions.

30 Joseph Goard a young child dyed of the same disease.

Month 4 day 3.   Hannah Seaver, daughter of Robert Seaver.

Month 11.   23.   Sarah Davis bro. Morel's daughter dyed, by ocasion of unheedfull taking cold upon an abortion.

1649.

Month 2 day 30.   Joshua Watson of 11 years old suddenly dyed of the belly ake.

Month 3 day 10.   John Mekins, 3 months afore baptized, now dyed.

2 infants borne & buryd un-⎫ Mʳ Prichard's
baptized, one.   ⎭   Bro. Peake.

Jeremiah ⎫ Dennison, sonns of Edward Deni-
Joseph   ⎭   son, dyed.   in one weeke

Also Joseph Patchin's child.

Month 6 day 2.   Abraham Morgan, a child not a yeare old.

      day 13.   John Stonhard a midle aged man or litle more.

      day 14.   Deborah Park daughter of Williā Park.

      day 28   Abigal Gardner, daughter of Thom: Gardner. died of a cough & feav̄.

Month 7 day 6.   Joseph Tory, a young child, of the cough & could.

        7   Alcock, a young child of Mʳ Alcock.

        9.   Thomas Weld a youth of about 17 y. old: sonne of Joseph Weld.

Month 8ᵗ day 21.   Joseph Weld, the infant of John Weld, a litle afore baptized, now dyed.

Month 9ᵗ day 2.   Hannah Hanshet, newly baptized, died of the cough & could.

      day 3.   Sister Bowles dyed of the small pox.

      day 8.   Sister Heli dyed in childbed wᵗʰ othʳ diseases wʰ cause her child to dy & was taken frō her by peeches.

Month 10   About the 16 day an infant of a sojoūrner at sister Lamb's dyed of the small pox.

Thankfull Perepoint the child of John Perepoint.

1650

Moneth yᵉ 3ᵈ day 23.   John Wooddie, a christian & godly brother dyed of yᵉ small pox.

Moneth 4ᵗʰ day 26.   Thomas Curtis, the son of William Curtis, dyed of a long & tedious Consumption.

Moneth 5ᵗʰ day 6.   Phebe Jones dyed of a scald.

Month , 6 day 16.   Anne Paison yᵉ daughter of Edw. Paison dyed.

      day 25.   Widdow Morrick dyed.

Month 7 day 13.   Thomas Wooddie son of Richard Wooddy dyed.

Moneth 9 day 20   This same child dyed [opposite entry of Baptism, Moneth 9 day 17, of   Morgan daughter of James Morgan.

Moneth 11 day 21. Our Sister Meakings wife to broth' Meakings the yonger, dyed in child bed. Shee was a gratious woman & left a good savour behind her.

The same day also dyed y.ᵉ daughter of Sister Culver newly borne.

Month 12 day 3. Sister Meakings the aged woman, mother to brother Meakings.

1651

Moneth 2ᵈ day 28. A servant to brother Porter dyed.
Moneth 4ᵗʰ day 28. Mʳ Goore's twins buryed. unbaptized.
day 18. Sister Mayes dyed, a very gratious and savoury christian.
Moneth 5ᵗʰ day 28. A yong child of brother Perepoint unbaptized.
Moneth 9 day 27. John Roberts dyed of a dropsy.
day 29. The wife of Neighbor Hawly dyed.
Moneth 11 day 2. An infant of Isaac Heath junior unbaptised.

1652

Moneth 3ᵈ day 29. William Heath an able godly & faithful brother dyed.
Moneth 5 day 10. Mary Baker, daughter to brother Baker.
Month 9 day 2ᵈ A youth servant to brother Hely.
day 3. Isaac Bowles, son of John Bowles. dyed.

1653.

Moneth 4 f 1. Deacon Parkes, his twins a son & daughter buryed.
An infant of Daniel Weld's still borne.
Moneth 5 day 3. Mary Griggs, wife to Joseph Grigs, daughter to brother Crafts, dyed.
day 22. Samuel Danforth sonn to Samuel Danforth dyed & buryed yᵉ day following.
day 31. being yᵉ Lds day, at night Thomas Dudley Esqʳ dyed & was buryed on yᵉ 6ᵗʰ day following.
Moneth 6 day 24. Peter Gardiner sonn of Tho. Gardiner buryed.
day 26. Samuel Weld sonn to Thomas Weld buryed.
Moneth 7 day 3. Obadiah Gore sonne to Mʳ John Gore buryed.
Moneth 11 day 17. Brother Potter.
day 25. Mʳ William Denyson.
Moneth 12 day 3. Hanna Seaver, the child of oʳ brother Robert Seaver.

1654

Moneth 2ᵈ day 2ᵈ John Hanchet, sonn to brother Hanchet, dyed
[Moneth 5 day 30. Gorton daughter to John Gorton baptized] [Opposite this entry is ' Within a short space it dyed.']

Moneth 7 day 22.   Hanna Glover aforesayd dyed [Opposite rec-
                   ord of baptism M? 7 day 3]
            29   Susana Pason daughter of Edwd Pason.
[Moneth 10 day 3.   Benjamin Goare sonne to broth^r Goare bap-
                   tized]   [Opposite this entry is 'This child
                   dyed within a short space after."]

1654 | 5

Moneth 1 day 10.   Elizabeth Williams, daughter to Sam! Williãs
                   buryed.
       day 24.   Goodwife Birchard.

1655

Moneth 4 day 9.   Margery Johnson, the wife of John Johnson.
       day 26.   Hanna Parke, daughter to Deacon Parke.
Moneth 5 day 7.   Elisabeth Bowles, daughter to Elder Heath.
       day 4.   Elizabeth Mattock, daughter to bro. Mattock.
Moneth 9 day 19.   Aaron Eliot, sonn to Mr Eliot dyed.

1656

Moneth 2^d day 5.   Anna Woodee wife to Rich Woody Senior.
Moneth 5 day 14.   William Park, son of Williã Park dyed
                   & was buryed ye day following. [Oppo-
                   site record of baptism M? 8 day 5 of
                   Samuel Griggs sonne of Joseph Griggs is
                   "This child dyed the next January fol-
                   lowing "]

1657

Moneth 4 day 2.   Mr John Gore dyed & was buryed the foll-
                   lowing day.
       day 9.   Sister   Seaver ye wife of Robert Seaver.
Moneth 6 day 9.   An infant of John Pierpoint dyed unbaptised.
Moneth 8 day 22.   Philip Eliot one of ye Deacons of this Church
                   dyed.

1658

Moneth 3 day 4.   Elisabeth Davis wife to Will. Davis.
Moneth 7 day 14.   John Dane dyed.
       day 15.   John Ruggles, Sergeant, dyed.
Moneth 8 day 7.   O^r aged Sister Gardiner was buryed.
Moneth 9 day 12.   Hanna Paul ye daughter of o^r Sister Woodee
                   buryed.
Moneth 10 day 7.   Richard Woodie Senior.
Moneth 1 day 15.   Anne Brewer.

1659

Moneth 7 day 30.   John Johnson, Surveyor Generall of all y^e
                   armes, dyed & was buried ye day following.

Moneth 10 day 5. Philip, sonne of Philip Curtis, was buryed.

day 5. Sarah Danforth dyed & was buryed yᵉ day following.

day 7. Mary Danforth dyed in yᵉ faith & was buryed upon yᵉ 9ᵗʰ day of yᵉ moneth.

day 15. Elisabeth Danforth dyed & was buryed yᵉ day followingᵉ.

day 15. Our aged Sister Heath yᵉ widdow of Will. Heath was buryed.

1660

Moneth 8 day 5. Hanna yᵉ daughter of Christopher Peake buryed.

Moneth 10 day 4. Benjamin, son to Joseph Wise, was buried.

Moneth 11 day 9. Joseph, son to Peleg Heath.

day 21. Mʳ Isaac Heath, Ruling Elder in this Church, dyed & was buryed on yᵉ 23 day.

Moneth 12 day 6. Martha, daughter to Samuel Williams.

day 8. Samuel, son to Tobias Davis.

day 20. Sarah, daughter to Peter Gardiner.

Moneth 1 day 7. Isaac son to Isaac Williams.

day 11. An infant of Daniel Brewer, still born.

1661

Moneth 9 A little infant of Will. Cheany jun: unbaptized.

day 13. Abraham Morrell died, being a hopefull young man about 21 yeares old.

Moneth 10 day 1. The wife of Goodman Gibson of Cambridge.

day 20. John Johnson, son to Capt. Johnson.

21. Isaac Morell, an aged brother.

1662

Moneth 4. Abraham Morrell of Salisbury fell sick in this town & dyed & was buryed upon yᵉ 20ᵗʰ of 4ᵐ.

Mayes to John Mayes jun.

Moneth 10 An infant of Benjamin Childe unbaptized.

Moneth 11 day 6ᵗʰ Widdow Homes was buryed.

1663

Moneth 3 day 4. John, son of Deacon Parke.

Moneth 4ᵗʰ day 2. A still born infant of Edward Denison.

day 18. Deborah, daughter to Edwᵈ Denison.

day 26. Daniel, son to Mʳ Thomas Welde.

Moneth 5ᵗʰ day 21. An infant of John Griggs unbaptized.

1663

Moneth 8 day 6.   John Ruggles Sen.
          day 23.   Jonathan, sonne to Robert Pierpont.
Moneth 9 day 7.   Robert Gamlin.

1664

Moneth 2 day 30.   Susanna, wife to John Polly.
Moneth 3 day 1.   Benjamin, son to Joseph Wise.
Moneth 4 day 12.   An infant of Edw.ᵈ Devotion.
Moneth 5 day 4.   An infant of Henry Bowin.
Moneth 9 day 1.   M.ʳ Samuel Eliot.
          day 12.   Sarah, daughter to Samuel Ruggles.
Moneth 11 day 10. Esther, daughter to John Weld buried.
          day 14.   Elisabeth Heath, Widdow of Elder Heath.
Moneth 12 day 6.   Joseph Ruggles, son to Samuel Ruggles.
          day 2.   Thomas Grocer, a stranger.

1665

Moneth 5 day 10.   John, son to Jonathan Peak.
Moneth 7 day .   Margaret, daughter to Henry Bowin.
Moneth 9 day 29.   M.ʳˢ Sarah Alcocke yᵉ wife of M.ʳ John
                   Alcocke, aged 44.
Moneth 11 day 11. An infant of John Polly unbaptized.
Moneth 12 day 3.   Robt. Prentice.

1666

Moneth 3 day 23.   Christopher Peak.
Moneth 5 day 22.   M.ʳ Daniel Weld aged 80, dyed and was buryeu
                   day 23.
          day 24.   Elizabeth Acrees, wᶜʰ was newly baptized.
Moneth 6 day 30.   Mary, wife to John Polly, dyed of yᵉ small
                   pox.
Moneth 8 day 25.   Sarah, yᵉ wife of John Leavins.
Moneth 10 day 19. Arthur Garee, having been distracted 18
                   weeks.
          day 29.   Rob.ᵗ Hawes aged about 84.
Moneth 11 day 7.   Jonathan Pason who dyed of yᵉ small pox.
Moneth 12 day 28. Rich.ᵈ Griffin.

1667

Moneth 1 day 29.   M.ʳ John Alcock Physician. He dyed at
                 Boston on yᵉ 27ᵗʰ day, but was brought
                 home and buried by his wife on yᵉ 29ᵗʰ
                 day. aged 40.
Moneth 2.ᵈ day 27. Deborah, daughter to Edw.ᵈ Denison.
Moneth 3.ᵈ day 13.   Smith, yᵉ wife of Francis Smith, aged
                 about 84.
Moneth 4.ᵗʰ day 8. John Remington.
Moneth 5 day 2.   William Cheany sen.

Moneth 9 day 28.   Rebecca, the wife of John Craft, who died
                            in child bed, not being able to be delivered.
Moneth 11 day 6.   An infant of Isaac Heath unbaptized.
Moneth 12 day 17.   An infant of Tho. Foster stillborn.
         day 24.   Abigail, daughter to John Welde.
                  Alice wife of William Davis who dyed in
                      child birth undelivered.

1668

Moneth 1 day 27.   Joanna, daughter to Edward Pason.
Moneth 2 day 28.   Edward Denison.
Moneth 3 day 14.   Mary Heath daughter to Isaac Heath
         day 30.   Jonathan, son to William Lyons.
. Moneth 4 day 9.   Elizabeth, daughter to John Hanchet.
Moneth 7 day 30.   Tatman, ye wife of John Tatman.
Moneth 8 day 1.   Joseph, son to John Chandler.
           3.   An infant of Samuel Ruggles newly born.
Moneth 9 day 20.   Joseph Buckmaster.
Moneth 11 day 2^d Thomas, son to Thomas Swan.
         day 27.   Edward Bughey, aged (as is said) above 80.
Moneth 12 day 1.   Silence, daughter to Henry Stevens.

1669

Moneth 1 day 17.   M$^{rs.}$ Anne Palsgrave, aged (as is said) 75.
Moneth 3 day 26.   Mary, daughter to John White, a maid of
                      about 17 yeares of age.
Moneth 7 day 2^d Elizabeth, wife to Edward Riggs.
         day 20.   Rebecca, daughter to Moses Craft.
         day 21.   Ezra, son to Robert Pierpoint.
         day 25.   Hanna, daughter to James Clark.
Moneth 8 day 24.   Day, daughter to   Day of Ded-
                  ham, servant to Saml Ruggles.
         day 26.   Hanna, wife to Samuel Ruggles.
Moneth 9 day 7.   Hanna, daughter to Samuel Ruggles.
         day 16.   Sarah, daughter to Samuel Ruggles.
Moneth 10 day 7.   Mary, wife to Edmund Chamberlain of
                  Chelmsford.   She died at Samuel Ruggles
                  house.
         day 18.   wife to Robert Seaver.
Moneth 11 day 16.   Benjamin, son to Robt Pepper.
Moneth 1 day 9.   Hanna, daughter to John Gorton.
         day 18.   John, son to Robt Pepper.

1670

Moneth 2 day 28.   John May senior aged about 80.
Moneth 3 day 5.   Sarah May, widow of John May.
Moneth 8 day 28   John Tatman.
Moneth 11 day 30.   Hanna, daughter to Nath. Garee was buried
Moneth 1 day 22.   Margaret, daughter to John Bridge.

.1671

Moneth 3 day 1.	John Parmenter aged 83 sometime Deacon at Sudbury.
Moneth 7 day 11.	John May aged about 40 who was blind seʋall moneths.
Moneth 8 day 23.	Abigail Gore, daughter to Mʳ John Gore.'
Moneth 9 day 18.	Peleg Heath who had a dangerous cutt on his knee & lay under yᵉ chirurgion's hand 13 weeks.

Also a litle infant of Nath. Homes born a cripple.

Moneth 10 day 12. John Cheanie who was found dead in our River. It was apprehended by yᵉ Jury that he slip. in accidentally as he was catching of Eeles.

Moneth 11 day 5. John Watson Sen.
Moneth 12 day . Gideon, son to Samuel May.
Moneth 1 day 5. Edward Riggs.

1672

Moneth 2ᵈ day 14. Thomas, son to Samuel Danforth who died the day before about noon.
Moneth 3ᵈ day 4. Moses, son to Moses Craft.
Moneth 4 day 15. Abraham Newel aged 91.
Moneth 5 day 19. George, son to Thomas Bacon, 3 yeares old
Moneth 6 day 7. Ralph Smith aged 95.
day 14. Joseph, son to Jonathan Peak.
Moneth 8 day 1. Francis Garee widow of Arthur Garee.
day 3. Benjamin, sonn to John Mayo.
day 18.   to John Mayo.
day 26. Elizabeth yᵉ daughter of Samuel Danforth, died of a putrid fever & was buried on yᵉ 28 day of 8ber.
Moneth 9 day 12. Sarah Sutton yᵉ wife of Richᵈ Sutton.
Moneth 10 day 9. William Curtis aged 80.
Moneth 11 day 9. Sarah, widow of Isaac Morrel, aged 72.

1673

Moneth 1 day 26. Alice Craft, aged 73.
day 27. Sarah Curtis, aged about 73.
Moneth 6 day 3ᵈ John, son to Abraham Newel.
day 23. Daniel Holdbrook, who was wounded 2 dayes before by the knife in his pocket, as he fell down, going oʋr a wall.
Moneth 8 day 4. A still born infant of Thoˢ Bacon.
day 6. Elizabeth Cartwright, Sister to Edwᵈ Morrice.
day 31. Elisabeth, daughter to Samuel Danforth. She died on yᵉ 30ᵗʰ day being a fortnight old, on the 5ᵗʰ day of yᵉ week about 3 in yᵉ afternoon.

Moneth 9 day 28. Ruth, daughter to John Griggs.
Moneth 11 day 27. Samuel Finch.
Moneth 12 day 4. Mary, daughter to John Harris.
          day 10. Joseph, son to Benjamin Childe.
Moneth 1 day 5? Abigail, daughter to Samuel Gore.

1674

Moneth 2 day 18. Sarah, daughter to Nathaniel Seaver.
Moneth 4 day 27. Margaret, daughter to John Welde, in the 17 year of her age.
Moneth 5 day 27. Elisabeth Williams aged 80 yeares, wife of Robert Williams.
Moneth 6 day 20. John Bridge, died of ye Winde Collick and was buried the day following. His body was opened. he had sundry small holes in his stomak & bowels, & one hole in his stomak y^t a man's fist might passe through, wch is thought was rent wth vyolent straining to vomit, the night before he dyed, for the watchers observed y^t something seemed to rend wthin him and he saide of it I am a dead man.
Moneth 8 day 19. Ebenezer, son to William Hopkins.
          day 31. Peter, son to Peter Gardiner. He died of a Consumption.
Moneth 9 day 19. Our R^d Pastor Mr Samuel Danforth sweetly rested from his labours, being sick of a putrid Fever 7 days, Who was interd ye 23 day of ye same moneth aged about 48 years
Month 10 day 6. Sister Ruggles wife to John Ruggles senior dyed. She was a meek & a godly christian, much lamented by her neighbors, her feav̄ & ague turned to a calenture, at last, disordered her head, but her very disorders w^r holy & sanctified & so she finished, buryed the 7th day of y^i month.
          day 9. Ebenezer, the infant of Isack Cardis, he dyed before y^{ei} had an oportunity to baptiz him.
          day 10. Joseph son to Widdow Heath, the relict of Peleg Heath. The child dyed of a great stoping at his stomach.
          day 18. I visited James Clark who had lived many years un̄d a bleeding of his lungs. I com̄ended him to God in prayre & about an hour after he dyed & buryed this 19^t day.
Month 12 day 14. Old Moth^r Roote who was Tho. Ruggles widdow afore. She lived not only till past use, but till more tedious y^n a child. She was in her 89 yeare.

1675

Month	3	day 16.	Rebecca, wife to John Curtis, dyed of hydropycal humors wch ocasioned the more speedy buryal of her, on the Sabath evening.

Month   3   day 16.   Rebecca, wife to John Curtis, dyed of hydropycal humors wch ocasioned the more speedy buryal of her, on the Sabath evening.

Month   4^t   day 11.   Sister Gardner, wife of Peter Gardner, was buryed.   She died in the Lord sweetly.

Month   5^t   23 day.   the wife of   Hadlock was buryed.

24 day.   The new borne infant of Samuel Gore was buryed.

John Druse dyed in the warrs & was there buryed. he acquited himselfe valiantly.

26 day.   Thomas Newel son of Abrā Newel he dyed suddainly

& Sarah a litle child of Sam. Dunkan.

Month   7   day 24.   Margret Corban

day 28.   Pete Swan.

Month   8   day 6.   Dorothy Swan, she exp^{re}ssed signes of faith above ō measure of such an infant being but 2 years and half old.

Here is a great empty space w^rin we had no buryals at home but we had many slaine in the warr, no towne for bigness lost more, if any towne so many.

1678

Month   9   day 17.   Jeremiah Wise, dyed of the pox.

day 30.   Elizabeth, infant of Jabesh Tatman dyed of the pox.

Month   10   day 13.   Stevens, dyed of the pox.

day 17.   Old Mother Wright dyed of old age, being neere an hundred years old.

day 18.   Williā Dàvis dyed of the pox at Boston, buryed in o^r burying place.

day 25.   Abrahā Nowell a youth of 18 years, of the pox.

day 26.   John Holbrook of the pox.

Woodward

day 30.   Jakob Newel, dyed of the pox, & left a poore weak familie.

Mon   11.   day 3.   Dorothy, daughter of Widdow Heath, dyed of the pox.

day 5.   Hannah, wife of Williā Hopkins, dyed of the pox.

An Indian boy of Holbrook's dyed of the pox

day 30.   Nathaniel Gary dyed of the pox & after his death his breast full of blew spots

Mon   12.   day 11.   A new borne infant of Robert Peirdoint dyed by falling out of lap of a girle y^t had it & slep, so leting it fall.

day 5.   Mary the daughter Jakob Newel dyed ō Pox.
day 8.   Theoda Willias ⎱ both dyed of the pox
         Mary Hopkins ⎰ buryed yⁱ day.
day 14. Marget, a child of Joseph Weld, dyed of the
         the pox.
day 17. Elizabeth, the wife of Joseph Weld, dyed of
         the pox.
day 18. John Goard, a young man, dyed of the pox.
day 21. Dorcas, infant of Widdow Nath. Gary, of the
         pox.
day 28. Phebe, the wife of Richard Goard, of the pox.

1679

Month 1 day 8.   Jonathan Winchester, dyed of a feav̄.
                 Deborah, daughter of Widdow Gary, dyed of
                 the pox.
      day 10.   John, infant of Sam. Gore.
      day 20.   Hanah Goss the infant last baptized.
Mon   2 day 10. Samuel, son of Toby Davis dyed of the pox.
      day 18.   Samuel, son of Isack Curtis, scaldd in wort &
                 dyed. An Indian girl of Mᵣ Dudly, neer
                 well of ō pox, fell a bleeding & bled to death.
Mont 4 day 30. Sister Scarbrow, she dyed of a consumption.
Mon   5 day 4.   Mary, the daughter of Caleb Lamb, she dyed
                 of the pox. the eyes of the child wᵣ forced
                 out of the head by the voleñce of the
                 disease.
      day 31.   An infant new born of John Scots. buryed.
M.   6.   An infant new born of Jabesh Totman, buryed.
M.   8. d. 27. Old John Moore, of 99 yeares old.
M.   11. d. 12. Mehitabel, daughter of Daniel Weld.
M.   12. d. 14. Benjamin, son of John Lyon, an infant lately
                 baptized, was buryed.

1680

M. 1. day 4.   A new born infant of   Wilson, buryed.
   day 19.   A new borne twin of Joseph Davis.
M. 2. day 4.   An Stebbin, wife of John Stebbin, buryed.
   day 17.   A new borne infant of Samuel Williams.
   day 23.   The infant of John Weld junioᵣ dyed.
M. 3. day 27.   A still borne infant of John Baker.
M. 5. day 29.   John, the infant of John Howard, was buryed
M. 6. day 18.   John, the infant of Mᵣ Dudley, buryed.
M. 7. day 1.   Old Davy Richards buryed.
   24.   Deare Bro. Bowles was buried, he hath bene
                 Elder above 5 yeare.
                 An infant of Sam. Gore ō same day buryed.
M. 8. day 8.   Sister Bishop, a godly prudent women buryed.
                 Also a new borne infant of Benjamin Gamlin
M. 11. day 15. A new borne infant of John Scot
   day 30.   Robert, the infant of Steven Williams.

1681

M.	3. day 20.	A young infant of Dorman Marcene an Irishman living at Muddy River, the child not baptized.
M.	5.	Father Portis of Boston dyed at his daughter Weld's in o.^r towne. y.^t day buryed.
M.	6. day 7.	Mary the infant of Jabesh Totman buryed.
M.	7. day 7.	A new born infant of John Howard's, buryed before it was baptized.
M.	8. day 17.	A new born infant of John Browne, dyed before it was baptized.
M.	9. day 17.	A new born infant of Isaak Heath junio.^r
M.	10. day 4.	Elizabeth, wife of Tho. Bishop buryed.
	day 7.	John Stebbin buryed.
	day 15.	Caleb Gardner son of Tho. Gardner, a v̄y hopefull youth.
M.	11. day 2.	Aged Sister Gamlin buryed.
	day 30.	Abigail, an infant of Andrew Gardner.

1682

M.	1. d. 10.	A new borne infant of Dan. Weld.
	d. 15.	The mother of y.^t infant dyed. the wife of Daniel Weld.
M.	7. d. 15.	Mahitabel daughter·of Jabesh Totman buried.
M.	8. d. 13.	Isaak, son of Isaak Curtis dyed of a flux.
	d. 18.	Margret, daughter of Tho. Bacon.
	d. 20.	Deborah Devotion buryed y.ⁱ day.
	d. 29.	An untimely borne infant of Joshuah Gadners.
	d. 30.	Isack Davis of a flux.
M.	10. d. 11.	Joen Peirpoint senior.
M.	11. d. 8.	A new borne infant of Mr Dudly's
	d. 9.	Nicolas Grace, a poore creature.
	d. 10.	A new born infant to Joseph Lyon.
	d. 16.	Moth.^r Newell neere 100 y. old.
	d. 19.	Mr Tho. Weld dyed of feav.
M.	12. d. 1.	Mary, the infant of Isaak Curtis.
	2.	Edward the 2.^d son of Mr Dudly.

1683.

M.	1. d. 17.	Old Mother Parmiter, a blessed Saint.
M.	2. d. 4.	A new born infant of Williā Lyon.
M.	3. d. 8.	Old Hugh Thomas who died in o Lord.
	d. 24.	Mary, ō infant of Joshua Seaver.
	d. 29.	A still borne infant of Sam. Williās Senio.^r
M.	4. d. 6.	Robert Seaver an aged Christian, buryed.
	d. 10.	Elizabeth ō infant of Joshua Lambe.
	d. 11.	Joseph ō infant of Caleb Lambe.
M.	6. d. 15.	Old Sister Johnson who dyed suddenly.
M.	4. d. 1.	Hannah, wife of James Clark.
	d. 21.	A still borne infant of John Gravner, it dyed in the birth.

d. 20. Blind Fath.' Goard buryed.
d. 25. Old mother Thomas buryed.
Goodwife Hankins of Boston.
M. 8. d. 5. An, the infant of Edward Dorr.
7. Hannah, infant of John Weld junio.'
10. Old Sister Finch
29. An infant, new borne of Joseph White.

1683.

M. 9. d. 3. Williā Meade an aged Christian, buryed.
d. 9. Old Sister Meade, his wife, was buryed.
d. 10. Benjamin Frizal, an hopefull youth, buryed.
d. 17. John, the infant of John Scot.
d. 21. Abraham How Senio.'
M. 10. d. 4. John, ō infant of John Weld junio.
d. 7. Edward ō infant of Edward Dor.
d. Jonathan Lyon, son of Tho. Lyon.
d. 22. William Davis, a slāv buryed.
d. 23. Edward Bridg, an aged broth.'
M. 11. d. 7. Old Sister Pepper a X^{ian} woman.
A new borne infant of Joh Davis senio.' was buryed wth Sister Pepp. in ō same grave.
d. 11. The wife of Joseph Grigs was buryed.
d. 15. The godly wife of John Davis senio.'
Abrāha How junior.
d. 30. Old blind godly fath.' Baker buryed.
M. 12. d. 23. Old John Hanshet buryed.

1684

M. 1. d. 12. Isaak White an hopefull son of John White junio.'
M. 2. d. 8. John, ō infant of Caleb Phillips.
M. 3. d. 11. John Crafts junior was drowned, about ō. oyster banks, y^1 day buryed.
M. 4. d. 10. Sister Polly wife of John Polly.
M. 5. d. 8. Robert Pepper, an old X^{istian} buryed.
d. 18. Ruth Hiuningway buryed
M. 7. d. 14. Joseph Wise buryed.
M. 10. d. 23. Isaak Heath junio^r
d. 28. A new born infant of Benj. Gamlin.
M. 11. d. 10. An infant of Edward Dor new born.
Widdow Ainsworth.
d. 31. John Parker of Muddy River.
M. 12. d. 7. An infant of Nath. San ger.

1685

M. 1. d. 10. A new born infant of John Searle.
M. 2. d. 2. Rebekkah Mayo died of a vomiting.
M. 4. d. 8. An infant of Josh. Lamb wch dyed by y^m in ō night.
M. 5. d. 29. An infant of Caleb Seaver.
M. 6. d. 6. Old Widdow Baker.

M. 7. d.   3.   John Crafts.
  d. 10.   Thomas Woodward buryed.
  d. 23.   Father Devotion buried.
M. 8. d. 29.   John, ō infant of John Mayes.
M. 9. d   7.   John ō infant of Mr John Page a stranger.
M. 11 d.   3.   An infant of Jakob Pepper.
M. 12. d.   3.   Old Widdow Hinningway buryed.

1686

M. 3. d. 16.   Phillip Tory was buryed.
  d. 10.   Abram Newels wife dyed, both mother & child
     bured together.
M. 4. d. 12.   An infant, grandchild of John Chandler.
M. 5. d.   3.   Aged Sist. Cheny buryed.
  d. 11.   Hannah, wife of Ralph Bradhurst.
  d. 20.   An infant of John Mayo junior.
M. 6. d.   1.   John Weld junior.
  d.   4.   Old Widdow Brand.
  d.   8.   A new born infant of Samuel Weld.
  d.   8.   A still born infant of Joshua Gardner.
M. 7. d.   2.   An infant of Steven Williams.
  d.   4.   Aged Widdow Bowles.
  d.   7.   An infant of Sam. Scarbro.
  d. 22.   Jabez Buckmaster buryed.
" 8. d.   6.   Hannah Corbin buryed.
  d. 15.   Richard Chik buryed.
M. 9. d. 27.   A still borne infant of   Parker's
M. 11. d. 10.   An infant o Joseph Bugby.
M. 12. d.   3.   An infant of Andrew Gardner.
  d.   5.   An infant of John Mayo.

1687.

M. 3. d.   5.   Ruggles wife of Jo. Ruggles senior
  d. 23.   Sarah, wife of John Bowles.
     Sarah infant of John Bowles.
  d. 24.   An infant of Jakob Pepper.
M. 5. d. 11.   An infant of Daniel Mashcraft
  d. 25.   John, infant of Jo. Mason.
  d. 31.   An infant of Nathaniel Page.
M. 6. d.   5.   An infant of Ben'min Gamlin.
  d. 14.   Pete an Indian.
  d. 27.   John, the infant of John Holbrook.
  day 20.   An infant of Thomas Cheny.
M. 7. d. 21.   An infant of Thom. Cheny a trader.
M. 9. d.   6.   Old Sister Gardner.
M. 11 or 12.   Hañab the wife of Mason.
M. 12 d.   8.   Doctor Thomas Swan.
  d. 11.   Sarah, child of Joseph Griffin.
  d. 22.   An infant of John Ruggls medius.
     An infant of Uriah Clark.
M 12.   Latter end,   An infant of Jacob Parker.
  Item.   An infant of John Heminway.

1688

March	d.	Nathaniel, the son of Caleb Seaver buried.
Apr.	d. 5.	John Park buried.
	29.	John Maio Senr buried.
Jun.	d. 8.	Mary Marscraft was buried.
July	10.	An infant of John Maio buried.

REV. JOHN ELIOT'S RECORDS OF THE FIRST CHURCH IN ROXBURY, MASS.

[Note. — The entries now printed commence on page 245 of the record book. The reader is advised to consult the admirable notes to these records, in the New England Historical and Genealogical Register in 1879 and 1880. — W. H. W.]

1642 m 4 d 12   Thos Wilson who had been excomvn'd received again into the Church & recommd to Chh at Hampton
  Isaak Johnson who had been admoinshed, left to a future time.
1643 mo 8.   Goodwife Webb reconciled to the Chh.
1643, month 8 day 29.   Robert Potter was excomvnicate, his sins wr first in the tims of mris Hutchinson, wn divers of or Church wr seduced to familesme & scizme, he was of theire side & company, & so fild wth them as yt he departed to the Ila'd rathr then would forsake them, & being there he refused to heare the church who had lovingly sent after him : secondly for that he was now tossed wth othr winds of new doctrine forsakeing the Ilaud & joyn-ing wth Gorton & yt not only in his heresys but also in his bereti-call blaspheamous & rep'chfull writings and publikly owned them in Court, & maide himselfe guilty of all those wicked ways :
  There happened (by Gods p'vidence) a dreadful example of God's judgment this yeare vpon one Willia Frankling who belonged to Boston towne, & take Mr Ting his farme above muddy river be-longing to Boston ; But he spent his sab: at or towne being neerer ; & after a season desired to joyne to or church : & had app'bation so to doe, & was received.
  But Satan p'sently did enter into him & having a boy whom he had bought some years time & p'ving sick & naughty ; alter he was joyned to the church he grew more passionate, crnel & feirce against him, though he had bene sharpe afore, yet vnknowne or vndisposed to vs, but now he grew out-raigeous, so yt by sundry cruel strips & othr kind of ill vseage the boy dyed vnder his rigor-ous hand, and yt (by a strange p'vidence of God & his own folly) at Boston, as if God ment to bring him on the stage for an example to all oth's for wch sin that day month yt he was admitted he was excomunicated & though much paines were taken to have brought him to repentance & reconciliation to the church, yet all in vaine he p'testing p'tly to deny & p'tly to mine his cruel actions towards the boy so yt in yt estate he was executed at Boston as publick records will show.

1644. A strange p'vidence of God fell out at Boston where a
peece of Iron in a dung cart, one was smote into the head & brains
of the daughter of Jakob Eliot deakon of the Church & brought
forth some of the braines ; and after more of the braines came forth,
& yet the Lord cured the child, the braines lying next the skin in
that place.

Soon after that one william Curtis of Roxbury was cast off fro^m
a cart of loggs vuto the ground wth such violence, y^t his head & one
side of his face were bruised, blood gushed out of his care, his braine
was shaken, he senseless divers days, yet by degres thro' Gods
mercy he recovered his senses, yet his cheeke drawne awry & p'alitik,
but in a quarter of a yeare, he was pretty well recovered, to the
wonder of all men.

1645. Toward the end of the first month call'd march ; there
happened (by Gods p'vidence) a very dreadfull fire in Roxbury
streete ; none knoweth how it was kindled, but being a feirce wind,
it suddenly p'vailed. And in this mans house was a good p't of
the Countrys magazine of powder of 17 or 18 barrels ; wch made the
people, y^t none durst come to save the house or goods till y^t none
durst come to save the house or goods till y^t was blowen vp, & by
that time the fire had taken the barnes & outhousing (wch were
many & great) so y^t none were saved.

In this fire were strang p'servations of Gods p'vidence to the
neighbors & towne, for the wind at first stood to cary the fire to
oth^r houses ; but suddenly turned & caryed it fro' all other houses ;
only carying it to the barns and out housing thereby. & it was a
feirce wind, & thereby drove the vehement heat fro' the neighbour
houses, wch in a calmer time would by the x'y heate heve bene set
on fire.

But above all the p'servation of all people fro' hurt & other houses
fro' fire at the blowing vp of the powder many being in greate
danger yet none hurt, & sundry houses set on fire by the blow &
yet all quenched, through Gods rich mercy in Christ.

1645. about the 16th of 5^t month was this anagrā sent to m^r
Dudley then Govno^r by some namelesse author.

> Thomas Dudley
> ah! old, must dye
> A deaths head on your hand you neede not weare
> a dying head you on your shoulders beare
> you need not one to minde you, you must dye
> you in your name may spell mortalitye
> younge men may dye, but old men these dye must
>   (or) it can't be long
> t'will not be long before you turne to dust.
> before you turne to dust! ah! must; old! dye!
> what shall younge doe, when old in dust doe lye?
> when old in dust lye, what N. England doe?
> when old in dust doe lye, its' best dye too.

This yeare we had sundry strange & p'digeous signes, a storme
of haile at Boston w^r the stones were as big or bigger than muskett
bullets, and fell terribly.

The week after the like was at Dedha', w^r some were in fash'on
like cross barr cañon shott, oth^{rs} like musket bullets. there was

also a feirce hirricane at Brantree soone after.   The Narragansets resolved a warr y^t yeare, but through mercy a peace was made.

Daulny y^t yeare tooke La Tours Fort.

Mr Hankins & anoth^r ship, great vessels both cast away at Spaine.   The country suffered many losses at sea, at least £10000 in lesse then 2 years besids many lives, yea some think twenty, or thirty thousand pound losse.

This winter we had much sicknesse at Roxbury & greater mortality then euer we had afore, in so short a time, 5 dyed in 8 days & more followed, as appeareth in the record y^{r}off; Wm Curtis who had that dreadful fall the year afore, excommun'd but upon his repentance received again.   Yet this mercy the Lord shewed N.E. this yeare, y^t the Iron w^{r}ks were brought to p'fection & tryall p'veing excellent well.

This yeare y^r was also a great scarcity of wine in the winter, wch had not so bene of 3 yeares afore, it was a gracious awakening the land, to conside^r of the excesse y^t hath here bene, that way.

1646.   This yeare arose a great disturbance in the country by such as are called the Petitioners a trouble raised by Jesuited agents to molest the peace of the churches & Com. w.

Gorton found favor in England, haveing none to informe against him what he was, but Mr Winslow was sent over whom the Lord direct, protect, & prosper.

A synod was held this yeare at Cambridg. & adjourned to the sūmer following, after some questions were discussed.

This yeare about the end of the 5^t month, we had a very strang hand of God vpon vs, y^t vpon a suddaine, innumerable armys of Catterpillers filled the Country all over all the English plantations, wch devoured some whole meadows of grasse, & greatly devoured barly, being the most greene & tender corne, eating off all the blades & beards, but left the Corne, only many ears they quite eat of by byting the greene straw asunder below the care, so y^t barly was generally halfe spoyled, likewise they much hurt wheat, by eating the blads off, but wheate had the lesse hurt because it was a little forwarder then barly, & so harder, & dryer, & they the lesse medled wth it.   As for rie, it was so hard and neere ripe y^t they touched it not, but above all graines they devoured Sylly oats. And in some places they fell vpon Indian Corne, & quite devoured it, in other places they touched it not ; they would goe crosse highways by 1000.   much prayer there was made to God about it, wth fasting in divers places : & the Lord heard, & on a suddaine tooke y^m all away againe in all p^{ts} of the country, to the wonderment of all men ; it was of the Lord for it was done suddainely.

This winter was one o' mildest y^t ever we had, no snow all winter long, nor sharp weath^r, but they had long floods at Conecticot, wch was much spoyle to y^r corne, in the medows ; we never had a bad day to goe p^{r}ch to the Indians all this winter, praised be the Lord.

1647.   This spring we of Roxbury wth some of Dorcheser ventured to sea in a small vessell but the master wanted sufficient experience, & the vessel overmasted & was over-sett, & many weeks after came whole allmost, ashore to shew the error of men to goe to sea so rawly : many m^r cast away in her, m^{ris} stoughtons eldest sonne, m^r Howards Eldest sonne wth many others.

This spring we heard p'bable tidings of New haven ship wch either was over sett, or foudered at sea, she was too tendersided, & therefore its to be feared she over sett. a very sad blow was y^t to N. E. to loose so many at once, of y^t to N. E. to loose so many at once, of y^t note & worth.

At the time appoynted the Synod assembled. But at that time the hand of the Lord was very strang among vs, by sickness ; it being an extreame hot time by thunder weather & vnwholsome.

At the begining of wc^{ch} weath^r, we had a great thunder storme in the night wch at Dorchester slew 3 oxen in the feild, wthout any remarkable signe, what it was y^t killed them.

Frō y^t time forward a great sicknesse epidemical, did the Lord lay vpon vs, so y^t the greatest p^t of a towne was sick at onc, whole familys sick young & old, scarce any escaping English or Indian.

The mañer of the sickneese was a very depe cold, wth some tincture of a feaver, & full of malignity, & very dangerous if not well regarded, by keeping a low diet ; the body solluble, warme, sweating, &c: at wch time of visitation, blessed m^{n} Winthrop the Govño^{rs} wife dyed. Also a lusty strong woman of Boston M^{ris} Stodder ; fondly eat greene peaches, wch set her to so vyolent a vomiting as y^t it burst her intralls, as its thought, & so she dyed.

Gods rods are teaching o^r epidemical sicknesse of colds, doth rightly by a divine hand tell the churches what o^r epidemical spr'l disease is. Lord help vs to see it, & to have such colds in the height of the heat of sumer, shews vs, y^t in the height of the means of grace, peace, liberty of ordinances &c. yet may we then fall into malignant & mortal colds, apostacys, & coolings, &c. This visitation of God was exceeding strange, it was suddaine, & generall : as if the Lord had imediatly sent forth an angel, not wth a sword to kill, but wth a rod to chastize ; & he smot all, good & bad, old & young, or as if there were a generall infection of the aer ; wch went frō North to South by degrees infect'g all, yea such as were on the seas neere o^r Coasts were so infected, & smitten : And this is remarkable, y^t though few dyed yet some did ; and generally those y^t dyed were of o^r choycest flowers, & most p'cious saints among oth^{rs} y^t were then taken to rest, was y^t worthy & blessed light Mr Hooker, who haveing a cold & p^{r}ched twice on the Sab: (Mr Stone not being at home) and ministred both the sac: the Ld^s supper in the forenoone, & Baptism in the afternoone, he was so over spent, & his spirits sunk, y^t he never could recover them againe.

God so graciously p'sp'ed m^r Winslows indeavours in England, against Gorton & his complices y^t all theire great hopes were dashed ; & they among vs, a little pulled in theire heads, & held theire peace.

About the end of the 10^t month of this yeare were very many colds againe among the people, though not so generall, nor so deepely seasing vpon theire spirits, as in the sumer time it was.

This winter we had a gracious p'vidence of God befell two brothers Edward & Georg Dennison, who had been pryude incendiarys of some trobls among us, & full of distemp', and disaffection. but the Lord left them to open and shamefull drunkennesse at Boston : espec'. edward. W^{ch} did so greatly humble them both y^t though George (being a memb^r) was excomvnicated, yet in a short time was taken in againe. And Edward humbling himselfe so effectually y^t he was also speedyly received in to the Church, this is the tryvmph of grace, to magnify grace by sinne.

This sumer we had notice of a very great & dismal storme at Newfound Land w^{ch}

[The remarks end thus abruptly on page 249. The following pages of the Roxbury Church Records, from 251 to the commencement of page 262, are taken up by the Register of Mr. Eliot's colleague, the Rev. Samuel Danforth. The last entry made by Mr. Danforth was 24. 7m. 1674. "A day of Publick Thanksgiving." We pass over Mr. Danforth's portions for the present, in order to have Mr. Eliot's record continuous.]

[1674] 15^d 9^m we first met & worshiped God in o^r new meeting house, but the l'd touched o^r thigh because yesterday my bro. Danforth fell sick.

19. 9^m. My bro. Danforth dyed in the Lord. it pleased the Lord to brighten his passage to glory he greatly increased in the pow^r of his ministry, especially ye last sumer. he cordially joyned wth me in maintaining the peace of the church. we consulted about the beautifying the house of God wth ruling elders, and to order the congregation into the primitive way of Collections.

22 9^m. a good Sab: & sac: blessed be the Lord, but sorrowfull, because o^r resp'ed Pasto^r was dead.

23. 9^m. the solemne funeral of my broth^r Danforth, whose departure the Lord brightened, as is above said & whose funeral was celebrated wth a great confluence.

29. 9^m. m^{rs} Burrows recommended & dismissed, she going for England and is advised to adjoyne herselfe to some church there.

6. 10^m. this sab. day o^r church had a pub. collection for o^r Sister Danforth, p'tly to pay the charges of the funeral, the rest to be given the widdow, the sume collected was [blank]. This day we restored o^r primitive practice for the training up o^r youth, first o^r male youth (in fitting season, stay every sab: after the evening exercize, in the Pub: meeting house, where the Elders will examine theire remembrance y^t day, & any fit poynt of catechise. Secondly y^t o^r female youth should meet in one place, where the Elders may examine y^m of theire remembrance yesterday. & about catechise, or what else may be convenient.

8. 10^m. a meeting held at Lyn by some of Sale^m, attempting to gather a church, but being found not fit matter, the assembly brake up, & the work p'ceeded not.

15. 10^m. a fast held at o^r church to humble o^{r}selves under the mighty & awfull hand of God, & to seek his favor & guidance of the church, for the healing o^r wounds, & beautifying Gods house,

in all things defective or out of order. God heard o^r prayre for sundry sicke, who y^t day began to mend.

20. 10^m. This sab: we had a pub: collection for Edward Howard of Boston, to redeeme him out of his sad Turkish captivity, in wch collection was gath^{r}ed 12lb. 18s. 9d. ob: wch by Gods favor made up the just su$\overline{m}$ desired.

[1674, 20. 10^m.] about this time I heard sad news fr$\overline{o}$ new york. where y^{ei} are p'pairing to reduce Southampton & Southhold on Long Iland by force of armes. because y^{ei} stand for theire liberty.

24. 10^m. m^r Oxenbridg was taken sick as he was p'ching the lecture.

25. 10^m being desired I went to watertowne to be p'esent at the euting b. livermore's daughter of a wonderfull great timpany. the op^{r}ation succeeded at the p'sent blessed be the Lord.

23. 10^m m^r Nehemiah Hubbard was ordained Pastor at Cambridg Village. an hopefull branch blessed be the Lord.

28. 10^m Mr Oxenbridg dyed. his disease was Apoplectical, he was mercyfully taken in his work. & the next lect^r day was his funeral day.

The above named woman cut of a timpany, the next day dyed, there were about 15 gallons of water taken fr$\overline{o}$ her p'tly afore she dyed, the rest after she was dead.

14. 11^m. Boston lect. turned to a fast, to seeke the Lord to make y^m a supply in ministry.

About y^s time m^r [Joseph] Gerish was ordained pastor at wenh$\overline{a}$. About y^s time m^r Woodrob a Scotchman, a scholar, had bene at Jamerca, & was too good for y^m he came hith^r, he is well accepted. The day y^t m^r oxenbridg was buryed, m^r Rob Gibbs of Boston, s iped at his owne dore, fell wth his breast upon the groundsell, bruised much, but was pretty well, untill 10 days after, & y^u he suddenly dyed.

14^d. 12^m. Hugh Clark was reconciled to the church.

one of the Duke of York his servants, in a ship at New York, in theire pots, drank an health to the Devil, he to w^m he drank saide, no, rather to his confusion, upon it was some apparition, wch terrified y^m. the p'ty sunke downe, but dyed not.

a distracted man at Hartford, stumbled or sliped at the dore, a child, by, laughed, he tooke an ax & killed the child, some say cut off the head, some say knoked it on the head & killed it

A fisherman about Pascatoway had 2 servants, who in an anger conspired to kill y^r master, did so, tooke his mony & fled, but were taken, & both executed.

1675. month 2^d. day 18. Sarah Cleaves wife of will. Cleaves received to full co$\overline{m}$union, penitently confessing.

day 25, we had a collection for m^r woodrobe a scotch man, y^t p'ched last lect^r a godly man, & we judged it charity to consid^r him. y^r was collected for him 3^l 14^s. 6^d, blessed be God

month 4^t. day 6. the church called bro: Bowles to the office of a Ruleing Eld^r & bro Peirpoynt also named but not yet called. left to consid^{r}ation.

This winter past, John Sossoman was murdered by wicked Indians. he was a man of eminent parts & wit, he was of late years conv^rted, joyned to the Church at Natike, baptized. & was sent by the church to Asowamsick in Plimouth Pattent to p^reach the Gospel. sine his death we heare by some godly English of Taunton, y^t he so ap'p'ved himselfe in theire neighborhood, as y^t he had the esteeme of a good Christian, & his death was much bewailed.

This June Court those y^t were suspected of the murd^r (being before bound over to this Court) were tryed, & 3 w^r found guilty, condemned, executed, the 3^d brake the rope & fell, revived, beged for life, he is repreived for one mouth.

11th day soone after the warr wth the Indians brake forth, the history w^roff I cañot, I may not relate. the prophane ludians p've a sharp rod to the English, & the English p've a very sharp rod to the praying Indians.

1676. on the 7^t day of the 2^d month, Capt Gookins, m^r Danforth & m^r Stoughton w^r sent by the Councill, to order matters at long Iland for the Indians planting there y^ei called me wth y^m in o^r way thithe^r, a great boat of about 14 ton, meeting us, turned head upon us, (weth^r wilfully or by negligenc, God he knoweth) y^ei run the sterne o^r boate w^r we 4 sat, under water, o^r boats saile, or something tangled wth the great boat, & by Gods mercy kept to it, my Cosin Jakob. & cosin Perrie being forwarder in o^r boat quickly got up into the great boat, I so sunke y^t I drank in salt water twice, & could not help it. God assisted my two cousins to deliver us all, & help us up into the great boat we were not far fro' the Castle, where we went ashore, dryed, & refreshed, & y^n went to the Iland p'formed o^r work, returned well home at night praised be the Lord. some thanked God & some wished we had bene drowned. Soone after, one y^t wished we had bene drowned, was himselfe drowned about the same place w^r we w^r so wonderfully delivered, the history w^roff is [Here ends the paragraph.]

month 2. day 27. Major Willard was buryed, an holy man, who left a gap on the Bench.

month 3 day 4. Election day, the people in theire distemper, left out Capt. Gookins, & put him off the Bench.

day 12. the Indians came off the Iland. Capt Gookins cars for y^m at Cambridg.

day 16. m^r Russel Buryed, a godly man, another gap on our Bench.

day 17. m^r Usher Buryed, a little afore m^r Lidget dyed.

18. m^r Atwater buried. 24. Cosin Jakob came home fro seakunk wounded in in his hand, his clothes shot through and through.

Capt Davis dyed. Capt Turner & 40 more slaine at or neere to Hadly.

month 4^t day 6. a sudden gust toward night, wch overset a boat coming fro' Noddls Iland, w^r were drowned m^r Bendal. & his wife, & a quaker maide, and a young man a factor.

day 8 at Boston lecter. at o^r meeting of elders, we p'posed for a fast, to move Authority for a gen: fast m^r math^r & Mr Allen had moved the gen: Court, but y^ei did not affect it, because the motion was not accepted wth the magistrats. the Governo^r p'posing rather for a day of thanksgiving. Mr Mather went to the Cover^r to p'mote the motion of a fast, but he refused, & would rather have a day of thanksgiving. Mr Hubbard of Ipswich concured wth the p'p'cio^n, whereupon the elders p^resent thought it necessary, y^t some p'ticular Churches should call a fast especially because now o^r Army to Coneticot w^r on y^r march, & Conecticot Army to meet y^m. Mr Mather was willing to call a fast in his Church & being next Sab before he should speak wth the Church, we agreed y^t the 4^t day come seavennight, wch was the 21 day of ye 4^t month should be the day of fasting and prayre, accordingly y^t church appoynted y^t day.

on boston lecture day following which was the 15 day of this month. Mr Foster a young scholar living at charlestowne w^r his parents live, had bene at Ipswich, & in the names of m^r Cobbet & m^r shephard did earnest p^re sse the eld's y^r p'sent, to move authority for a day of thanksgiving. we discoursed the poynt, we thought y^t God called to fasting & prayre but we could joyne wth o^r brethren in a day of thanksgiving, but for the p'sent, because the North church had all ready appoynted next 4^t day to be a day of fasting & prayre, we would stay untill next 5^t day, the day after the fast, & y^n we will consider of moving for a day of thanksgiving, & consider what causes to p'pound, y^r answ^r we desired m^r Foster to returne to m^r Shepard.

10 day some captive women & children w^r set downe, shipped to be sold for slaves.

12 day capt Tom having rendered himself, was brought downe, a great rage was against him.

14 day I was at the Court, called to be there. Cowel & oth^rs testified y^et saw him at Sudbury fight, he denyed and saith he was y^n sick & nev. ingaged agst the English, only when y^et were surprized by the enemie a devil put it into his hd. to be willing to goe wth y^m knowing the rage of the English.

[1676 mo. 4] 15 day I visited the p'soners, everything looketh wth a sad face. God frowneth.

19 day Capt Tom was tryed on his life, but I had not the least knowledg of it, & y^rfore was not p'sent, he was condemed, upon Cowells oath, & the others

20 day I went to the p'son to comfort y^m I dealt faithfully wth him, to confesse if w^r true, w^roff he is accused & for wch he is condemned. I believe he sayth the truth.

The same 20 day was Court at charlstowne, thither the Gov'no^r went to keepe Court, because they want magistrates in ye county two being dead, & a 3^d left out.

There y^et did appoynt the day of thanksgiving, to be held the 5^t day seavennight after, viz. on the 29^t of this month.

21 day was the fast at the North church, where we saw a mighty p'senc & assistanc of the spirit of grace. m^r Allins prayre & m^r Math^rs prayre & sermon w^s sad p'phesys to sick sick new England.

afore the worship began I visited to p'soners & after it was done, I went to the Gov'no^r & intreated y^t Capt Tom might have liberty to p've y^t he was sick at the time w^n the fight was at Sudbury, & y^t he was not their, it might not be, but he did exp^resse how bad a man Tom was. I told him, y^t at the great day he should find y^t christ was of anothe^r mind, or words to y^t purpose, so I dep'ted.

22 Boston lecture, afore sermon the marshal gave me a paper y^t is the printed ord^r for the day of thanksgiving, & after sermon he hurried away the p'soners to execution. I accompany^d him to his death, on the Ladder he lifted up his hands & said, I did never lift up hand against the English, nor was I at sudbury. only I was willing to goe away wth the enemise y^t surprised us. W^n the ladder was turned he lifted up his hands to heaven prayre wise & so held y^m till strength failed, & y^n by degres y^{ei} sunk downe.

m^r Stoughton & m^r Bulkly were sent to England to agent for the Country. Lord p'ty y^m !

month 9, day 26   the x'n b^{rn} in Dublin in Ireland sent a gracious gift of charity to relive such as suffered in o^r late warr, the ship arrived y^t day at night the master was at Boston on the Sabboth.

day 27. next morning a dreadfull fire broke forth in Boston, wch consumed many dwelling houses & many rich shops & warehouses, & the north meeting house, in 2 hou^{r}s time, by reason of a v^{r}y feirce wind. the history w^{r}off I leave to oth's to describe. but this is observable y^t so much p'visions was consumed, & so many pore aded to such as were made pore by the war, y^t (though the gift was only dispenced according as it was given to such as w^r made pore by the warr) yet the seasonablenesse of their charity was very much magnifyed, and a crowne of beauty was set upon the head of their charity thereby.

So soone as we condescended to impr've o^r praying Indians in the warr. frō y^t day forward we allwayes p'sp'd untill God pleased to teare the rod in peeces, p'ly by conquest, p^{tly} by theire sicknesse & death, & hath brought us peace, praised be his name. But no sooner was y^t rod broken, p'sently the Northeastern warr broke forth the history whereoff I leave to others to relate.

God also drew forth anoth^r rod upon o^r backs in epidemical sicknesse wch tooke away many of us. And yet for all this it is the frequent complaint of many wise & godly y^t litle reformation is to be seene of o^r cheife wrath p'voking sins, as pride, covetousnesse, animositys, p'sonal neglecte of gospelizing o^r youth, & of gospelizing of the Indians &c. drinking houses multiplyed, not lessened, quakers openly tolerated.

1677, month 2, about the 10^t of this month Boston was much indangered, by a chimuy going on fire. in a very windy day, but the Lord did succeed the indeavors of men, so y^t it was quenched. about the middle of this month a blazing star appeared in the east.

The Indian war now about to finish, wherein the praying Indians had so eminent an interest in the recording whereoff I thought not my selfe so fitting. I desisted frō this work of recording p'ticular matters, & knowing y^t it was comited to oth^{r}s I declined it, but now on 2^d thought I blame my selfe for it, Lord p'don all my many omissions. the successe of o^r Indians was highly accepted wth the souldiers, & y^{ei} now welcomed where ev^r y^{ei} met y^m y^{ei} had y^m to the ordinarys, made y^m drink, & bred y^{r}by such an habit to love strong drink, it p'ved an horrible snare unto us. y^{ei} learned so to love strong drink y^t y^{ei} would spend all y^r wages & pawne any they had for rumb or any strong drink; so drunkenesse in creased & quarreling fighting & were the sad effects of strong drink. Praying to God was quenched, the younger geneiation being debauched by it, and the good old generation of the first beginers gathered home by death. So y[t] Satan imp'ved y[s] op'tunity to defile, debase, & bring into contempt the whole work of praying to God. a great apostasy defiled us. And yet through grace some stood and doe stand, and the work is on foot to this day, praised be the Lord. when the Indians were hurried away to an Ilaud at half an bou[r]s warning, pore soules in terror y[ei] left theire goods, books, bibles, only some few caryed y[r] bibles, the rest were spoyled & lost. So y[t] w[n] the wares w[r] finished, & y[ei] returned to y[r] places y[ei] w[r] greatly impov'ished, but y[ei] especially bewailed y[r] want of Bibles, y[s] made me meditate upon a 2[d] imp[r]ssion of o' Bible, & accordingly tooke pains to revise the first edition. I also intreated m[r] John Cotton to help in y[t] work, he having obtained some ability so to doe. he read over the whole bible, & whatever doubts he had, he writ y[m] downe in order, & gave y[m] to me, to try y[m] & file y[m] over among o[r] Indians. I obtained the favor to reprint the New testam[t] & psalmes, but I met wth much obstruction for reprinting the old testam[t], yet by prayre to God, Patience & intreatye, I at last obteined y[t] also, praised be the Lord.

RECORDS OF REV. SAMUEL DANFORTH.

[NOTE. — Rev. Samuel Danforth, M.A., second son of Nicholas Danforth., of Cambridge, Mass., was born in Framingham, co. of Suffolk, England, in September, 1626. He came to New England with his father, in 1634, his mother having died when the son was three years old. He graduated at Harvard College in 1643, in the same class with the Rev. Samuel Mather, son of the Rev. Richard Mather, of Dorchester. He was made a freeman in 1647, and on the 24th of September, 1650, was ordained as colleague to the Rev. John Eliot, pastor of the First Church in Roxbury. Mr Danforth married Mary Wilson, daughter of the Rev. John Wilson, of Boston, Nov. 5, 1651. They had twelve children, two of whom were ministers of the gospel, John, who settled at Dorchester, and Samuel at Taunton. Rev. Samuel Danforth, the father, in addition to his services as a minister, was of some note as an astronomer, mathematician, and poet. For several years he published almanacs. John Farmer states that he had seen "those from 1646 to 1649, inclusive," and that "some of them are valuable for the chronological tables at the end." The ministry of Mr. Danforth continued twenty-four years. He died Nov. 19, 1674, at the age of 48. His colleague Eliot, who outlived him more than fifteen years, said, " *My Brother* Danforth *made the most glorious End that ever I saw!* " The widow of Mr. Danforth married Joseph Rock, or Ruck, of Boston, where she died, Sept. 13, 1713, in the eighty-first year of her age. See REGISTER, vii. 317; American Quarterly Register, viii. 135–137; Sibley's Harvard Graduates, i. 88–92. The Danforth items which follow commence on page 251 of the book from which these church records are printed. — W. H. W.]

1849.

John Winthrop Esq. late Governour of Massachusetts deceased march 26. & was buryed Aprill 3.

August. 25. m[r] Thomas Shepard Pastour to the Church at Cambridge rested from his labours.

Septemb: A generall visitation by the small pox, whereof many dy.·d.

Novemb 3. our sister Bowles the wyfe of John Bowles dyed of the small pox.

Jan. 13. on the lords day the lord sent a great storme of snow & wind, which was so violent as that a certain vessell suffered shipwrack, and all the p'sons that were therein perished.

March 17.   A collection for yᵉ poor distressed Church at Bahamah & yʳ was about 28   gathered in ōr little Congregation.

1650.   m͛ Pen & mʳ Palmer were sent as Messengers fro yᵉ chs in oʳ Bay to Bahamah.

march 26.   mʳ Samuel Haugh ordained Pastour to the church at Redding.

May 23.   John Wooddie dyed of the small pox.

Aug. 21.   mʳ Jonathan Mitchel was ordained Pastor to yᵉ church at Cambridge.

July 28.   This Church Elected S. Danforth to the office of a Pastor amongst them.

September 13.   The church of Boston ordained 3 Ruling Elders, mʳ Colbron, mʳ Jacob Eliot & mʳ James Pen and three Deacons.

Sept. 24. 1650.   Samuel Danforth was ordained Pastor to this church at Roxbury.

Novembʳ 21.   A gᵗ burning at Charlestown.

1652.

June. mʳ Samuel Phillips ordained Teacher to yᵉ Church at Rowley.

Octobʳ 12. A church gathering & ordination at Medfield.   m͛ John Wilson junior was ordained Pastor.

9ᵗʰ 10ᵐ. There appeared a Comet in yᵉ heaven in Orion, which continued its course tow'd yᵉ zenith for yᵉ space of a fortnight viz. till mʳ Cottons death.

23ᵈ 10ᵐ. mʳ John Cotton B. D. Teacher to yᵉ church at Boston rested fro his labours.

1st march.   A dreadfull Conflagration at Boston.

16. march. Rumours of yᵉ Indians Conspiracy agsᵗ yᵉ English.

13ᵈ 12ᵐ. Nath Garee was admonished.

Anno 1653.

31ᵈ 5ᵐ. Thomas Dudley Esqʳ dyed & was buryed yᵉ 6ᵗ day following.   His death was on yᵉ Lords day at night.

Anno 1655.

In the beginning of the 5ᵗʰ moneth God sent an Epidemicall sicknes & faintnes : few escaped, many were very sick severall dyed. as Elisabeth Bowles &c. in oʳ towne, mʳ Rogers of Ipswich the Revd Pastor there, mʳ Samuel Eaton at Newhaven & his wife [late mʳˢ Haines].

Añno 1655.

26^d 6^m. Lydia Eliot cast out of ye church.
2^d 9^m. 1656. Received again.

Anno 1656.

23^d 5^m. m^r John Norton was ordained Teacher to the church of Boston.

8^m. m^r Hook late Teacher to ye ch. at New haven set saile for England.

8^m. m^r Noice that blessed light at Newbury, rested frō his labours.

2^d 9^m. m^r Eliot our Teacher having been exercised wth ye Sciatica, & endured much anguish, dolour, & by that meanes detained frō the house of God, & we deprived of his pretious labours, & that for ye space of 10 weekes, this day came abroad into the assembly (through Gods mercy) & gave us a taste of Gods gratious remembrance of him in his low estate.

Anno 1657.

2^m. Certaine Elders & oth^r messengers of ye churches in ye Bay went to Hartford & endeavoured to compose ye differences betw. ye church there & ye dissenting Brethren.

1657   This Winter m^r Garrets ship was lost, w^rin was m^r Thomas Mayhew Preacher to ye Indians, m^r Davis sometime schoolmaster at Hartford, m^r Jonathan Ince, m^r Nathaniel Pelham wth many others.

1657 Augt 30   Elizabeth Hagbourne cast out of ye Church.

m^r [Theophilus] Eaton Governour at Newhaven dyed.

1658 moneth 1 day 28   Rec^d again.

[1658] moneth 2.   much rainy & intemp'ate weather wch was a g^t hindrance in seed time.

month 6 & 7. The season intemp'ate, rain imoderate, much wheat corrupted, ye getting of fodder for ye Cattel much hindred. Generall agues in ye southw^d p^{ts} of ye Countrey. Fevers & fluxes in ye bay; w^rof not a few dyed.

moneth 12. 11^d. At midnight y^r happened a great Burning. The fire began in ye outside of Henry Farnham's work-house next ye orchard & it burnt up his work house & his dwelling house & consumed a g^t p^t of his Timber, some of his goods & corne & all his Tooles, but it pleased God not to suffer it to proceed any further.

March 9. 1658–9 m^r Peter Bulkley Teacher to ye Church at Concord rested frō his labours.

1659.

✦ April   The greatest part of ye 2^d moneth was cold & rainie weather.

April. 13^{d.} m^r Thomas Shepherd was ordained Teacher to ye church at Charlestowne.

3^m 1^d. John Matthews was excommunicated.

7^m 26. The Councill began to set at Boston, consisting of ye m̄bers of 9 ch's. viz. Boston, Dorchester, Roxbury, Dedham Charlestowne, Cambridge, Watertown, Sudbury & Ipswich.

9^m & 10^m. The Lord sent a general visitation of Children by coughs & colds, of wch my 3 children Sarah, Mary & Elisabeth Danforth died, all of y^m within ye space of a fortnight.

10^m. m^r Norrice Teacher to ye church at Salem rested frō his labours.

12^m 22^d. A fast in ye Bay in reference to ye state of England.

1660.

11^m. The Lord was pleased to visite vs, with epidemical colds, coughs, agues, & fevers.

21^d. Elder Heath dyed of a sore throat, being ye issue of his cold wth fever.

23^d. m^r Ezekiel Rogers. Pastor to ye church at Rowley rested frō his labors,

31^d. In ye evening about 7th hour there was a great Earthquake, besides y^t wch was about 9 weeks before.

March 23 (60) m^r Thomas Welde sometime Pastor to this Church dyed in London.

1661 April 28 Lydia Smith publicly admonished by the Church.

Decr 29 John Matthews released frō censure.

This year also in ye moneth 10th died m^r Dalton of Hampton.

This yeare 1661. April 22^d o^r Soveraigne Lord, Charles y^e 2^d was Crowned.

January 1. 1661. The Generall court agreed to send m^r Bradstreet & m^r Norton to England to solicite his majesty in y^e behalfe of this Countrey.

Jan. 31. Here fell a very great & deep Snow.

1661. Feb^r 10th m^r Bradstreet & m^r Norton wth m^r Davis & $m^?$ Hull took ship & set saile y^e next morning.

Feb 23 Lydia Smith reconciled to the Church.

March. [20.] m^r [Nathaniel] Vpham, who sometime preached at Malden died at Cambridge.

1661-2. March ii. The Synod began, which sat at Boston the Messengers being sent frō y^e seuerall churches according to ye order of ye general Court. The Quest'o's discussed were 1, who are ye subjects of Baptisme? 2. whether according to scripture there ought to be Consociat'o' of churches & what is ye manner of it. The Assemblie continued vntill ye 21 of March & then adjourned unto ye 10th of June next.

1662.

1662. March 30. m^r Samuel Hough Pastor of ye ch. at Reading, to ye Synod, fell sick at Boston & died.

1662 April 20 Joshua Seaver servant to m^r Eliot was brought before ye church & convicted of lying & stealing wch he confessed.

1662.

It pleased the L^d this spring to exercise ye Country wth a very severe drought wch some were so rash as to impute to the sitting of ye synod; but he was pleased to bear witnesse ags^t y^r rashnes; For no sooner was ye synod mett June 10. but they agreed to set ye next day ap^t to seek his favourable presence & to ask raine, & ye day following G^d sent showers frō heaven, & frō that day following visited ye Land wth seasonable showers of rain week after week vnto ye harvest.　The synod also agreed upon several propositions in answer to ye first Question ppounded by ye Generall Court.

This Sūmer several came to vs frō England.　m^r James Allin, minister. m^r Franciss Willowby, m^r Leveret. m^r wheelwright, m^r Leverich, m^r william Stoughton.

August 1.　m^r William Colbron, ruling Elder of ye church of Boston died.

Sept. 3.　m^r Bradstreet & m^r Norton returned from England, bringing wth y^m a Gracious letter frō his Majesty confirming our Charter & liberties.

Sept. 9. was ye 3^d Session of ye Synod who agreed upon propositions concerning ye subject of Baptisme & Consociation of churches wch are since printed by order of ye general Court.

Jan. 26. about 6 o'clock at night there happened an Earthquake wch shook mens houses & caused many to run out of their houses into the streets, & ye tops of 2 or 3 chimneys fell off, or some p't of y^m likewise there was another earthquake about midnight. also in ye morning once or twice ye earth trembled & mens houses were shaken.

Jan. 28. about 10 o'clock in ye morning there was another earthquake.

1663.

1663.　Aprill 5. m^r John Norton, teacher to the church of Boston, rested from his labours.　His death was suddaine.　The night before about midnight he awakened with a pain vnder his left pap. yet he went to meeting in ye forenoon (it being ye Lords day) and made account to preach in ye afternoon, but his wife & friends perswaded him to stay at home.　after meetinge freinds came in to visite him & he walked vp & downe ye room & discoursed pleasantly after his wonted manner.　About shutting in, as he was walking up & down in his parlour, he went to ye fire side & leaned his head forward, as if he meant to vomitt.　his wife & m^r Duncun stept to him to help to hold him & he sunk downe vnder them & never spake more.

June 14. m^r John Miller Preacher of ye Gospell at Groyton, sometime Pastor to ye Church at Yarmouth rested frō his labours.

July 5. m^r Samuel Newman Teacher to ye Church at Rehoboth rested frō his labours.

This spring may 24 Came m^r Walley a Preacher frō England. And m^r Williams.　This Summer came m^r Brewster.

July 20.　m^r Samuel Stone Teacher to ye church at Hartford rested frō his labours & sorrows.

The Churches in yᵉ Bay kept a weᵏly fast in p't of 6ᵐ all yᵉ 7ᵗʰ moneth & most of yᵉ 8ᵗʰ moneth.

Novemb. 4. A church, was gathered at Topsfield & mʳ Gilbert was ordained.

11. A church was gathered at Billerica & mʳ Samuel Whiting jun, ordained Pastor thereof.

Decemb. 9. The ordination of mʳ Benj. Bunker to yᵉ office of a Pastor in Maldon.

10. A church was gathered at Wenham & mʳ Antipas Newman ordained.

The churches of yᵉ Bay began a monethly fast, one one moneth another another moneth.

Jan. & Febr. It pleased G. to visit vs wᵗʰ general Colds & coughs. In some they were accompanyed wᵗʰ fevers.

March 9. There was dreadfull thunder & lightning in yᵉ night, wᶜʰ smot yᵉ house of one Wakefield in Boston tore two of yᵉ rafters of yᵉ house & yᵉ gᵗ Corner post of yᵉ House frō top to Bottom & rent of yᵉ boards yᵗ end yet there were 3 men lying in yᵉ chamber, one who lay wᵗʰ his head neer to yᵉ said post yet they had no hurt, onely they smelt a gᵗ stink of Brimstone.

1664.

1664. The churches set up their monethly fasts.

May 27. mʳ Encrease Mather was ordained Teacher to yᵉ ch: last gathered at Boston.

June 15. there was a solemn fast kept in the ch's throughout yᵉ jurisdictiō by order of yᵉ Genᵋ Court.

[1644.] June 26. About this time began yᵉ blasting of yᵉ wheat to be p'ceived.

July 13. A church gathered at Groyton & mʳ Willard ordained.

July 20. A church gathered in yᵉ bounds of Cambridge & mʳ John Eliot jun. ordained Pastor & mʳ Thō Wiswall Ruling Elder.

July 22. The kings Comissioners arried here, viz Colonel Nichols, mʳ Cartwright, Sʳ Robᵗ Carr & mʳ Maverick.

31. They departed for Long Island & Monhados [Menhaden.]

Sept. 1. Wee had a solemn & publick Fast throughout yᵉ Jurisdictiō.

2. A great storm of Wind that beat down much of ōr fruit, & yᵉ nipping Cold & frost did much hurt amongst yᵉ Indian Corne.

Octob. 30. Major Daniel Denison had his House fired at Ipswich & burnt down.

Nov. 16. A solemn Publick fast throughout this jurisdiction.

Nov. 17. About this time there appeared a Comet in yᵉ Heavens the first time I saw it wᶜʰ was yᵉ 5ᵗʰ of 10ᵐ. It appeared a little below the Crows Bill in Hydra in yᵉ Tropick of Capricorn or neer to it. on yᵉ 18ᵗʰ day it appeared in Canis Major 2 degrees below yᵉ Tropick On yᵉ 19ᵗʰ day I observed it to passe on yᵉ upper star in yᵉ Hares foot about 2 degrees & ½ above the tropicke. It continued till Feb. 4.

1664. December 18. Robert Pepper publickly admonished

restored again.   Isaac Heath also was admonished but reconciled again.   June 13. 1665.

Feb. 4.   m^r Samuell Torry was ordained to ye office of a Pastor in ye Church at Waymouth.

we had a very mild & moderate winter till ye middle of February.

Feb. 19 & 21.   Bitter Cold weather.   Feb. 22 Snow & Feb. 27 Snow.

March 5.   John Harris was publicly dealt with.

March 11.   Another Comet appeared in ye East in ye constellation of Antinous.

15.   Our aged Governor m^r John Endicot dyed.

1665. 22.   A publick fast throughout this Colony.

5 May.   In this moneth were our debates wth ye k's Comissioners.

June 3.   was a g^t battell betw. England & Holland.

June 20.   At shutting in happened a burning in Roxbury in ye dwelling House of Abrahā Newell senior, & June 23, his old barne fired by his girle.

June 22.   A publick Fast.

This moneth y^e lord smot our wheat both winter & summer wth Mildew.

July 5.   There happened a very sad accident at Situate.   lieftenant Torry, having rec^d order frō the Governor of Plimouth (by reasō of the kings letter y^t informes of y^e Hollanders coming $^{ag}_{st}$ vs) to look to y^e powder & ammunition of y^e Towne,   He went into y^e House of Goodmā Tickner where y^e Magazine of y^e Town was, wch was but two barrels of powder & opened y^m & while y^e said lieftenant was drying some of y^e powder, abroad upō boards & doores, by some accident, G. knows what, ye powder was fired both that in ye house & and that abroad, & ye house blown up & broken in pieces, And y^e woman of y^e House Goodwife Tickner miserably burnt esp'ly on her belly (for it seems she was at that instant stepping upō y^e barrell y^t was in y^e house to reach something) & a little childe also was sadly burnt & buryed amongst y^e rubbish & Timber, but y$_e$ woman & childe lived sev'rall houres after about 10 or 11.   Also y^e lieftenant was sadly burnt esp'ly on his breast, face hands & armes, yet he lived till y^e next day and then dyed.

July 15.   There was dreadful thunder [&] lightning.   A stream of fire was observed to fall upon m^r Benj. Gilhams House, wch shattered his chimney & some of ye principall beams in ye house, wounded & hurt his daughter mrs More, stupifyed ye rest that were in ye house.   Also at charlstown ye lightning rent a Mast of a little Vessell.

And at ye Castle it wounded 3 or 4 men In so much that they cryed out some honres after, some that y^{ir} tooes, others y^t their legs were falling off, and ye Captain of the Castle, m^r Rich. Davenport, a man of a choice & excellent sp't, having bin hard at work, was layd down upon his bed in ye Castle, there being but a Wainscot betw. ye bed & ye Magazine of Powder, the lightning came in at ye window & smot ye Captain on ye right eare so y^t it bled, bruised his flesh upon his head, wounded & burnt his breast & belly, & stroke him dead that he never spake more: but it pleased God ye powder escaped ye fire.   likewise there was a dog lay at ye gate & a boy, one of ye Captains sons was not far from him : the lightning stroke ye dog & killed Him, but ye boy through mercy had no hurt.

The same day about ye same time y^r was a whirlwind betw. Dedham & Dorchester wch took water out of ye River & spouted it up in ye air, cast down many trees & carryed away many cocks of Hay, & other hay that lay in ye swath & in windrows.

About ye same time also at Malbury was a storm of Haile, some as big as an Egge, some long & flatt, some Cornered, some neer as big as a ma's fist.

July & August. A great Drought wch burnt up ye pastures & threatned ye Indian Corn.

The Anabaptists gathered y^ms, into a church, prophesied one by one, & some one amongst y^m administred ye Lords supper, after he was regularly excomunicated by ye ch. at Charlestown. They also set up a lecture at Drinkers house, once a fortnight They were admonished by ye Court of Assista[ ].

10th 7^m 65. Hugh Clark was called before ye church & charged with telling a lye in ye face of ye Court, slandering Authority in saying that his son in law was Committed for Murder which was proved 1. By his own Confession to ye Elders y^t [t]he court had reprehended Him for so speaking, & y^t ye foreman of ye Jury affirmed y^t he had so spoken. 2. By ye Testimony of Samuel Williams, who heard Hugh Clark speak those very words in open court. But Hugh Clark in ye church denyed y^t y^e [he?] spake these words & that the court or any of ye magistrates imputed it to him y^t he had so spoken or reprehended & blamed him for it : By all wch it appeared to ye church y^t his soul was sick & needed medicine & therefore dispensed a publick admonition vnto Him. It doth appear y^t Hugh Clark did herein tell a notorious lye agst ye light of his Conscience. 1. Bec: ye Court laboured to convince Him of his error in so speaking & argued ye matter with him to shew him his error & yet he stood to justify what he had said [attested by Samuel Williams.] 2. bec. Hugh Clark told myself y^t his aim & intent in what he said in ye Court was to get some satisfaction & recompence for ye wrong y^t was done to his son in law.

7. 7. 65. m^r Adam Blakeman Pastor to ye church at Stratford rested from his labours.

5th 8^m 65. About 10 a clocke at night there happened an Earthquake.

9^m 65. Contributions were made in several churches for ye relief of ye distressed by reaso of ye Sicknes in London.

27th 9^m 1665. Mrs Sarah Alcock dyed, a vertuous woman, of vnstained life, very skilful in physick & chirurgery, exceeding active yea vnwearied in ministering to ye necessities of others. Her workes praise her in ye gates.

8th 9^m 65. A solemn Thanksgiving.

15. 9^m 65. m^r Samuel Shepard was ordained Pastor to ye church at Rowley.

m^r Shore was ordained to ye church at Taunton. Gilhams Vessell, wherein was Colonel Cartwright one of ye k's Comissioners, was taken by ye Dutch, and all his writings agst ye Countrie, made void.

22. 9ᵐ 65.   A solemn Fast in reference to yᵉ Sicknes in England &c.

8ᵗʰ 10ᵐ 65.   A great Storm of Winde, Wherein mʳ Shoot & all his Company were cast away at Marble-head.

This moneth yᵉ churches in yᵉ Bay set upon a Course of Fasting and prayer.

1666.

·5ᵗ 2ᵐ 66.   All the churches in this Jurisdiction kept a solemn day of fasting & Prayer.

Cristophers Island was taken by yᵉ French inhabiting there & yᵉ English dispossest.

It pleased God this Summer to arm yᵉ Caterpillers agst vs, wᶜʰ did much damage in our Orchards, and to, exercise yᵉ Bay with a severe drought.   The churches in yᵉ Bay sought yᵉ Lᵈ by Fasting & Prayer, our Church of Roxbury began, yᵉ 19ᵗʰ of 4ᵐ   The Lᵈ gave rain yᵉ next day.   The rest of yᵉ churches in like manner besought yᵉ Lord 21ˢᵗ of 4ᵐ   And it pleased God send rain more plentifully on yᵉ 23ᵈ day following.   At wᶜʰ time happened a sad accident at Marshfield. for in that town a certain woman sitting in her house (some neighbours being present) & hearing dreadful thunder crackes, spake to her son & said Boy, shut yᵉ door, for I rem'ber this time 4 yeares we had like to have been killed by thunder & lightning   The Boy answered, Mother, its all one wᵗʰ God whether yᵉ door be shutt or open; The woman said ag'n, Boy shut yᵉ door: At her command the Boy shut yᵉ door: but imediately yʳ came a Ball of Fire frō heaven, down yᵉ chimney & slew yᵉ old woman (whose name was Goodwife Phileps) & yᵉ Boy, and an old man, a neighbor that was present, & dog yᵗ was in yᵉ House, but a little child yᵗ was in yᵉ armes of yᵉ old man escaped: and a woman wᵗʰ child being present was soor amazed.

It pleased God that our wheat was Mildewed & blasted this year also.

10ᵗʰ 5ᵐ 1666.   There happened a dreadful burning at Andover. mʳ Bradstreets house & yᵉ g'test p't of his goods were burnt.   The occasion of wᶜʰ burning was yᵉ Carelesnes of yᵉ maid, who put hot ashes into an hogshead over yᵉ porch: the tub fired about 2 o clock in yᵉ morning & set yᵉ Chamber & house on fire.

29. 5ᵐ 66.   Divers strangers yᵗ came from Christophers Island being in yᵗ necessitie & distress by sicknes lameuesse &c besides yᵉ p'vision made for yᵐ by yᵉ Generall Court, the severall Churches contributed towards their relief.

26. 5ᵐ 66.   Tidings came to vs of Forreiners invading our Coast. Two French ships lying at Martins Vineyard & having taken Plumbs ship & another Sloop, lay at Martins Vineyard.

31. 5ᵐ 66.   The next week we vnderstood that it was one Dutch man, a man of war, with 12 guns & a prize wᶜʰ he took upo' yᵉ coasts of Virginia who took Armstrong & Plumb & A shallop: & after he had taken out wᵗ he saw good, set yᵉ men at liberty with their vessels, & carried away none but a Boy, & so left our coasts.

7ᵐ & 8ᵗʰ.   Wee heard of a dreadfull Heracano at Barbados & yᵉ neighbouring Islands wherein many vessels p'ished & my Lord

Willoughbey fleet in his expeditiō agst ye French at Christophers, were lost.

21. 8^m 66.   Hugh Clark had a solemn admonition dispensed to him.

25. 9^m 56.   Hugh Clark was forgiven by ye church.

It pleased ye Lord this Summer to visit ye Countrey with ye small pox, which greatly encreased in the Winter & proved very afflictive & mortal vnto many.

12. 10^m 66.   m^r William Tompson Pastor to ye church at Braintree departed this life in ye 69 year of his age.   He had been held vnder ye power of melancholy for ye space of 8 yeares.   During wch time He had diverse lucid intervales, & sweet revivings, esp'ly ye week before he dyed, in so much that he assayed to go to ye church and administer ye Lord's supper to them, but his body was so weak that he could neither go nor ride.

30. 10^m.   An Earth-quake was perceived by severall.

2^d 12. 66.   m^r Henry Withington, Ruling Elder in ye Church of Dorchester.   A man that excelled in Wisdom, meeknes and goodnes, being aged 79, departed this life, and was buryed on ye 5^t of 12^m.

4th 12^m 66.   Terrible & dreadfull Tidings came vnto vs by ye way of Mevis & Jamaica concerning the taking of Antigea. & ye burning of ye city of London.

11. 12^m 66.   Tidings came to vs from Connecticot, how that on ye 15th of 10^m 66. Sergeant Heart ye son of Deacon Heart and his wife & six children, were all burnt in their House at Farmington, no man knowing how the fire was kindled, neither did any of ye Neighbors seè ye fire till it was past remedy.   The church there had kept a Fast at this mans house 2 dayes before.   One of his sons being at a farm escaped this burning.

This Winter there was a house burnt at Piscataque w^rin 3 p'sons p'ished.

Also at ConCord ye House of m^r Woodies was burnt & his onely son p'ished in ye fire.

21. 1^m &frac67;.   There was a publick Fast throughout ye Jurisdictson.

This day o^r church made a Collection for m^r Wigglesworth, 4^{lb} 17^s

27. 1^m 67.   Mr John Alcock Physician, dyed.   His liver was dryed up & become schirrous.

8. 2^m 67.   Our Church made a collection for ye relief of our Brethren & Countrymen who were reduced to extremities at Cape-Feare.   The sum was about 7^{lb}

25. 3^m 67.   There was a dreadful crack of thunder.   Samuel Ruggles happened at that instant to be upon ye meeting-house-Hill with oxen & horse & cart loaden with Corne.   The horse & one ox were strucken dead wth ye lightning, the other had a little life in it, but it dyed presently.   The man was singed and scorched a little on his legs, one shooe torn a pieces & ye heel carrried away, the man was hurled of frō ye cart & flung on ye off side, but throcgh mercy soon recovered himself & felt little harm.   There was chest in ye cart w^rin was Peuter & linnen, the peuter had small holes melted in it & the linnen some of it singed & burnt.

19th 4^m 67.   A sad accident happened at Boston to one Wakefield a boatman, who helping ye rope maker about a Cable had his head splitt & his braines beaten out.

7th 6^m 67.   About two of ye clock in ye Morning, my honoured Father, m^r John Wilson, Pastour to ye church of Boston, aged about 78 years & an half, a man eminent in Faith, love, humility, self-denyal, prayer, soundnes of minde, zeal for God, liberality to all men, esp'ly to ye s^{ts} & ministers of christ, rested from his labors & sorrowes, beloved & lamented of all, and very honourably interred ye day following.

28. 8^m 67.   About break of ye day there happened dreadfull thunder & lightning, whereby an Hay cock of 4 Load of Hay belonging to Robt. Seaver, was fired in our Marishes & burnt up.

5th 9^m.   A day of publick Thanksgiving vnto God for ye Continuance of o'r peace & liberties.   The Day before God sent vs tidings of the Cessatio. of war & ye Conclusion of peace betw. England & ye neighbouring Nations. viz Capt. Martyn, and ye week after both ye Prontz & Harrison, & Skarlet & a while after Christopher Clark.

4th 10^m.   A Publick Fast throughout ye Jurisdictio.

12^m.   Strange noises were heard in ye air like guns, drums, vollies of g^t shot at Waymouth, Hingham &c.

This winter many women died in childbirth not being able to be deliv'd, as [blank] Craft, Alice Davis, in our Town, and severall in other Townes.

29th 12^m 67.   There appeared a Coma or blazing Stream wch shone frō ye western horizon & extended to a small star in ye river Eridanus, but ye Head or star itself was occult & hidden by reason of its propinquity to ye Sun.

This winter was very moderate, little snow or hard weather.

15. 1^m. 6⅞.   Edward Bugbey admonished by the church.

22. 1^m. 6⅞.   Sarah Chamberlain was excomunicated.

1668.

26. 1^m 1668.   A publick Fast throughout ye Jurisdiction appointed by ye Council.

3. 2^m 68.   An Earthquake.

7th 2^m 1668.   m^r Samuel Shepard Pastor to ye Church of Christ at Rowley, rested frō his labors.

14 & 15. 2^m 68.   A publick Disputation by order of ye Council for ye Conviction of Tho. Goole, John Farnham sen. Tho. Osborn & their Company, who schismatically withdrew from ye Comunion of these churches & set up another assembly in ye way of Anabaptism & boldly intermeddled with those institutions of ye Ld Jesus, wch are proper to office trust. showing that their practice is not justifiable by ye word of God nor to be allowed by ye government of this Jurisdiction.

14. 2^m 68.   m^r Thomas More's Vessel cast away at Cape-Cod in ye storm. w^{rin} 4 persons perished, and much wealth lost.

27. 2^m 68.   m^r Henry Flint, Teacher to ye church at Braintrey, aged 61, deceased.

29. 2^m.   The general Court of Elections.   This Court banished

Tho. Gool, John Farnham & [William] Turner, schismatical Anabaptists.

22. 3^m. A frost w^{r}by y^e Corn & fruit suffered Damage. Tidings came concerning y^e Burning of y^e Bridge at Barbados.

16. 3^m 68. There were prodigies seen in y^e heaven in y^e night before y^e Lords day by 500 p'le, in this forme. $+$ $|X|$. This spring was a time of much infirmity & sicknes, many were visited with feavers & some dyed.

3^d 4^m 68. One Stratton at Boston stabbed & murdered himselfe. It pleased God to restrain the Palmer worm amongst vs in y^e Bay & to spare o^r fruit trees.

15. 4^m 68. John, y^e son of John Gorton about 12 yeares old, going into ye water to wash hims^{lf} in ye companie of several little boyes, was drowned & perished in ye river.

16. 4. 68. After much dry weather, wch scorcht ye fruits of ye earth, it pleased G^d to send us rain, even showres of blessing

4^m 68. m^r Tho. Wells of Hartford one of their Magistrates, fell down frō one of his cherri trees and so died.

6^t 5^m 68. [blank] Robinson, a brother of ye Ch. at Dorchester was drawn through by ye cog-wheel of his Mill & was torn in pieces & slain.

9th 5^m 68. m^r Jonathan Mitchel, Pastor of ye Church at Cambridge rested from his labors.

5^m 68. A Council of 4 churches called by ye Elder & major part of ye church of Boston in reference to their dissenting Brethren. Their advice was to dismiss them in order to ye propagatio. of another church in Boston.

13th 8^m 68. m^r John Eliot jun. Pastor to ye Church at Cambridge-village rested frō his labors.

17th 8^m 68. John Web, alias, Everit, pursuing a Whale, was caught in ye rope, twisted about his middle, & being drawn into ye sea, was drowned.

5. 9^m 68. One of Salem was Executed for murdering her childe, born in fornication. Doctor Emery & ye mother of ye woman sat upō ye Gallows an Hour.

9. 9. 68. m^r Waltam, ye minister at Marblehead, who died of an Apoplexie, was buried.

20. 9. 68. A notable conjunction of ♀ & ☽ wherein y^r was a visible contact.

9. 10^m 68. m^r John Davenport was ordained Pastor to ye Church at Boston and m^r James Allin was ordained Teacher.

11^m 68. m^r [blank] Wings·Catch cast away at Cape Ann.

13. 11^m 68. Bro. James Humphryes was ordained Ruling Elder in Dorchester.

25. 1^m 69. A Publick Fast throughout ye Colonie.

13. 2^m 69. A great Assemblie of Elders & Messengers of several Churches in ye Bay, who upon ye Call of y^r Dissenting Brethren at Boston, met together to consider & advise y^m what to do. They judged that the Dissenting Brethren might seasonably make vse of their xtian libertie vnto a regular coalitio. in another churchbody.

22. 2^m 69. m^r Richard Mather Teacher to ye Church at Dor-

chester, aged 73, rested from his labors & sorrowes, having been greatly & grievously afflicted with ye stone.

20. 2^m 69.   m^r John Reyner senior dyed.

12. 3^m 69.   The Dissenting Brethren aforementioned, made a Secession frō ye Church at Boston & gathered y^ms. into a new ch. estate at Charlstown having the approbation of 7 of ye magistrates & ye right hand of fellowship frō ye Elders & Messeng^rs of 5 churches.

26. 4^m (69).   Mr William Woodward, Minister of ye Gospel, dyed at Dedham.

This moneth several persons were cast away & drowned in their passage frō Martins Vineyard. In ye 5^t moneth we had many showres & rain & much wet weather, esp'ly two great stormes of rain wch raised great floods & drowned ye meadows in inland townes.

5^m.   m^r Eleazar Mather Pastor to the church of x^t at North-Hampton dyed.

7^m.   It was a very sickly time, many being visited with gripings, vomiting & flux, with a fever, which proved mortal to many infants & little children, esp'ly at Boston & Charlstown, and to some grown persons.

26. 7^m 1669.   Thomas Lyons was excommunicated.

17. 9^m 1669.   A publick thanksgiving.

20. 9^m 1669.   An Earthquake.

26. 9^m 1669.   m^r Richd Champney, one of the Ruling Elders at Cambringe, died.

2. 12^m 1669.   m^r Benj. Bunkur Pastor to ye church at Malden died.

16. 12. 1669.   m^r Thomas Thatcher was ordained Pastor to ye 3^d church in Boston, and m^r Rainsford Ruling Elder.

This winter was very sharp & tedious, we had much 'snow & cold weather, ye wayes difficult & vnpassable.

10. 1^m.   A youth of Charlstown [blank] set up ō Gallows, & had other corporal punishment for Attempting to comitt Buggery.

Thomas Hawly a youth was drawn vnder both y^e mill-wheeles, but one of y^e ladders brake & so his life through Gods merciful providence was preserved.

$\frac{69}{70}$ 1^m 13.   m^r John Davenport, Pastor to the first Church at Boston was taken with y^e dead palsey on y^e right side and 2 dayes after, viz on y^e 15th of y^e first moneth died, and was buried on y^e 22^d of y^e same. Aged 73.

1^m.   m^r Warham Pastor to y^e church at Windsor died.

70. 2^m 11^d.   m^r Peter Oliver died and was lamented by all men.

21^m 4^d.   m^r Howchin died

3^m 4^d.   m^r John Oxenbridge was ordained Pastor to ye first church at Boston, & mr John Wiswall Ruling Elder.

70. 4^m 20^d.   A solemn Council of 6 Churches, viz y^e Elders & Messengers of y^e first Church in Boston, of Roxbury of Dorchester waymouth, Cambridge & Watertown, met at Braintrey upon y^e request of y^e church there, for y^e hearing and healing of their Divisions & distractions in reference to y^e choice of Teaching Elders amongst them.

70. $\{^{4m\,30}_{5m,\,1,\,2.3}\}$ The Fish in y^e fresh Pond at Watertown in great abundance came to y^e shore, faint drooping, pining & dying, many scores of cartloads were observed by y^e shore on the south side of y^e pond, but within 4 or 5 dayes they were rotten & much consumed.

A great drought this summer : little rain frō ye time of ye Election vntil ye 9th of 5^m except a good shower on ye 9th of 4^m. else none but sprinklings once or twice vntil ye 9th of 5^m then G. sent a solid & soaking rain.

70. 7^m. many visited wth Ague & fever.

70. 5^m 31. Sarah ye wife of William Cleaves solemnly admonished Mary Baker also solemnly admonished.

70. 9^m 24. A Day of publick Thanksgiving.

A sad accident at Lancaster of a yong girle.

A sad accident at Boston of a man that was shingling a house & fell down ye ladder & was killed.

A sad accident at Woburn of three men y^t were digging a well & ye earth caved in & swallow^d up two alive & the third hardly escaped but was digged out, his head not being covered wth earth.

70. 10^m. 4. Isaac Heath solemnly admonished.

29. 11^m. 70. Sarah Cleaves forgiven by the Church.

4th 12^m 70. m^r Zacharie Symmes Pastor to the church at Charlstown dyed. Frō 19th of 1^m to ye 28th was rainie, stormie, & tempestuous weather.

3th 2^m 71. m^r Francis Willoughbey Deputy Govr, died, & was interred on 7th of 2^m.

3^m 71. The first fortnight was rainie & wet weather.

9. 4^m. A sweet and seasonable rain.

11. 4. 71. Thomas lyons upon his repentance was absolved frō ye sentence of excom̄.

11. 5^m 71. m^r Joshua Moody ordained Pastor to y church at Portsmouth.

12. 5^m 71. m^r John Reyner ordained Pastor to the church at Dover.

18 5^m 71. A Council frō sev'all churches out of ye Bay met at Newbury.

26. 6^m 71. m^r John Allin, Pastor of ye church at Dedham died & was interred ye 29th of ye same.

29. 6^m 71. mrs. Katharine Allin his wife died also. buryed in the same grave by her husband.

8th 7^m 71. An Indian executed & hung up in chaines for murdering an English maid at Woburn.

This summer many were visited with ye ague & fever.

30. 7^m 71. m^r James Pen Ruleing Elder in ye first church in Boston deceased.

19. 8^m 71. A day of solemn Thanksgiving.

21. 8^m 71. We heard ye sad & heavy Tidings concerning ye captivity of Capt. Foster & his sonn at Sally.

8th 9^{ber} 71. m^r Vrian Oakes ordained Pastor to the church at Cambridge.

27. 10^m 71. m^r Josiah Flint ordained Pastor to the church at Dorchester

14. 11^m 71. 21. 11. 71   o^r brother Giles Pason was elected & called to ye office of a Deacon & ye Sabbath following he was solemnly ordained by prayer and impositio. of ye hands of ye Elders.

15. 12. 71.   Ales Thomas, mr More, Goody Langborough, [blank] Jeffrey [blank] Read, stood on y^e Gallows, &c.

19. 12, 71.   Charles Chauncey, B. D. President of Harvard Colledge rested from his labours & was solemnly buried on y^e 21 day of Febr. m^r Oakes makeing a Funeral Sermon and m^r Alex. Nowel a funeral Oration.

10 1^m 7$\frac{1}{2}$.   Shubal Seaver solemnly admonished.

1672. 3m.   A severe drought all this moneth.

1. 4^m.   Rain with thunder & lightning, wrby Benjamin Gamlin's Barn was fired & burnt down.

2. 4^m.   Elizabeth Parker cast out of the church.

3. 4^m.   It pleased God to send most seasonable & plentiful showers of rain   This summer we were visited wth agues & fevers, both yong and old.

12. 5^m.   m^r Edmund Frost Ruling Elder in Cambridge dyed.

13. 5^m.   m^r Alexander Nowell (aged 27) one of ye fellows of ye Coledge, after long sicknesse and furious destraction and madnesse, dyed.

12. 6^m.   A great Eclipse of ye Sun, ^{Wch} at ye eastward was total & central, insomuch that ye stars appeared about ye Sun.

25. 6^m.   Caleb Seaver solemnly admonished.

30. 6^m.   A great spring tide together with a g^t storme of rain, wch did much damage to ye hay in ye meadows For ye space of 12 dayes together it was cloudy & rainie weather.

11. 7^m.   m^r Moses Fisk was ordained Pastor to ye church at Braintrey.   Agues & fevers prevailed much among vs about ye Bay, & fluxes & vomiting at Boston. The spotted feaver at & about wenham.

15. 8^m. m^r Antipas Newman Pastor to the church of wenham died.

2^d 8^m.   m^r Jeremy Hubbard ordained Pastor to the church at Topsfield.

5. 9^m.   A Committee of ye General Court sat at Newbury & composed y^r diff. & reconciled y^m one to another.

7. 9^m.   A great storme of raine & winde.

10. 9^m.   Another dreadful Tempest, wch made g^t spoil esp'c. at Boston & charlstown & some vessels were wracked and lives lost.

12. 9^m.   Major Eleazar Lusher died.

20. 9^m.   A Day of publick & solemn Thanksgiving.

7. 10^m.   Richard Bellingham Esqr Govr aged 81, died, & was honorably interred on ye 18th day of 10^m.

1672. 10th 10^m.   Dr Leonard Hoar was solemnly Installed into his office of President of Harvard Colledge.

24. 10^m.   A publick Fast throughout this Jurisdiction.

5^t. 11^m.   Isaac Heath upon his penitent Confession, released from Censure.

28. 12^m.   News from New York of a sad prodigie, ye raining of blood. but some thought it might be y^e muting of Birds.

6. 1^m.   Abraham Newels house was burnt. o^r congregat'o. made a Collec'o. for him of 14^{lb}.

This spring the churches in y^e Bay set vpon a Course of fasting & prayer in their several Congregat'ons. Coughs & colds & sore eyes frequent distemp's amongst vs.

21. 1^m 7$\frac{2}{3}$ our castle was burnt.

Tidings also came concerning a g^t fire at Barbados wch burnt up y^e street called N. E. street.

23. 1^m beinge y^e Ld's day there was a very stormy & tempestuous Winde, wch blew down m^r Perponts Barn in y^e morning while y^e family was at prayer, but y^e Cattle escaped & suffered no hurt, tho'· tyed up in ye house.

24. 1^m. Alice Craft smitten wth Apoplexie & died next day.

1673. 29. 1^m. m^r Thomas Prince, Governor of Plimouth Colonie died. In ye spring frequent Fasts in ye several churches.

1673. 13. 2^m. Esther Gravener was excomunicated.

3^m. Tidings concerning the redemption of m^r Foster of Charlstown frō captivity after neer 18 moneth slavery and his return to London, his sonn william coming home to his mother at Charlestown, having been his father companion in bondage.

18. 3^m. one Goldsmith of wenham slain by lightning in m^{rs} Newman's house & his dog: div'se others being in ye room & escaping.

This sumer we had excessive raines, much wet weather and several stormes.

8. 4^m. Hugh Clark was solemnly admonished.

21. 4^m. m^r waltem ye ministers son, at Marble head beinge in his boat, was smitten with thunder & ligtenings his leg & back bone broken, & within a few dayes, dyed.

14. 5^m. Nathaniel Mitchel, Eldest son to m^r Jonathan Mitchel was slain by a fall frō his horse, as he was running a race.

1. 6^m. Tidings frō Virginia of ye Dutch taking 6 & destroying & burning other 6 of ye English fleet.

3^d. 6^m. Tiding of ye Dutch assaulting New York: wch awakened ye Bay to put y^{m}s, in a posture of war, p'pare fortificatio' and seek ye face of God.

14. 6^m. A publick & solemn Fast at Boston upon that account.

17. 6^m. Old goody Bird of Dorchester falling down at a Trap door in her own house, broke her neck & nev. spake more but 2 dayes after, died. ·

21. 6^m. Daniel Holbroke going over a stone wall, fell down upon ye stones & ye knife in his pocket, pierced his bowels & two dayes after, he died.

28. 6^m. A publick Fast through this Jurisdiction.

3^d. 8^m. A dreadful burning, at Hingham. The house was all on a flame while ye inhabitants were asleep, but at length awakened by ye howling of a dog in ye flames, but a child of 8 yeares old was burnt to death, and a little infant fearfully scorcht.

7. 8^m. About 9 aclock at night ye house of Robt. Seaver was fired through ye Carelessness of a maid y^t went up into ye chamber to order the cheeses, her light fired ye thatch & ye house was burnt down, but much of ye goods preserved, as also ye Barn.

2^d. 9^m. Esther Gravener was reconciled to ye church & solemnly owned ye Covenant.

17. 9^m. Forrest & Piccard executed for Conspiracy against ye master of ye ship.

20. 9^m. A publick Thanksgiving.

1. 10^m. Captain Foster returned home after his Captivity.

3. 10^m. m^r. William Adams ordained Pastor of ye church of christ at Dedham.

11. 10^m. A publick fast in reference to the Genl Courts consultation about an Expedition ag^st ye Dutch

28. 10^m. Thomas Hanchet was solemnly admonished.

15. 1^m. Benjamin Goad a youth was excommunicated.

1674. 27. 1^m. A publick Fast throughout ye Jurisdiction.

2. 2^m. Benjamin Goad was executed.

5. 2^m. Shubal & Caleb Seaver were released by ye church.

24. 3^m. Margaret Cheany widow having been long bound by Satan vnder a melancholick distemper, (above 10 or 11 yeares) wch made her wholly neglect her Calling & live mopishly, this day gave thanks to God for loosing her chain, & confessing & bewailing her sinful yielding to temptation.

13^d. 7^m. Ruth Hemingway was excommunicated.

24. 7^m. A day of Publick Thanksgiving.

INDEX

TO

ROXBURY LAND AND CHURCH RECORDS.

INDEX

ROXBURY LAND AND CHURCH RECORDS.